Still Waters
for
Shallow Shores

Still Waters for Shallow Shores

A THROUGH THE YEAR JOURNEY FOR REDISCOVERING THE GOD OF THE BIBLE

XULON PRESS ELITE

Jabez Abraham

Xulon Press Elite
2301 Lucien Way #415
Maitland, FL 32751
407.339.4217
www.xulonpress.com

Xulon ELITE

© 2021 by Jabez Abraham

All rights reserved solely by the author. The author guarantees all contents are original and do not infringe upon the legal rights of any other person or work. No part of this book may be reproduced in any form without the permission of the author. The views expressed in this book are not necessarily those of the publisher.

Due to the changing nature of the Internet, if there are any web addresses, links, or URLs included in this manuscript, these may have been altered and may no longer be accessible. The views and opinions shared in this book belong solely to the author and do not necessarily reflect those of the publisher. The publisher therefore disclaims responsibility for the views or opinions expressed within the work.

Scripture quotations taken from the King James Version (KJV) – public domain.

Printed in the United States of America

Paperback ISBN-13: 978-1-6628-3472-1
Hard Cover ISBN-13: 978-1-6628-3473-8

Ebook ISBN-13: 978-1-6628-3474-5

Dedication

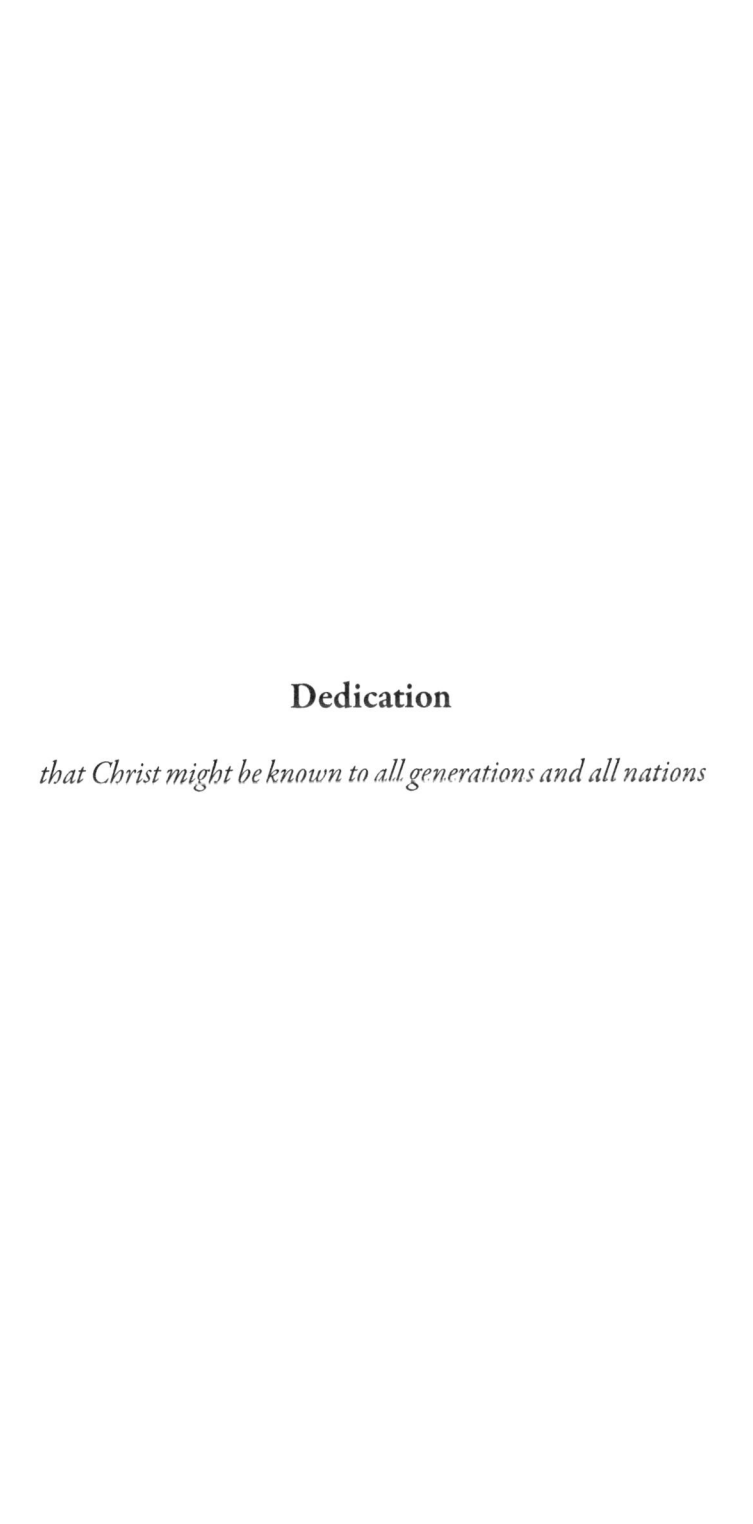

that Christ might be known to all generations and all nations

Contents

Introduction ix

January **1–31**
   GOD 1
   HOLY SPIRIT 18

February **32–61**
   HOLY SPIRIT 32
   HOLY SCRIPTURES 33
   MAN 41

March **62–92**
   SIN 62
   THE GOSPEL 74

April **93–123**
   THE GOSPEL 93
   DISCIPLESHIP 121

May **124–154**
   DISCIPLESHIP 124

June **155–184**
   DISCIPLESHIP 155
   PRAYER 175

July **185–216**
   PRAYER 185
   HOLINESS 193

  WORSHIP.....................................209

  REVIVAL 216

August 217–247

  REVIVAL 217

September 248–277

  REVIVAL 248

October..................................... 278–308

  REVIVAL 278

  THE CHURCH 282

November.................................. 309–338

  THE CHURCH 309

December................................... 339–371

  THE CHURCH 339

  EVANGELISM 340

  RESTORATION.............................355

Additional Resource for Consideration.......... 372

Title Index 387

Introduction

For the Lord is good; his mercy is everlasting; and his truth endureth to all generations.—Psalm 100:5.

Truth is like a dying fire; unless it is stoked, it will die out. In consideration of writing a book, to put in words all the avenues that God used to birth these truths in my heart by His Spirit and through the word such as Divine Providence, through human agents, and so forth will be impossible. The greatness of the book of Romans is not the Apostle Paul, but the God of the Apostle Paul who wrote it, God using weak human instruments of clay. The realization of the Sovereignty of the Holy Spirit, who moves men to pray and brings them to a deeper understanding of God by the scriptures, is essential to assimilate the meat of these teachings. It is the intrinsic desire of God for the conveying of truth from one generation to the next, and where needed to bring to remembrance the truths that exist eternally but have been forgotten or at times forsaken at the altar of convenience. As with any generation, it is God who is the author and finisher of our faith, and these are dedicated to the sole glory of God and for the fulfillment of God's desire that He might receive the praise in bringing us unto Himself. Unto Him be glory and praise now and forever, amen.

Holy, Holy, Holy
Reginald Heber

Holy, holy, holy! Lord God almighty!
Early in the morning our song shall rise to thee.
Holy, holy, holy! Merciful and mighty!
God in three persons, blessed trinity!

Holy, holy, holy! All the saints adore thee,
casting down their golden crowns around the glassy sea;
cherubim and seraphim falling down before thee,
which wert, and art, and evermore shalt be.

Holy, holy, holy! Though the darkness hide thee,
though the eye of sinfulness thy glory may not see,
only thou art holy; there is none beside thee,
perfect in pow'r, in love, and purity.

Holy, holy, holy! Lord God almighty!
All thy works shall praise thy name, in earth, and sky, and sea.
Holy, holy, holy! Merciful and mighty!
God in three persons, blessed trinity!

Public Domain

January

January 1

God, our Supreme Goal

Who is like unto thee, O Lord, among the gods? who is like thee, glorious in holiness, fearful in praises, doing wonders?– Exodus 15:11

There are good teachings that can come from men who love the Lord and love the truth. But there is a grave danger in building on another man's foundation for personal convictions. Historic truths by others who have gone before us can benefit us, but they are never the standard upon which to stand therein. It is the word of God and the Spirit of God who has the supreme authority over any man-made interpretations of the scriptures. A humble maid in love with God and desiring God in all His fullness can know more of the scriptures, theology, and interpretations than the most learned theologian of our day. We are to strive to learn the deeper things of God that are imparted by the Spirit of truth and instilled by the fear of God. Though with all sincerity a godly man may teach, it is still one frail man teaching another, and standing on another man's convictions can cause one to be a follower of men at the expense of a personal walk with God. The anointed man who preaches in the power of the Spirit becomes hidden to the hearers where the people hear God and follow Him instead.

GOD

January 2

Desiring God Alone

And he is before all things, and by him all things consist.– Colossians 1:17

Our motives are always tied with our actions. Whether good or bad, there is a purpose for what we do that has the hidden root of why we do it. It is the "why" we do that matters since that is the reason for what we do. We need to examine ourselves regarding why we desire revival more than what we would like to see happen. God, who sees the secret motives of man's heart, lays bare our shallow asking if God is desired for accomplishing our goals and using Him for our purposes. In true revival praying, our motive should be to desire God Himself for who He is and not for what He can do for us. God, who is Sovereign, knows all things, and He can accomplish infinitely more with His vessels when we have that pure motive of desiring God Himself. To Abraham, God Himself was his great reward. And until God becomes all we want, our asking for revival will be a distant dream and wish that one asks for but never attains since God is not at the center of the asking. God must be the central attraction of our asking, and true revival is about desiring God alone. Even when asked with good intentions, anything else will come short of seeing God come and walk among us. It is a joyous occasion when God comes when we have longed for Him more than anything else.

GOD

January 3

The Triune God

Now unto the King eternal, immortal, invisible, the only wise
God, be honour and glory for ever and ever. Amen.
–1 Timothy 1:17

The doctrine of the Trinity is not about wrapping the understanding of the infinity of God and logically approving of it in human terms. A man who has a low view of God and tries to find some similarity will try to wrap words for transcendent unknowns that will make him look smart. But the reality of God as "I am God, and there is none else" is just as true as when God said, "let us make man in our image" or "I and my Father are one." Man is confined by time, space, and knowledge, but God is unlimited in all those areas and has an understanding beyond those areas that man is not privy to. To think that we can know God by hacking Him down to intellectual progress of the senses is to call ourselves as god and fall into the delusion of Lucifer, who declared, "I will be like the most High." To have one God in three persons and yet exist perpetually unchanging and be inimitably unique in substance, form, and purpose should cause us to fall down and worship the glory of this eternal Being of whom we are privileged to adore and utter "let God be true, but every man a liar" and be content to bask in His presence.

GOD

January 4

Interwoven with Christ

For in him we live, and move, and have our being–Acts 17:28a

The fundamental construct of life itself reveals that man is a being who is not a product of mindless evolution. He can reason, build, and organize cities and work for the betterment of things he is put in charge of. With that comes the great divide that a man apart from God is lost and has no desire to seek after God but realizes that he is faced with uncertainties such as death, fear, enemies, and so forth. On the other hand, God, who created man, has life, purpose, love, and so on that span time and eternity, for they are based on the eternal nature of God. When they intersect in the act of regeneration by the Spirit, everything falls in place of interweaving one's perspectives with God's truth. Thus, the scriptures paint the picture of the lost man, the eternal God, and the regenerated man. When we read the scriptures and intersect everything we do in light of God, man's life has a purpose, and we can see a beautiful tapestry that God is weaving and a life worth living for. It is a picture of the God-called man woven with the threads of purpose, faith, grace, victory, suffering, joy, sorrow, peace, and a myriad of others to form a picture that displays the glory of God and the praise of heaven. Such purpose can only be fully realized by the crucified life of one who is filled with the Spirit.

GOD

January 5

Starting Point

I am Alpha and Omega, the beginning and the ending, saith the Lord, which is, and which was, and which is to come, the Almighty.–Revelation 1:8

Having a wrong starting point will lead us to the wrong destination. It affects everything we do and how we do it, and why we do it. It affects our reasoning, our world around us, our view of life itself, and ultimately how we view death. When we apply this to truths of immense consequences such as God and who He is, it is tremendously vital that we have the right starting point. To see the scriptures as one book with many scribes given by the same God represented in the Old and New Testament; to know the working of justice, judgment, righteousness, holiness, and love by the Triune God displayed consistently in any portion of scripture. Our starting point matters. Christ was not born, as in origination, with the event celebrated as Christmas; He always was, is, and will be. He put on the shell of human covering during His incarnation and became God in human flesh while being God a very God and man a very man. He put on mortality to subject Himself to human limitations while never losing His eternal Godhead. When we look at Christ through the lens of the Old and New Testament, then we have the proper view of God to know that He is eternal and the same yesterday, today, and forever; where He makes that grand declaration of "I am the Lord, I change not."

GOD

January 6

Jesus and Jehovah

Jesus saith unto him, Have I been so long time with you, and yet hast thou not known me, Philip? he that hath seen me hath seen the Father; and how sayest thou then, Show us the Father?–John 14:9

While we wrestle with the profound doctrines of the Triune God and its far-reaching implications of that truth; One God, three in persons, the same in substance, not diminished in any singular representation of Himself unto us; we come to the Old Testament and look at the greatness of God, the majesty of His Creation, the restoration through repentance of the people of God and His care and love for His children, and to those who followed His ways even of the gentiles such as Ruth, Rahab, and Nineveh. When we approach such greatness of our God, we are further expanded in our learning of Him when He stepped into humanity, in mortal flesh and lived among us as God in the flesh, Jesus Christ who always has, always been, and always will be. But His life was in complete accordance with the Old Testament truth of God's dealing with man, for Christ was the face of Jehovah, His hands, His feet, and His life on earth. And yet as we grapple with truths that are hidden, such as the Godhead in the union of the Father, Son, and the Holy Spirit, we desire to stay silent as we fall down and worship Him in the stillness of eternity, this great God who loves us so, leaving truths that are too lofty for mortal minds to the wisdom and counsel of God.

GOD

January 7

The Holiness of God

And one cried unto another, and said, Holy, holy, holy, is the Lord of hosts: the whole earth is full of his glory. –Isaiah 6:3

Can a man approach God? Can God, who is absolute in perfection and incorruptible in holiness, interact with the fallen man who desires to be his own god? Can man comprehend God before whom the heavens are not clean in His sight, who putteth no trust in His saints, where man is as a worm before His Creator? Can a regenerated man truly comprehend the command of "Be ye holy; for I am holy"? If eternity cannot exhaust the nature of God and our knowledge of Him in fresh and anew in perfection, then how insignificant is our understanding of Him now on earth, we who are bound by time and limitations; if the best of us who seek Him are of unclean lips, and dwell in the midst of a people of unclean lips, can mortal man ever learn of the perfection of God? If we cannot enter into the treasure of a snowflake, how greatly do we fall short in knowing the vastness of the God of the oceans and galaxies? The holiness of God brings us to the place of nothingness and the unapproachableness of God, the One the seraphims fear to look upon but cry, Holy, holy, holy, is the Lord of hosts. Words cannot continue to expound further on the holiness of God. Such is the unexplainable beauty of holiness. And unless we have the proper view of God, history will rise to condemn our generation for our low view of the most High.

GOD

January 8

The Existence of God

The fool hath said in his heart, There is no God. They are corrupt, they have done abominable works, there is none that doeth good.
–Psalm 14:1

The outcome of a reaction is based on the input of the source and the empirical data that is produced. And the reality of the Imago Dei that is imprinted in every man is the outcome of the nature of the Creator when God said, "Let us make man in our image, after our likeness", though now he is in this fallen state. To know the difference between right and wrong, though skewed it may be, nevertheless shows the seed of a moral element. How did right and wrong evolve? How did conscience evolve? How did dreams evolve? How did the power to reason, emotions, intelligence in ideas, love, and so forth evolve if there was nothing to evolve from because of the lack thereof at the source? The natural laws, chemical laws, psychological laws, moral laws, observable patterns in life, all proclaim loudly and reflect the handiwork of God. For those regenerated by the Spirit, the existence of God is not reflections as seen around them, but it is an experience that is supernatural where one who hated now loves, one who was gripped by the vices of sin now lives in victory over sin, one who sought to fill that void now speaks of the nearness of Christ who has taken abode in their hearts. In Christ, the reality of God and the nature of God is imparted in that great transaction where at one time, they were a child of the devil have now become the children of God.

GOD

January 9

The Study of God

For thus saith the high and lofty One that inhabiteth eternity, whose name is Holy; I dwell in the high and holy place, with him also that is of a contrite and humble spirit, to revive the spirit of the humble, and to revive the heart of the contrite ones.
–Isaiah 57:15

There is no greater purpose nor a loftier goal in life than God. One must desire to employ all the faculties of their mind, soul, and body to get to learn and study this glorious Being of immortal, invisible, the only wise God. Such study ought to be undertaken with fear and trembling due to its immense consequences; to find the Truth lest we believe a lie in a self-imagined view of God. There are five crucial pillars that one can build upon in this grand endeavor, which is to be undertaken by a genuine Christian, being led by the Spirit through the word. First, the nature of God such as His holiness, unknown-ness, Godhead, and so forth; Second, the attributes of God such as His Omnipotence, Omniscience, self-proclamations, and many others; Third, the goodness of God as seen in Creation and Divine Providence such as long-suffering, mercy, love, and grace; Fourth, the justice of God that is very different from the human perception of fairness; Fifth, God's effectual interaction with mankind. In so doing, we fully need to realize that the infinite God can never be fully understood or comprehended by the finite man now or in eternity by all of Creation put together. After a lifetime of such depth, it would be but as a singular dew upon a flower which shows a glimpse of the heavens where it came from.

GOD

January 10

Created for His Pleasure

Thou art worthy, O Lord, to receive glory and honour and power: for thou hast created all things, and for thy pleasure they are and were created. –Revelation 4:11

The tendency of Christians who like to rationalize the happenings in their life as following the familiar narrative of "for their good and for God's glory" can come to the place of formulating trials and tragedies as something that should be looked at from their point of view alone, that it is for their good. But that is the wrong starting point, for such tendencies can quickly move one to look at life and events as benefitting them in the realm of other decisions such as making money, buying a car, and such. Our solidarity in seeing the outlook of life should begin from the viewpoint of God's original intent for creating us, for His pleasure. And if I can see all events that happen as bringing me to the place of that which brings Him the greatest pleasure from me in my response of it, then that is the correct viewpoint. The grand theme unveiled is that God desires to bring us unto Himself and purge what hinders that one goal as we respond in reciprocal love, realizing the good God that He is and that nothing better exists apart from Him. Such truths will allow us to see life in the proper view of pleasing God. To enjoy this relationship in unadulterated purity and a perfect friendship with the God of the Universe should be our motivation to love and adore Him.

GOD

January 11

Retribution

It is a fearful thing to fall into the hands of the living God.
–Hebrews 10:31

The character of God to give just reward for those who have earned it speaks of the justice of God to demand truth at all costs. For the perfect moral Being who has no shadow or turning will do right as the judge of all the earth. To punish evildoers is not only the reality of God's nature but also the response of men and women who have been made in the image of God and thus bear in them the mark of requiring accurate judgment for crimes that have been committed. The perfection of God as the righteous judge speaks of Himself, whose judgment will be based on His perfection and not ours. The accountability of being His Creation speaks of the need to acknowledge the God of the Bible who not only loves but judges those who have rejected His way of pardon through Jesus Christ. And such is the nature of those who face the wrath of Almighty God for all of eternity. The reality of Hell is not about a fear factor; instead, it is the place of justice that is perfectly meted out at the culmination of man's sin to reject His Creator and spurn the grace of God that has been shown forth; in Creation, Divine Providence and from those who have preached the truth in love.

GOD

January 12

Fingerprints of God

The heavens declare his righteousness, and all the people see his glory.—Psalm 97:6

In any investigation, there's a need for irrefutable evidence in solving a mystery to be able to come to a conclusive verdict. When we look at the world around us, there is a definite pattern portrayed in the grandeur of the variety of things we see in nature. Be it the myriad of colors in a petal, the beauty of a sunset, the changing of the seasons, the variety in birds and animals, the treasures of a snowflake or the patterns of fishes, extreme intricacies and uniqueness of organs that perform various functions in the human body, the language of DNA, the vastness of space, stars and planets, the infinite number of things that are seen and unseen that we touch, hear and feel every single day that evoke our emotions. It overwhelmingly speaks of a reflection of an all-wise Creator God who splattered in purposeful intent a myriad of variations in the canvas of His handiwork. While man's sin brought the consequences of corruption seen from aging to sickness and the finality of death, the remnant is still a declaration of the glory of God and His care for His creatures.

GOD

January 13

Creation

In the beginning God created the heaven and the earth.
—Genesis 1:1a

Christians believe that Jesus fed the five thousand because they read it in the Bible. Still, some, applying the reasoning of their minds influenced by the corrupt "theories" of this world, deny that God created all things in six literal days around six thousand years ago as God records it. The "day", which is associated with evening and morning, always means a twenty-four-hour literal day (Genesis 1:5,8,13,19,23,31). If we don't believe Genesis as recorded, why believe the rest of the Bible, and when did truth have to bow down to the god of the secular worldview, which is science falsely so called? "For the wisdom of this world is foolishness with God. For it is written, He taketh the wise in their own craftiness."–1 Corinthians 3:19. Sir Isaac Newton, one of the most influential scientists of all time, wisely stated, "When I look at the solar system, I see the earth at the right distance from the sun to receive the proper amounts of heat and light. This did not happen by chance."

GOD

Means to an End **January 14**

Thou shalt have no other gods before me.–Exodus 20:3

There is a sobering warning given in the scriptures regarding the tendency of man to worship the creature more than his Creator. There is a constant battle that rages in our hearts to see the here-and-now and look away from the underlying source of where it came from. Elijah had the means for the provision of water by using the brook, but the source was God; an occupation is the means to an end for the sustenance of our body, but the source is God; an officer is the means for the enforcement of the law, but the source is the law. The challenge one has when doing something like a profession is to keep looking at God and doing the task given to them with all their might and fulfill their duties; at the same time, not depend upon their job for their provision but rather depend on God who is the provider of the job and food through the financial provision of that job. For therein is how a man can ensure that he does not take his eyes off the source and make the means an idol. Anything that we give preference to in place of God is an idol.

GOD

January 15

God, Our Great Reward

I am thy shield, and thy exceeding great reward. – Genesis 15:1b

In a fallen world, we are often used to a tangible way of praising or rewarding something good. There is a danger in applying results and physical rewards to spiritual things in the hope of gaining worldly pleasure. To Abraham, God was his exceeding great reward. It was not that God would reward him with wealth, but God Himself was going to be Abraham's crown jewel that he got to enjoy. Our desire needs to be not what God can give me; instead, our supreme desire should be to desire Him for who He is and not for what He can do for us. When God Himself becomes our reward, then everything else becomes secondary. A Christian in Iran who worships God in prison with no earthly possessions has the greatest riches when he enjoys God. Today, there is a danger of prevalent teaching that implies that when you get God, you get everything as in earthly goods; this is a fallacy that God is primarily associated with temporal blessings. In the New Testament, God was associated with deprivation, prison, and crucifixion, but the early Christians enjoyed God as their reward, for they had nothing else. Possessions become as the dew upon the grass, and God alone remains. He must become our greatest desire.

GOD

January 16

Enshrined Captivation of God

Who among us shall dwell with the devouring fire? who among us shall dwell with everlasting burnings?—Isaiah 33:14b

Deep in the depths of every human breast is a place that is sacred to him where he worships a god. It could be money, possessions, self, religion, imaginative god, and so forth. Thus, the manifestation of his sinful nature, which rebelled against God, has created a false god and has placed him in that inner sanctum known only to that man. Though the rightful owner of that shrine is his Creator, man is content to pollute it with anything other than the Light who can give that true purpose for their existence. For the Christian, the living God, the Creator of heaven and earth, will not share His glory with another nor allow joint ownership of His rightful place. The need for the Christian to deny everything that supplants God in that inner shrine, including self and the little foxes that spoil the vine, is crucial for living with the abiding presence of God in their lives. Such sacred courts are constantly purified and perpetually made ready for the One who occupies them. Any threat to Him is violently dethroned by putting to death the danger in the power of the Spirit and the aul of His word. Anything less than this will cause one to lose the sweetness of His coming and give place to apathy, and a life tossed to and fro with every wind of doctrine.

GOD

January 17
The High View of God

I have lift up mine hand unto the Lord, the most high God, the possessor of heaven and earth,—Genesis 14:22b

Everything rises and falls on our view of God. The Apostle John who leaned on the breast of Jesus, fell at His feet as dead in Revelation when he saw the glorified Christ (Revelation 1:17). Whether it was Isaiah, David, Job, or John, there was the crushing weight of the infinite greatness of God and the infinite corruption of man. There is an unknownness of God that we often forget. God is infinite, and the mortal man is a finite creature swimming in the pool of ignorance. There are portions in the Scripture where we just utter "let God be true, but every man a liar" and move on, lest we bring God to the harsh scrutiny of human reasoning and put Him in a box; for we see darkly through a clouded glass through the veil of the Lamb of God who was slain, and the Spirit imparting to us a glimpse of what it means to approach the burning altar of God's holiness as revealed in the scriptures.

GOD

January 18

Holy Spirit and the New Birth

Jesus answered, Verily, verily, I say unto thee, Except a man be born of water and of the Spirit, he cannot enter into the kingdom of God.–John 3:5

The active agent of the Holy Spirit who wrote the scriptures and birthed in the womb of Mary the Christ Child does a similar transaction of rebirthing the natural man who has no light in him to seek the true God off himself. The natural man will much rather flee from the Light as Adam did when confronted by God. Being the children of wrath by nature and further solidified by our choice to love and commit sin, the wonder of regeneration is captured with such significant impossibilities where it can only be wrought by God when He conquers the soul of man. Impossibilities such as being born again, the replacing of the heart of stone for the heart of flesh, the quickening of that which was dead to life, the adoption of one who was a child of the devil to become a child of God, being adopted into the family of God, the indwelling witness of the Holy Spirit and so on. The nature of such operation demands immediate change on the part of the sinner who has been born of the Spirit of God and has been made alive, just as iron immediately gets affected when it comes in contact with the furnace; anything less is damnation and not salvation.

HOLY SPIRIT

January 19

Striving against God's Spirit

The Lord looked down from heaven upon the children of men, to see if there were any that did understand, and seek God. They are all gone aside, they are all together become filthy: there is none that doeth good, no, not one.–Psalm 14:2,3

You must have the high, which is the proper, view of God for having the correct view of man. You begin with God and not the man when dealing with God and trying to understand what is happening in the world around us. Fundamentally it is the battle of 2 G(g)od's, the God of truth with His original claim on man through Creation against the god of self who is diametrically opposed to the living God by nature and by choice being dead in sin with no desire to seek the living God. While Satan offers the distractions of this world to the pleasure of a man who seeks to suppress the truth in unrighteousness, man is held accountable for his response to God just as Adam was in the garden. The goodness of God who has prepared a way of escape, while is merciful and long-suffering, does not disclose how long He is willing to suffer the man who spurns the grace of God. For the Christian, beginning with God's truth with a desire for God can help reject the lies of men who have given ear to the deceptions of the evil one. The judgment of the righteousness of God that condemns a man into Hell is not primarily about the response of God for sinful men; instead, it is about the response of man to the righteousness and holiness of God.

HOLY SPIRIT

January 20

Baptism of the Holy Spirit

he shall baptize you with the Holy Ghost and with fire:
–Luke 3:16b

With every great move of God, it is to be noted that it was always through men and women whom God raised who had the baptism of the Holy Spirit upon their lives. It was an experience separate and different from salvation. The baptism of the Holy Spirit is not about tongues or sinless perfection. Instead, it is the pouring of God's Spirit in a greater measure into a vessel that has been sanctified and meet for the Master's use. Being filled is an event that must be done by something external that pours its content into a vessel that can receive it since the vessel lacks it, the act of baptism by immersion into the Spirit. Whether Elisha with the double portion, Samson and the jawbone, Paul and Elymas, Hudson Taylor, Wesley, Whitefield, Frances Havergal, A. W. Tozer, or many others, there is always a time that you will find when this event happened in their lives, and their works do follow them. D. L. Moody, after he was baptized with the Spirit, said, "I was all the time tugging and carrying water, but now I have a river that carries me." We can produce a lot of "results" without the Holy Ghost, but God's plan has always been "Not by might, nor by power, but by my spirit, saith the LORD of hosts."

HOLY SPIRIT

January 21

Penetrating the Veil

And you hath he quickened, who were dead in trespasses and sins;
–Ephesians 2:1

There is an ally for the preaching of the gospel inside the man who is dead in trespasses and sins; it is his conscience that has been implanted into every man by the mercy of God for the moral well-being of His creatures. The Holy Spirit takes the law of God and breaks it upon the heart of stone to reveal that hidden, vulnerable man. When the Spirit of God thus confronts a man in light of the law of God, the conscience is made alive where what he once thought as trivial such as taking God's name in vain, becomes as life-and-death where he stands guilty before that perfect law and the penetrating eyes of a Holy God who gave those laws. Unless a man is revealed the vileness of his sin, he is not ready to repent, and unless he repents, he cannot believe, and unless he believes he cannot be saved. Conviction of sin is God's Spirit crushing man's righteousness by God's law to lay him bare before the eyes of a Holy God while causing him to see the danger of where it will lead him to. When man thus convicted repents and turns to believe on the only way of hope, Jesus Christ, he is born anew by the work of the Spirit in regeneration. Thus, Jesus said, "except ye repent, ye shall all likewise perish" and that "Ye must be born again."

HOLY SPIRIT

January 22

The Inward Witness

The Spirit itself beareth witness with our spirit, that we are the children of God:–Romans 8:16

Every religion has some adherence to the teaching of its leaders of some sort. Even those who profess to be atheists have adherence to some tenet of what they believe. The strongest proof of one who has passed from death unto life is not in its teachings but in that sacred inward witness of the Holy Spirit. It is with that witness we cry "Abba, Father" of sonship. It is a cry of relationship and not of religion. Without this inner illumination of truth by the Spirit, the word alone cannot give us that assurance since many believed, but Jesus did not commit Himself unto them. It was a belief in Christ for carnal benefits. That divine witness who gives credibility that someone is an adopted child of God must be given first place before any assurance can be shown from the word. The Spirit itself beareth witness with our spirit that we are the children of God. To conclude someone as a believer and give them assurance because they believed in some key passages from the Bible is to grossly undermine the work of the Spirit and substitute it with human reasoning, leaving them lost. It may give temporal comfort to the hearer, but it will never stand in the eternal scrutiny of God.

HOLY SPIRIT

January 23

Divine Discontent

He that believeth on me, the works that I do shall he do also; and greater works than these shall he do; because I go unto my Father.
–John 14:12

To be desirous of God to work in our midst is a term that is subjective to how one perceives that. But there are areas that we have never entered in our generation, something that we can read off from the past that we look to and use as a guidepost of what God has done. Unless we are discontented with where we are and desire God for the ways He had moved in the past, God will let us be content with what we are used to in our services week after week. Though there may not be any supernatural moving of the Spirit in manifest presence and power, we can be content with it as "always has been" and expecting nothing more. But being discontent of the stagnation and desiring more should produce a divine discontentment which causes us to ask for what only God can do. A community touched, services that go well into the night, and days where the world has stopped and taken notice of it, sinners crying out to God for mercy and saints in speechless adoration in worship, where people sense the presence of God miles away as they come closer to the sanctuary and other workings of the Spirit. These events have happened in the past, and as long as we don't expect more and are content with where we are today, God will restrain His arm and leave us to our devices. In the end, we would have been the jest of this world which sees us as nothing more than just a religion.

HOLY SPIRIT

January 24

Proclamation of Truth

But his word was in mine heart as a burning fire shut up in my bones, and I was weary with forbearing, and I could not stay.
–Jeremiah 20:9b

There is a grave responsibility in hearing the voice of heaven and having been touched by the coals from the altar, of bringing that truth and preaching it with a burning heart. One who is in the place of declaring "thus saith the Lord" needs to realize the difficulty of truth being able to penetrate the hardness of the heart of man and into his conscience. This sense of helplessness is crucial for the message bearer to look unto Jesus, desire death to self, methods, and ability, but rather desire the revealing of the Person of truth, Jesus Christ. Coming to meet God and to hear from Him is the privilege of the hearer, and there is no distinction between a beggar or a king who may be present to listen to it. The Spirit who rested upon Christ when He was on Earth is the same Spirit who can break through this dichotomy of states, the truth of an eternal God, and the inability of the message bearer to convey it by human words. And this cannot be learned from an academic institution but from the unction that is from above. Thus, the proclamation of truth is the ability to embrace the weakness of man and rely wholly upon God for the fulfillment of "Not by might, nor by power, but by my spirit, saith the Lord of hosts."

HOLY SPIRIT

January 25

Make Alive

t is the spirit that quickeneth; the flesh profiteth nothing: the words that I speak unto you, they are spirit, and they are life.–John 6:63

For God's truth to be made into reality in hearts of stone, it needs to be made effectual by the One who gave us the truth, the precious Spirit of God. God breathed the word into existence and preserved this revelation from God. The One who inspired the word is the One who can effectively convey the word. These are treasures in earthen vessels of clay, and those desiring truth to be heard must listen to truths that are given in the still small voice of the Spirit of God and preach in that realm of the Spirit. Anyone can put words together, but God is the only one who can make it alive. It is called the living word because it reflects the Word made flesh and dwelt among us. And it is the Holy Spirit who has been given the office of making alive the word of God where the hearers hear the God of the word, and it becomes that living Word. Faith cometh not by reading but by hearing the word of God, and for ears that are deaf to be able to hear, only the Spirit can do that. My son once said that the word "ritual" is part of the word spiritual. Without the Spirit, it is just a ritual.

HOLY SPIRIT

January 26

God of the Word

zeal of God, but not according to knowledge.—Romans 10:2b

There is a great falling away that we see today because of our zeal to teach the word of God without desiring the audience for themselves to reach beyond that veil to the God of the word by the Holy Spirit. Such misplaced zeal causes a constant exodus of people who leave their teachings of the word of God and find alternatives in education, religions, and philosophical persuasions. In response, those in doubt must be constantly assured that the Bible is the very word of God using science, historical evidence, archeological discoveries, prophecies, etc. Though these are true, and they do carry the fingerprints of God, they are secondary to the believer. The source needs to be the God of the word who has revealed Himself to the penitent man, one who has passed from death unto life. It is like the blind man, who when the Pharisees cast doubt about Jesus after he was made whole, replied, "one thing I know, that, whereas I was blind, now I see." Without that experience of regeneration, we have to be constantly relying on looking at opposing views and proving one wrong to justify the truth that this is the word of God. When a man has an illumination of God by the Holy Spirit, he is not evaluating the validity of the word of God; he knows that they are the very words of God.

HOLY SPIRIT

January 27

The Flow of the Spirit

But God hath chosen the foolish things of the world to confound the wise; and God hath chosen the weak things of the world to confound the things which are mighty;–1 Corinthians 1:27

When God speaks, He chooses to use weak vessels, vessels that have been set apart and consecrated for the Master's use. To stand before men on behalf of God is a fearful place to be in lest we touch the Ark with unclean hands. A conduit does not adjust the message for the likes of the people; instead, for the conduit to work effectively, it must die. It must die to self, sin, and head knowledge. Head knowledge that does not get transformed by the Spirit into heart knowledge will not penetrate the heart of the hearers. Heart knowledge that the Spirit does not anoint will die on the vine. A man can have great oratory, energy, and words and may even get the people to the altar, but it will die before someone leaves the auditorium. But the Spirit wrought preaching wraps itself as it were a barbed wire in the heart of man and gives him no rest wherever he goes; until he falls on his face before God and obeys what God says or quenches it to his peril. The desire of every sincere preacher should be that they would be a conduit of God and that the Spirit who rested upon Christ would rest upon them as they die to self that God's truth may reach man's ears where man hears the voice of God.

HOLY SPIRIT

January 28

The New Creature

My sheep hear my voice, and I know them, and they follow me:
–John 10:27

The beauty of the gospel is in its outcome. All religions give some sense of hope for what's next, whether reincarnation, nirvana, or meeting your deity in the afterlife. But hope without truth is just a fantasy to help live this life and ease one's need to fill the void that is in the heart of every man. And the truth that does not bring enduring change is a lie. The act of regeneration is an act of God on behalf of man to sever the heart of stone and transplant into him the heart of flesh. And for someone to claim to be a Christian and show no evident change by nature of this great work of the Spirit is just deceiving themselves. Millions claim to be speaking the truth; to the causal hearer, it can cause confusion and aversion when seeing the gross sins of those who claim to preach the truth but not live it. The active work of the Spirit, who bears the primary inward witness, the dramatic change of one who was blind but now can see, the secondary witness of scripture, are all essential aspects of the true nature of the gospel. Anything less than that is just man's opinion and doctrines of the devil. The call of God to repent and believe the gospel and the role of the Holy Spirit are pivotal for that change to happen and to bear evidence. The evidence of the reality of the relationship that is established and not a religion that is followed.

HOLY SPIRIT

January 29

The Holy Spirit

And when he is come, he will reprove the world of sin, and of righteousness, and of judgment:–John 16:8

The Sovereignty of the Holy Spirit, the sufficiency of the Holy Scriptures, and the necessity for Holy Supplication are three pillars that one needs to pay careful attention to. Among these, we see the work of the blessed Spirit of God, who, as the third person of the Trinity, has the paramount role in all areas of our lives. He works in effectual calling; convicts of sin; accomplish that great work of salvation with repentance, faith, and regeneration; He indwells the believer; He bears witness that we are the children of God; He empowers the Christian for service as He did on the day of Pentecost; He makes alive the word of God and guides us into all truth; He reveals the God of the word to open blinded eyes and deaf ears to hear the voice of God; He instructs, reproves and rebukes; He does that magnificent life-work of conforming us to the image of the Lord Jesus Christ; He maketh intercession for us with groanings which cannot be uttered; He speaks of Christ and not of Himself; He directs the Church as it pleaseth the Father for fulfilling the desire of the Son; He is given the place of honor where the blasphemy of Him is the unpardonable sin; He enables us to hold fast unto the end in working out our new life in Christ with fear and trembling.

HOLY SPIRIT

January 30

Two Veils

But the natural man receiveth not the things of the Spirit of God: for they are foolishness unto him: neither can he know them, because they are spiritually discerned.–1 Corinthians 2:14

In the supernatural, when dealing with the heart of man, there are two veils that we are immediately confronted with. There is the veil of heaven where nothing penetrates unless it is anointed by the Holy Spirit, has the right motive, and is aligned with the will and mind of God. Then there is the veil of man where nothing penetrates unless it is carried by the Spirit's anointing, has heaven's message that reflects God's desire to the hearers, and has been bathed in prayer. The first purpose of preaching is to penetrate the veil of man by proclaiming the truth that is carried by the power of the Holy Spirit and quickened by Him into the hearts of the people, penetrating their conscience and bringing alive the word in their hearts; the second purpose is to move the people from where they are to where God is so they can experience God and get to know Him or quench Him to their peril. The first purpose of prayer is to stand before God and penetrate the veil of heaven by the Spirit and reach the ear of God, knowing the heart and mind of God; the second purpose is to see faith become sight in seeing the response of God no matter the outcome. Thus, preaching and prayer are about penetrating two veils. America is doomed to continue her downward trend unless we have a Divine intervention and God raises up such men of preaching and prayer and put to rout the forces of evil.

HOLY SPIRIT

January 31

Without the Holy Spirit

For our gospel came not unto you in word only, but also in power,
and in the Holy Ghost, and in much assurance
−1 Thessalonians 1:5

There are certain things in life that one cannot be without, and the lack thereof, though it may not be realized, when ignored it becomes the death knell for the person allowing its demise. Such is the case of neglecting the crucial role of the precious Spirit of God as revealed in the Old and New Testament continuing until today. Without the Spirit, we would have no word of God, no gifts or fruits of the Spirit, no intercessory prayer, no conviction of sin, no repentance, no regeneration, no effectual calling, no awakening of the conscience, no direction as the Comforter, no exploits against the powers of darkness, no assurance of sonship, no directing of truth through the Word, no Pentecost, no turning the world upside down, no boldness, no penetrating power into the hardness of man's heart, no empowerment, no prevenient grace, no guiding into all truth, no spreading of the gospel, no forgiveness of sin without His drawing, no revelation of the Person of Christ, to name a few. The precious Spirit of God as the third Person of the Triune Godhead, is the executor of God's purpose and the fulfiller of God's desire on earth, as it is in Heaven.

HOLY SPIRIT

February

February 1

The Gospel Witness

And the woman said to Elijah, Now by this I know that thou art a man of God, and that the word of the Lord in thy mouth is truth.–1 Kings 17:24

The truth of the gospel is not in the declaration of it but the result of it. The gospel is the power of God unto salvation. But it must be preached with the Spirit of Christ and not in the spirit of Adam. The Spirit of Christ brings life, the spirit of Adam brings death. A cult that adheres to some semblance of Christianity but teaches strange doctrines is simply God's word overlapped with man's word and preference given to man's interpretation of it, resulting in dead works. If you emphasize more on the will of man, then you will focus on the word only; but if you realize the need for the work of God more than the will of man, you will recognize the need for the Spirit of Christ. The demonstration of the gospel is not in word only, but also in power, and in the Holy Ghost, and in much assurance. A man who has submitted to the claims of the gospel and seen God's work in regenerating him will never be the same again. A lack of change on the part of someone who believes the gospel witness is given the admonition in the scriptures to examine himself whether he be in the faith. It is high time that we as a Church exhort those who show no evident fruits of regeneration to examine themselves as unbelievers rather than give them assurance and inoculate them to the truth by calling them Christians.

HOLY SPIRIT

February 2

The Implication of the Gospel

For whosoever shall call upon the name of the Lord shall be saved. –Romans 10:13

Christ has been the central theme from the Old Testament to the New Testament in scarlet red and revealed from Adam to the end of time. From pictures of the Trinity in Jehovah, Yeshua, and the Spirit of YHWH, we see that history is His story. Though the birth of Christ signifies His incarnation to come to earth, He always is and was one with the great I AM. Many played a role in His coming, but none was to receive honor as some have done with the deification of Mary, who was just as sinful as anyone born into this world and needed a savior. The gospel witness is universal, where for the Jews and Gentiles, there is only one way which is through Jesus Christ. And the prominence for the nation of Israel in the world scene is because of Christ, who split history into BC and AD and continues to show that He is the Alpha and the Omega. The significance of the Jewish people is because of the truth that God chose Abraham and made a covenant with him, and Christ was to come from his seed. And we love the Jewish people just as we love the Muslims, Hindus, Atheists, and others, desiring all men to be saved and to come unto the knowledge of the truth. The truth remains that there is none other name under heaven given among men, whereby we must be saved.

HOLY SCRIPTURES

February 3
One Book, One Message

For the prophecy came not in old time by the will of man: but holy men of God spake as they were moved by the Holy Ghost.
–2 Peter 1:21

The significance of an Omnipotent God who, through the act of preservation of the truth, gave us sixty-six books of Holy Writ. This should cause us to be sober when dealing with holy things when handling the word of the living God. The scriptures though separated by vast periods of time, had their beginnings in the mind of God. With the many scribes over the centuries, though varied by cultures, circumstances, and revelations, they all shared God's one message to mankind and the priceless truth of redemption by the Lord Jesus Christ. The truths of the Old Testament and the New Testament speak of the same God in three Persons. And each book is a portrayal of His revelation to man in irradiant beauty. Those who see the Bible as written by a human author and leave out the Holy Spirit, who was the source of that author, cannot see the eternal nature of God who created time and space but always has, is, and will be, world without end. It shows their low view of God to conform Him to their harsh interpretations. The importance of the scriptures is to be pondered upon and gleaned, as it were, jewels for a crown that shines forth its beauty and uniqueness in each given book. And to know that each has its place interwoven with purpose as a tapestry of this love letter from God about God Himself. The question is not which portions are true; the scriptures are truth, infallible and inerrant; the question instead is if one believes it or not in its entirety.

HOLY SCRIPTURES

February 4

The Word of God

For all those things hath mine hand made, and all those things have been, saith the Lord: but to this man will I look, even to him that is poor and of a contrite spirit, and trembleth at my word.
–Isaiah 66:2

The self-existence of God who revealed Himself to Abraham, Isaac, and Jacob through His voice and by His actions shows the reality of God taking the initiative to reveal Himself to man. God who always was, is, and will be, in a desire to give, though as a glass, darkly, to put into language who He is and what He is like and so forth speaks of His willingness to reach down to fallen man. By giving man the representation of the voice of God, the spoken word made into human language and preserved for all generations, and apt for all people groups for all eternity, causes us to realize the precious nature of the Holy Scriptures. Though the word of God is not an end of off itself, it is a means to learn of God, and to the worshipping heart, it is made where they hear the voice of God, which forms the basis to understand the nature of the word of God. It is not that God can be limited to His word; instead, God has given sacred portraits of who He is for us to know through the word. The Spirit in making alive the word makes it the Word who lives forever, and man is made to hear and touch and know the God of the word, which is its final intent. The word of the Lord that abides forever is not that written word of ink and paper, but rather the God behind that word who speaks and man trembles at His voice and in solemn worship bows down and fears Him.

HOLY SCRIPTURES

February 5
Social Media "Christianity"

Study to shew thyself approved unto God, a workman that needeth not to be ashamed, rightly dividing the word of truth.
−2 Timothy 2:15

The inundation of information and the overwhelming streams of people's opinions in the matters of Christ and His dealing with men seems to have taken a new form by good sincere, and thoughtful Christians who have gotten their theology from social media instead of the word of God. Christ's revelation of Himself reaches the highest peaks and the loftiest mountains in the scriptures that the Holy Spirit of God has breathed into human language. His illumination brings us to the expanse of unlimited space when we take the preserved text that has been done so in a word-for-word translation and let the Spirit Himself guide us into all truth. One of the tools for lowering down the proper and high view of God is when we don't heed the word and its preserved purity and try to go after the myriad of translations that cater to man's laziness in giving him thought representations of the original texts. Such shallow views show themselves in the new doctrines and theology given by priests and priestesses who are found in abundance representing their point of view and desiring the praise of men for their tearing down of the exalted view of God.

HOLY SCRIPTURES

February 6
God's Word vs Man's Response

There is none that understandeth, there is none that seeketh after God.—Romans 3:11

Over the centuries, man has justified using his selfish motives by misusing the word of God. In desiring truth in the inward parts, one must come to the conviction of what God has given compared to what man has portrayed or responded in lies. God created us in His image while man desires to tout evolution and be as gods; God gave life while the man tries to find where life came from or kills it in the womb; while it is appointed unto men once to die, man perverts truth by reincarnation; God holds man accountable while man denies the existence of God and final judgment; while Jesus is the only way to God, man denies the deity of God's Son; while God gave man true freedom while submitting to authority, man oppresses with slavery and bondage; God created us as Male and Female while man denies gender and embraces gender choices; while God calls marriage as one man and one woman, man fulfills his sinful predispositions by giving into homosexuality and other lifestyles; while God gave absolute truth in the word of God man questions it and "bends" it as he pleases; and the list goes on. No matter how much we blend or justify a position, God's truth will always remain, while man's attempt to fulfill his lusts will fall by the wayside.

HOLY SCRIPTURES

February 7

God, the Final Authority

For the Father judgeth no man, but hath committed all judgment unto the Son:—John 5:22

During times of unrest, there is always the blurring of the lines by those in leadership or in authority to control their domain where they have not been given the power to do so. In government, there is the overreach; in the home, there is the distortion of what makes up a home and marriage; in the church, there is the leaven of the false gospel and a low view of God. In all these three God-ordained institutions, one needs to realize that authority comes from God, and what has been given is "imparted" authority that is subject to the God who has given it. These three areas need to be looked at through the lens of scriptures, where when the particular entity rejects the role that God has provided for them, they have immediately lost the authority that God gave to them. In such cases, we do not despise them, speak evil of them, or resist using violence and rebellion. Rather we dissent using the truth, for we will be held accountable to the God who gave us the truth to see if we obeyed God rather than men. We go the path of God's truth where He stands alone and supreme in being the final Authority. Our alignment to the truth must always be based on being subject to God's law, and we submit to man's demand as long as it aligns with God's law.

HOLY SCRIPTURES

February 8

The Seriousness of the Gospel

With men it is impossible, but not with God: for with God all things are possible.—Mark 10:27b

There is a warning in the scriptures that states that "strait is the gate, and narrow is the way, which leadeth unto life, and few there be that find it." We have cheapened grace when we make it easy enough where no one realizes the seriousness of the gospel. Just come forward and pray a prayer and repeat after me so you can go to Heaven; where is the conviction of sin where the sinner cries out to God for mercy? Where is the plowing of the heart by the word and the Spirit? Where is the godly sorrow that worketh repentance to salvation? A gospel of accommodation that is attractive to the flesh is not the true gospel, a gospel that does not bring the change of a new creature whom the Spirit has regenerated is not the true gospel, a gospel that does not bring the condemnation of sin upon the sinner to cause him to turn from his sin is not the true gospel, a gospel where the Spirit does not bear witness by Himself that one has passed from death unto life is not the true gospel, a gospel that exalts the importance of man against the price God paid in crushing His Son for wretched unworthy man is not the true gospel. The true gospel is bad news because it shines light on the corruption of men.

HOLY SCRIPTURES

Amazing Grace
John Newton

Amazing grace (how sweet the sound)
    that saved a wretch like me!
I once was lost, but now am found,
    was blind, but now I see.

'Twas grace that taught my heart to fear,
    and grace my fears relieved;
how precious did that grace appear
    the hour I first believed!

Through many dangers, toils and snares
    I have already come:
'tis grace has brought me safe thus far,
    and grace will lead me home.

Public Domain

February 9

The Missing Link

In whom the god of this world hath blinded the minds of them which believe not, lest the light of the glorious gospel of Christ, who is the image of God, should shine unto them.
–2 Corinthians 4:4

In his fallen nature, man has created a myriad of delusions to satisfy the inner longing of the void that he finds present in his bosom. Since the garden when Adam and Eve sewed fig leaves to cover their nakedness, man has been in a headlong race to fill that void with religion, relationships, gender choices, pleasure, careers, technology, evolution, pets, fantasy, entertainment, and whatever else that comes in his way. Sadly, it has made man more miserable where; though some of these may have filled his void to an extent or at least deafened its voice, he is still left wondering for his purpose on planet Earth. Thus, he lives blinded to the correct solution until he faces death, and the reality of what life is all about hits him, in most cases when it is too late. God, the benevolent Creator, desires that all may know Him, for we were created for Himself, and nothing other than the restoration of that relationship will ever satisfy the longing of one's heart if one is willing to be honest enough to find out. This is the reconciliation of the gospel, of God reaching down to man, for man can never be complete apart from union with the living God through Jesus Christ.

MAN

February 10

The Quantum Breakthrough

Where wast thou when I laid the foundations of the earth? declare, if thou hast understanding. —Job 38:4

We are continually reminded of how little we know of things around us with the fascinating discoveries that bring us to new frontiers. God who created time and space also created the laws of quantum entanglement where one particle mirrors another in behavior though disjointed from each other. With the limited information we have, man feels enlightened that he has come across something so radical that it seems to have jumped out of a science fiction story and contemplates building theories around it. He seems to share the excitement similar to when mankind found the property of steam to produce kinetic energy and run massive locomotives of iron by the 19th century and ushering in the "modern age". It was always there, but it was just a discovery. But this aligns perfectly with an Omnipotent God who created these and many other undiscovered awe-inspiring marvels of Creation that man is yet to uncover. We humbly bow down in worship to our God who gave man the understanding to discover His Creation in such mind-bending ways that declares His glory, for Christ is before all things, and by Him, all things consist.

MAN

February 11

Defilement by Association

Wherefore come out from among them, and be ye separate
−2 Corinthians 6:17a

How we use sacred words speaks a lot about our view of God. The use of the word "holy" in its proper implication is exclusive to be attributed in similarities to the nature of God. Using it in sentiments such as holy "roller", the salvation of dogs to go to Heaven, using things that are polluted like Hollywood and trying to convey scriptural truths, swallowing goldfishes to tout the gospel; cute or well-intended as it may be, is still defiling the high view of God and shows the casting of pearls before the swine and the defilement of holy things. The lost have no sense of the magnitude of the word holy, and they used it in profanity and suggestive comments; why should the so-called Christian church allow such degraded representation of the word? Having such a low view of God causes one to walk into the sanctuary, not considering the seriousness and implication of worshiping a thrice Holy God. The seraphims and elders in Heaven fall down in worship and adoration and cry out Holy, holy, holy, whereas Christians on earth with unclean hands and minds, though claim to be worshiping the same God, cry out holy "cow", sanctified cats, and regenerated dogs; the creature worshiped and served more than the Creator.

MAN

February 12

Opportunities and Outcome

The desire of the slothful killeth him; for his hands refuse to labour.—Proverbs 21:25

Fallen man has always found ways to express his sinful desires, and through the centuries, has named it with many names as a facade for the actual intent. The chief end of man is to fear God and keep His commandments, for God is not a respecter of persons. And those who have oppressed another "using" the word of God have done it to their peril for satisfying their greed and lust to rule over men unjustly. To teach equal outcome by force or equity is not Biblical, for an outcome is based on consequences for what was done with the provided opportunity. For the slothful man who buried his talent instead of working according to the rules of labor and reward, to reward with equity would unjustly remove him from the consequences for his actions. Instead, it would foster the victim mentality for acquiring another man's reward to feed their sin of laziness. There is an absolute standard, and it is God and His word that He has given; that in all things He might have the preeminence, for we are His handiwork who are held accountable for what we will do with that which has been given. Social justice, which is loosely tied with man's perception of oppression, is not Biblical justice, for it is antithetical to the Law of God and man's accountability to obey it. And in the realm of the eternal, there is only one way to God, and it is through His Son, the Lord Jesus Christ.

MAN

February 13

Diversity and Inclusion

And this is the condemnation, that light is come into the world, and men loved darkness rather than light, because their deeds were evil. –John 3:19

In a day where diversity and inclusion are the mantras of our society, man has desired to create for himself a world where he is excluded from his responsibility to his Creator God. In the area of diversity as an example, when choosing to change his gender, man assumes that he knows what is good and that no one can judge his actions or choices; in wanting to be inclusive, man desires that no matter how contradictory his lifestyle may be to the truth he is to be included without question at the expense of suppressing the voices of truth. Though it may sound good considering man's desire to be friendly with fellowmen, God holds exclusivity to absolute truths of immense and eternal consequences. There is one true God Jesus Christ, who is part of the Godhead; one true way of salvation, through the blood of the Lamb; it is appointed unto men once to die, but after this the judgement; one biological gender for life, male or female; one instituted marriage covenant, between one man and one woman and so forth. Though God never discriminates based on a person's color, gender, traits, or status and is not willing that any should perish, but that all should come to repentance, God does govern man according to the principles of His word and desires exclusive obedience to His laws given for the good of man.

MAN

February 14

Nothing New Under the Sun

Let us hear the conclusion of the whole matter: Fear God, and keep his commandments: for this is the whole duty of man.
–Ecclesiastes 12:13

Solomon, in his day, uttered with the wisdom given by God that there was no new thing under the sun. Today with all the "enlightenment" and technological advantages, fallen man is still the same as he was when he walked on the face of the earth six thousand years ago. Nothing has changed, and sin has not changed regarding how it manifests itself. In America, we call it racism; in India, they call it the Hindu caste system; in the communist regime, there is the oppressor and the oppressed. Man killing man and exploiting the weakness of another, whether in slavery, cannibalism, human trafficking, wars, jihads, or so on, have followed us thousands of years since the fall of man. While man is struggling to comprehend and feels like he has finally found the answer in law, politics, education, protests, or religion, every generation finds out that the problem remains. We may try to fix the fruits that manifest themselves, but the root remains, and only Jesus Christ who came to destroy the heart of the problem "sin" can give this true freedom, to be freed from sin and finally break the vicious cycle, one person at a time.

MAN

February 15

Gender Wars

So God created man in his own image, in the image of God created he him; male and female created he them.
—Genesis 1:27

In Creation, we see the uniqueness of God's signature in every individual who is stamped with the image of God. A God who desired good for all humankind and wanting to shield them from harsh consequences created boundaries that defined gender, role, intrinsic desires, and so on. God holds exclusive rights to His creatures by designing the biological classification of males or females for their lifespan through Creation. As the rightful owner of the Universe, He holds us accountable to Him whether we like to accept it or not, and in death, everything is made plain in finality when we meet God, our Creator. In the fall, because of man's sin, this desire of God became corrupted where sin gave into rebellion. Since then, humankind has been trying to find satisfaction apart from God in defining gender and classifying it with foundational shifts such as LGBTQ+ and so on. Though there may be a temporal satisfaction that one may feel to think they are not the biological gender that their Creator endowed with them, deep within, there is a void that only God can fill. Nothing or no one can satisfy that God-shaped vacuum in the heart of every individual and be able to fulfill the purpose they were created for.

MAN

February 16
Wealth Distribution?

For even when we were with you, this we commanded you, that if any would not work, neither should he eat. –2 Thessalonians 3:10

The law of labor and reward is not based on how much one makes over another; it is the principle of getting rewarded for what you do and are promised. At the core of the socialistic belief that everyone must share their wealth irrespective of the labor or the intensity of the craft it demands is the hidden root of covetousness and self. Thus, God gives us an accurate diagnosis for the underlying cause. We see similar patterns in other areas as well. In feminism, we see self and pride; in the welfare state, we see entitlement and laziness; in the redefining of marriage, we see self and rebellion towards the law of God and nature; in racism, we see self and pride over fellowman, in the destruction of another at the cost of self-exaltation we see self and jealousy, and so forth. The common denominator in all of mankind is sin, and the impetus is self. In the eyes of God, all are created equal and belong to one race from our first parents Adam and Eve, and subject to the reality of whatsoever a man soweth, that shall he also reap. In its finality, Jesus did not come to deal with surface issues or form a religion. He came to deal with the root issue of sin that separates us from God and to restore that relationship, and for us to realize that there is no other name given under heaven that men might be saved.

MAN

February 17

Cancel Culture

My son, if sinners entice thee, consent thou not. –Proverbs 1:10

When one expresses their beliefs, which causes neither bodily harm nor threat of lives but just voicing their conviction could be labeled as microaggression based on the amoral climate of our day. It is not considered a possibility of truth but drowned out in the rowdy noise of "intolerance" at the expense of allowing only one view. Thus, the individual can be quickly brought to public shaming and thrust out from everything that the law-abiding citizen continues to uphold. As an example, someone proclaiming the truth of God's word in love, while desiring the best for the other, and preaching about the sin of homosexuality in a Church outside of their work context can be considered as homophobic and producer of hate speech and cause their employer, who has not been part of this proclamation, to terminate the employee even though they were in excellent standing in their job. The more significant proposition remains, for Christians to discern the hidden forces of darkness that constantly seek to undermine God's truth, that these hidden forces will be manifested more and more openly in a society that moves further and further away from God.

MAN

February 18

Sickness and Fear

And as it is appointed unto men once to die, but after this the judgment:–Hebrews 9:27

Death is a great motivator, and in fear of death, people are made willing to give away freedoms that they fought and died for in the place of security. But safety comes from God, and every man is subject to God's truth in that grand declaration of "it is appointed unto men once to die, but after this the judgment." This has been true since Creation for over six thousand years. Yet, in a moment of fear and in the vain desire to prolong one's life, men give in to whatever comes their way and place their faith in the media or government, which sinful men run. While being subject to the powers that God has put over us, every follower of Christ needs to ask the question of whether the law of man contradicts the law of God, for God's law always supersedes the law of man. And when in contradiction, we ought to obey God rather than men. Despite being cautious, if we die young because of sickness, our desire to be with Christ has been fulfilled in His timing; if we die a natural death because of old age, then our desire to be with Christ has been fulfilled in His timing. In either case, being prepared for death is only possible through Jesus Christ. And the call of God is to repent and believe the gospel, for, without that remedy, there is no hope whether we die of sickness or we die in our sleep.

MAN

February 19

Naming and Shaming

He that sitteth in the heavens shall laugh: the Lord shall have them in derision.—Psalm 2:4

The trend of bullying someone who has a different viewpoint seems to be prevalent today. But in reality, it is the rejection of light by darkness. Those who reject the false narrative of those who promote homosexuality as a healthy lifestyle or as "normal" are called homophobic. Though there is nothing phobic about calling truth as truth, any rejection of error is immediately labeled as right-winged or extremist and intolerant. We see such name-calling in many areas such as religion, politics, and so forth. The absolute truth of the scriptures is not to be believed because they can be true, but they are believed because it is the truth and exclusive in its message that there is but one true God and knowing Him is only possible through Jesus Christ. While shaming someone because of their beliefs to suppress their viewpoint can be abused by anyone when it comes to absolute truth, truth always remains, and God always has the last word.

MAN

February 20

Chasing Careers, Losing Homes

And if it seem evil unto you to serve the Lord, choose you this day whom ye will serve; whether the gods which your fathers served that were on the other side of the flood, or the gods of the Amorites, in whose land ye dwell: but as for me and my house, we will serve the Lord. –Joshua 24:15

The modern family has no time for stillness, meditation, and discovering the deep things of God. There is entertainment, sports, and trivial joys that rob us of eternal rewards, yet the chaos is amplified by the roles that have been misplaced and the self-life that has been put on the pedestal of popularity and pride. Man is to be the leader of the home, to provide, show Christ-like love in the house and fulfill his responsibility as he submits to his Master, a servant-leader putting the preferences of his family before his own. The wife is to submit to the direction of God upon her life and complete her husband in love and enjoying companionship in things that have meaning and purpose for life, with the children in obedience to their parents. But such is the deception of sin where careers have become the driving force, and the mantra of self-ability to make money and reject what God desires to help nurture their children has tragic consequences. In the end, the age-old wisdom of God will find itself calling out to the one who finds herself robbed of the very thing that she longed for when money and power did not afford what she thought she could have but finds herself left empty. At the same time, the husband languishes in his failure to be the father he ought to have been to his prodigal children, while the vicious cycle continues.

MAN

February 21

The Hardening of the Heart

He, that being often reproved hardeneth his neck, shall suddenly be destroyed, and that without remedy. –Proverbs 29:1

What does God have to do to harden one's heart? Nothing. Man is bent towards sin, and the heart, in its fallen nature, is in a perpetual state of hardening. It is the grace of God that softens it as oil is fed into a lamp for the sustenance of the burning wick. Man, who is dead in trespasses and sins, is shielded before being brought to the savior by the mercy of God, which preserves the soul lest he should plunge into Hell. The natural man who despises the grace of God will self-destruct just as surely as Pharaoh, who said, "Who is the Lord, that I should obey his voice to let Israel go?" The heavens declare the glory of God, and men are consistently given seeds of grace where some find their way into the good ground for a harvest. It is by grace through faith that we are saved, and we tremble at the thought of a man who scorns the grace of God, who is his only hope, to the point where he is suddenly destroyed and that without remedy.

MAN

February 22

The Quest for the Origin of Life

For by him were all things created, that are in heaven, and that are in earth, visible and invisible, whether they be thrones, or dominions, or principalities, or powers: all things were created by him, and for him:–Colossians 1:16

The reality of the natural man suppressing the truth in unrighteousness is seen beyond doubt when men spend billions of dollars in perfecting a mission that can have zero margins for error and call it a marvel of engineering with precision in space, size, weight, and maneuverability for adaptation in a foreign terrain like Mars and yet turns around and looks at the most incredible display of engineering in the human body with its nervous system, self-healing defense systems, emotions, hormones, self-awareness, structure, brain, and the complexity of everything it supports, and to look at it all and say that it happened by blind, purposeless and random chance of evolution. And yet, in spending billions, man is attempting to find where he came from and other life forms, in his desperation to find an alternative to the origin of life other than God, while even traveling millions of miles away trying to find it. Instead, he could just go to a bookstore and spend a few dollars and get a Bible given by the Creator of life and the truthful witness, which tells him where he came from, where he is going, and his purpose for life on earth is.

MAN

February 23

Religion, Cults, and Identity

And they made their lives bitter with hard bondage, in morter, and in brick, and in all manner of service in the field: all their service, wherein they made them serve, was with rigour.
–Exodus 1:14

In the enslavement of the human soul, there are many ways that men are subject to fellowmen in bondage. And such is the tragedy of those who find themselves unable to reason for themselves but are forced into the mold of religion or a cult that has the oppressive behavior of control and are led to believe their identity as "what they are" in that system. Since the dawn of Creation, man has always tried to find ways and means to bring other men into subjection of the mind by various philosophies and theories. But such is the wickedness of the human heart that desires to be like the most High, playing out the original promise of Satan in the garden. But Christ came to set men free to worship their Creator in spirit and in truth, and not through religion, cult, or any other forms of man. And who we are in Christ, our Creator, defines who we were meant to be when God created us around six thousand years ago. In redemption, the spirit of man is set free to serve his Maker and enjoys the communion with God void of oppression, force, fear, or manipulation, but out of love for our Kinsman. Where there will be acts of charity "out" of that love, it will never be "for" attaining love which has been freely shed abroad in their hearts by grace through faith.

MAN

February 24

Social Justice and Absolute Truth

Wherefore, as by one man sin entered into the world, and death by sin; and so death passed upon all men, for that all have sinned:–Romans 5:12

In a world where social justice is seen as a motivator for committing crimes against individuals and other entities, the definition of "good" is seen as subject to one's private interpretation. In truth, only God is perfect and the definer of good, truth, love, morality, sexuality, etc., because He is the One who created us in perfection. Man chose to rebel against God and found out that the "good" he defined and saw around him are seriously flawed. God deals with absolutes while the fallen man tries to blur it with relativism. Thus, the moral construct of what defines a marriage, gender, equality, social justice is all blurred into what feels good and right in the eyes of fallen man. There is an absolute good, truth, and right, and it is God. The problems in this world do not come from color, inequality, wars, or poverty, but rather it is because of sin, man's sin. To blame God for the sin of man and its consequences is the epitome of foolishness. In its finality, all lives matter to God, and no one is above the law of God, for God established it.

MAN

February 25

The Answer to Questions

For who hath known the mind of the Lord? or who hath been his counsellor?–Romans 11:34

In an effort to solve truths that stun his intellect and reduce it to manageable terms, man is forced to ask questions to negate what he sees as unreconcilable. Questions such as the Triune nature of God, God having a Son, the death of God who cannot die, the seeming paradox of the Omnipotence of God and the presence of evil in this world, and so forth. Yet, in so doing to the response of the finite man to comprehend the infinite nature and wisdom of God, the man settles for less and solidifies what he can concur by explainable terms and ends up with a god of his own making. And man misses out on the richness of God and the wisdom of God that is eternal and past finding out, which can only be grasped in a minuscule way by those whom the Spirit of God has regenerated. Thus, the regenerated man is brought, as it were, into a new dimension of spiritual awareness that he was blind to and experienced the God of Creation and his redemption. Such revelation brings man to the edge of understanding where he is content to fall down in adoration and worship the God invisible, immortal and the only wise God, going forth in the satisfactory realization of what it means to be known of God and enjoy the privileges of sonship.

MAN

February 26

"Freedom" for All?

For, brethren, ye have been called unto liberty; only use not liberty for an occasion to the flesh, but by love serve one another.
–Galatians 5:13

In the name of freedom, there seems to be an insane amount of confusion over a person's rights based on what they choose to do instead of what is to be protected. The early founders of our Nation realized that our rights come from God, and what we choose to do with what He has given to us was considered with reverence, even in relating to the time when God brought them from England and made them prosperous in the founding of America. Regarding this, they said "that all men are created equal, that they are endowed by their Creator with certain unalienable Rights" in their Declaration of Independence. And our Creator has given us off Himself the right to life, to live to the fullest as what He has created us as, whether we were born as male or female. Sin has a way of perverting reality and giving cause for seeking after an error in the name of "freedom" for choices people make that are condemned by our Creator. And to placate someone who has chosen their way and has the loudest voice, be it homosexuality, transgender, or any other, and allow for the perversion of rights given by God is not true freedom. Still, instead, it will bring bondage and the judgment of God upon our beloved land. We are all held accountable to God, as it is appointed unto men once to die, but after this the judgment.

MAN

February 27

Masculinity and Femininity

Know ye not that the unrighteous shall not inherit the kingdom of God? Be not deceived: neither fornicators, nor idolaters, nor adulterers, nor effeminate, nor abusers of themselves with mankind, Nor thieves, nor covetous, nor drunkards, nor revilers, nor extortioners, shall inherit the kingdom of God.–1 Corinthians 6:9,10

There always has and always will be the distinction of sexes that God has ordained. No matter how much people decide to blend the lines with the transgender movement, God has affirmed in the Old and New Testament that He has created us as male and female. The uniqueness of gender is not a curse but a blessing to bring forth the beauty of God in Creation and fulfill one's purpose in life. Men are called to be the providers of the Home while women are to be the keeper of the Home, and children are to obey their parents in the Lord, while parents are not to provoke their children to wrath but rather bring them up in the nurture and admonition of the Lord. Such order of the Home is not meant for forcing one's authority over another but rather a love relationship to complete each other and thus portray the order and unity of the Godhead. Such distinction needs to be a conviction for those who find themselves in a society that desires to make men feminine more and more and women masculine and cause confusion. And there is one being who brought chaos from the order when he tempted Eve to partake of the tree of the knowledge of good and evil, plunged humanity into sin, and likewise tempts this generation to reject God.

MAN

February 28

Abortion

My substance was not hid from thee, when I was made in secret, and curiously wrought in the lowest parts of the earth.
—Psalm 139:15

Dealing with the life of another that is protected in the womb is about ownership. If we realized that God, who created us, has the original claim of ownership on us, it changes our whole perspective of what abortion is dealing with. If I am not my own, but I am bought with a price, then every gift given by God is precious. And the life that forms in the womb of a mother is precious in God's sight and considered as a unique human being created in the image of God. If that is the foundational truth of life, then abortion becomes the extinguishing of life of that individual no matter where they find themselves in, inside the womb or outside the womb. The premise of abortion that it is convenient for the mother or because the child has perceived disabilities as the cause of having one are all secondary. The primary foundation is God and His rightful claim on us. The miracle of life in conception, gestation, and birth speaks loudly to a Creator, God, and the need for us to consider the sacredness of intimacy to be within the bounds of marriage and as a privilege, and not as a right to one's exploration of chemical response; and walk in gratitude toward our benevolent Creator.

MAN

February 29

Education and Self-Reformation

O Timothy, keep that which is committed to thy trust, avoiding profane and vain babblings, and oppositions of science falsely so called:–1 Timothy 6:20

A fallen man tries to cover himself with many "layers" of self-ability when trying to better himself. Adam chose fig leaves in a desperate effort to hide his rebellion. In denying the need of the inner man to be reconciled with His Maker and follow the path of Adam, the depraved man tries to satisfy this yearning with religion, good works, charity, sexual exploration, and spiritual experiences. One of the other key areas is to try to convince himself that education, as good as that can be for helping acquire actual knowledge, can eradicate the fruits of sin he faces. In taking someone who lives out his baser desires by cannibalism, man thinks that by covering him with a layer of education, one can be civilized and produce a moral society. But without dealing with the root problem of sin, education becomes another layer of fig leaf that could not curtail the mass wickedness of educated men, even Stalin, Lenin, or Hitler. Though desirous in attempting to make his world a better place for the benefit of his flesh, man inevitably finds out the darkness lurking within his bosom that comes out when given the right impulse and force. While neither education nor self-reformation can remove the depravity of man, God came in human flesh to restore that broken relationship with our Maker through Jesus Christ.

MAN

March

March 1

All we need is "Love"?

[Charity or Love] Rejoiceth not in iniquity, but rejoiceth in the truth;–1 Corinthians 13:6

To the movement today that states that all we need is "love" to combat racism, social justice, and so on, the question that needs to be asked is whose definition of "love" do we base it on? One person may feel like love is not bound by moral laws, and thus he can defile a child and commit crimes against that individual in the name of "love". We had the whole "free love" movement in the 60s, and what did that produce? Venereal diseases, abortions, and the drug culture, of which we are still reaping the consequences today. When we come to a question and answer it without a standard, man is left to fend for himself and, by his definition, come up with a perspective without a guiding compass. God, who is the Creator and the only absolute standard of love, a love that was unveiled at the cross, gave us an example of love that is selfless and one that rejoiceth not in iniquity. And iniquity is sin as God has defined it and not as man classifies it. Our loving God gave us His truths in the scriptures for all to know the perfection against which we will be judged, for we are appointed once to die and after that to face God who claims exclusivity as the only way, the only truth, and the only giver of eternal life.

SIN

March 2

Sin's Nature to Multiply

But every man is tempted, when he is drawn away of his own lust, and enticed. Then when lust hath conceived, it bringeth forth sin: and sin, when it is finished, bringeth forth death.—James 1:14,15

In the realm of the flesh, where the wickedness of man's heart is unfathomable, one is reminded of the grave danger when sin is left unchecked where it has an inherent tendency to multiply. Where one may give into pride, it leads to arrogance, anger, disobedience, rebellion, and so forth. What God has condemned man desires to exalt, in keeping with the nature of a heart that is lifted with pride and trying to fulfill the original deception of "ye shall be as gods." Where one sin leads to another in the progressive hardening of the heart, the finality finds itself in death and facing the unbridled wrath of Almighty God. But where sin abounded grace much more did abound, for the penitent sinner to fall on the mercy of God, one who has been revealed the holiness of God and the sinfulness of sin, for such a one, grace is ever-present to plunge him under the blood of Jesus and bring the good grace of forgiveness and cleansing, to go in freedom and sin no more. Throughout the seasons of the times, enlightenment, technology, and so forth, the undercurrent of sin has not changed but manifests itself in many forms, where one may begin with lust but end with murder. Sin exerts its influence in darkened hearts, destroying lives, homes, and nations.

SIN

March 3

Tolerance and Truth

Wherewithal shall a young man cleanse his way? by taking heed thereto according to thy word.—Psalm 119:9

A society that has a skewed view of truth will eventually end up in bondage. In the name of inclusion and promoting a sinful lifestyle, anyone who challenges the movement on the foundation of truth is seen as intolerant. It is the most sensible thing to tell someone who is on the path to destruction to turn from their ways so they can be safe. To warn someone who is driving onto oncoming traffic is not about being intolerant or discriminating against them based on their behavior; it is telling the truth in light of the law that they are breaking, which is detrimental to them and dangerous for others. And there is a law of God that we are all subject to, which supersedes the law of man, which has been given to us in the scriptures by our Creator, to show us the way of right and wrong. Denying facts does not negate the danger, and denying truth does not remove the consequences. Those who preach tolerance should take solemn account into the standard by which they are holding that scale. The most intolerant person is the one who believes in being tolerant as long as the other agrees to follow as he does at the expense of the truth of God; God, who is the only true standard of truth.

SIN

March 4

The Trap of Socialism

It is better to trust in the Lord than to put confidence in man. It is better to trust in the Lord than to put confidence in princes.
–Psalm 118:8,9

Removing our dependence upon God is the fundamental principle of Socialism which leads to Communism. God, who as our benevolent Creator gave man all things richly to enjoy in the realm of good and right. When a man desires control over other men, having an outlet of what feels good without thinking about the long-term ramification of where that path leads can have the outcome similar to feeding the man but never teaching him how to fish. Thus, the man stays bound by his own perceived inability, a false sense of freedom and equality, in exchange for security and food. The law of God is about labor and reward, and what we sow is what we will reap. In a society of hidden motives, the constant desire of government is to bind its people to a system that defines its laws apart from God, and giving in to this construct brings with it the bondage of slavery. The God who raised up the slave Joseph from prison to become the second-in-command ruler of a nation is well able to lift up anyone irrespective of their social standing, color, race, or background. Dependence upon government is a crucial requirement for establishing the one-world government that will come to pass as prophesied, and we are seeing it being played out before our very eyes.

SIN

March 5

Born "this" Way?

And he [Jesus] answered and said unto them, Have ye not read, that he which made them at the beginning made them male and female,–Matthew 19:4

Since the beginning of time for over six thousand years, it has been and always will be as the predetermined counsel of God to be fruitful and multiply by procreation. At birth, God gave the laws of nature to have the only two genders of male and female for life. The times of unnatural affection towards another of the same sex or the desire to change one's biological gender is not justifiable as being born "incorrectly" in the gender given by God at birth; instead, it is because of the effects of sin that lieth in every person born on earth. There is no valid reason for anyone to change gender. Instead, it shows the greater need to seek God, change the feeling, and be aligned with Creation and the Creator. Yet fallen man is bound by his sin and blinded by the god of this world to desire that which pertaineth to their own destruction. God in His mercy has made the way of escape through Jesus Christ to not only restore that broken love-relationship with Him but also to be able to have the accurate view of life, death, and the endowment of God's purpose in their biological sex. Changing this construct would be the epitome of foolishness because it presumes that we know better than an all-knowing, infinite God.

SIN

March 6

Judgement Upon Sin

But God said unto him, Thou fool, this night thy soul shall be required of thee: then whose shall those things be, which thou hast provided?–Luke 12:20

The history of the human race is about the reality of God's interaction with His Creation. From the first judgment upon Adam to the subsequent judgments upon sin in history and culminating in the book of Revelation, sin will be judged and must be paid for before a thrice Holy God who requires the wages for sin. We saw the same judgment in the Old Testament against the pollution of the land and were destroyed in mercy, lest sin in its fullness goes to the point of no return and destroy mankind. Joshua, in his conquest, was the arm of judgment executing the wrath of God upon sin. The same judgment was seen upon Israel when they sinned against God, and in Ananias and Sapphira when they sinned against the Holy Ghost and were struck dead in the early church, all the way to the Pastors who were warned in the book of Revelation. We serve the same God of the Bible who has not changed before the beginning of time or now in the act of time and after in the demise of time into eternity. The judgment of sin fell upon Christ on Calvary on our behalf, and for those regenerated by the Spirit of God, this transaction is made complete where they are set free from the bondage of sin to serve the Savior. No nation, wealthy or poor, can get away with sin in this life but will answer for them either now or in the judgment that is to come.

SIN

March 7

Modesty and Character

Lust not after her beauty in thine heart; neither let her take thee with her eyelids. –Proverbs 6:25

By giving in to the temptation of desiring ease and wanting results at the cost of nothing, man is lured to seek the path of least resistance to attain his perceived end. Be it that the goal may be reached by crook and deception. In one's scheme to attract the other, the end goal of wanting attention, to have absolute control over another, we see the trend of hiding their true character and revealing their body by a woman to attract the forbidden desires of sensuality when dealing with the opposite sex. With mini-skirts and bikinis to appease the lusts of men, women have taken their lessons from the world and wore garments of fashion and pomp, which are nothing more than trinkets of cheap attraction for sacrificing purity at the altar of pleasure. The desire of God to attract attention to the face, displaying beauty in character and holiness, is exchanged for faster results by bringing attention to the body and that which pleases the flesh. While it may suffice for the now, the externals will wither away with age and what is left, which is of the true worth of character, is what that will remain.

SIN

March 8

A Real Enemy

Woe unto them that call evil good, and good evil; that put darkness for light, and light for darkness; that put bitter for sweet, and sweet for bitter!–Isaiah 5:20

The romanticization of evil through Hollywood and the acceptance of events such as Halloween have conditioned us to see evil as something to play with. The subtlety of the enemy is not in his outcome but his strategy. That fallen angel of evil, Satan, and his demons have the singular desire of destroying the soul of man because we are made in the image of God. Anything that God loves, Satan hates, and anything that God desires to do, Satan counterfeits. Even during seasons of revival, there is always the supernatural moving of God. Still, at the same time, there are the supernatural workings of Satan to bring dishonor to the name of Christ with excesses and displays of the flesh. We are to try the spirits, whether they are of God, and anyone who is seriously considering the matter of an encounter with the eternal God better be prepared to seek God for discernment and reject the advances of the enemy to cause the righteous to stumble. The more one sets their heart to seek God, the more the enemy will attack personally and collectively to thwart the believer's progress. But our God can keep us faithful in this journey of faith as we stay near to Him and walk in His way one day at a time.

SIN

March 9

Irrevocable Damage

Then shall they call upon me, but I will not answer; they shall seek me early, but they shall not find me:–Proverbs 1:28

In the realm of maturity, one is confronted with the real condition of a child as a minor who cannot make decisions that take into account the realities of the world and how it affects them. Such is the nature of a little child who, at a young age, may feel like there is a better world out there, and many who run away from their homes based on their immature judgment are exploited and abused for the pleasure of another. Thus, they are faced with the consequences of their lack of discernment and mistake, and in many cases, too late. The parent's admonition to see such patterns and help their children navigate through life and restrain them from such mistakes would be heralded as proper, and the responsible thing to do, and a lack thereof, is seen as not being in the interest of the child but as bad parenting. Such is the case of a child's propensity who has contrary tendencies of their sexes as part of growing up, which eventually solidifies to what they were created as, male or female. In today's parenting, the utter horror of a parent giving in to such immaturities of their child and putting them through life-altering surgeries and gender therapy which are irreversible and detrimental to the child, speaks of the desire of the enemy of the soul to get them at an early age, to steal, kill and destroy.

SIN

March 10

Sinful Lifestyle and Influences

Woe unto them that are wise in their own eyes, and prudent in their own sight!–Isaiah 5:21

Rejecting influences of those practicing sin as their "normal" way of life is not about being intolerant; instead, it is the commonsense way to avoid following the same path since it tends to influence us to do the same and reap the fruit that sin produces. Above all, God has warned us regarding evil communications that corrupt good manners and God has given us His absolute truth. Though we don't discriminate against the person created in God's image, we condemn the sinful practice and their voice of calling evil good, whether as an individual or in media, politics, big tech, etc. Be it racism, LGBTQ+, pornography, pride, prostitution, abortion, or anything that is condemned in the word of God, for therein is the means where our loving Creator has given to us what is truth and right. With mercy and truth and in love, these crucial topics are seen through the eyes of one who has been redeemed by the blood of the Lamb to be set free from sin as God sees it and not how man has chosen to re-define it.

SIN

March 11

Drawn unto Death

Thou lovest evil more than good; and lying rather than to speak righteousness. Selah. –Psalm 52:3

With the reality of man's inability to control certain things, he comes up with manageable ways to reconcile them so he can try to reduce the need to deal with them. Death means separation, and man has various ways to represent it while living out the original sin that Adam committed. We see it in the display of skull art to invoke a false sense of security of being tough or "defying" death, Halloween with its symbols of death and evil, movies on horror with sadistic twists that validate the depravity of man, the gothic culture of black with body piercings to inflict pain, tattoos that symbolize the darkness of man, the coming-out of man's lust in the storyline of a movie, hallucinogenic drugs to induce a feeling of temporal euphoria and so on. In all this, man is bent on desiring to hide from the unavoidable eventuality that looks at him, death. It is a suicidal way to help alleviate the finality of death and the reality of being flung into a Christless eternity forever. God is light, and in Him is no darkness at all, and only He can bring us to that blazing light of original intent for the creation of man, to glorify God and to enjoy Him forever.

SIN

March 12

A Stark Reminder

That they all might be damned who believed not the truth, but had pleasure in unrighteousness. – 2 Thessalonians 2:12

In our generation, where sin is being downplayed, the need for adjustment of "truth" to fit into our generation is seen in the open, where sins done in secret are now done openly. It could be a scantily clad woman in billboards, in public, or at the magazine rack in a grocery store, or a Hollywood movie that is filled with thrills of the flesh desensitizing the conscience. Sin becomes acceptable and considered the norm where doctrines of the victorious Christian life are attacked to make way for sin to become accepted in the life of a believer or the Church. But when we look at the scriptures, they paint a very different picture. The judgment of God by the slaughter of thousands including women and children by the hand of Joshua, the killing of millions in the day of Noah when God judged sin, the destruction of Sodom by brimstone and fire, the literal place called Hell where those without Christ are plunged daily, the wrath of God that is poured out in the lake of fire that burns forever and ever, are but a small representation of the wrath of God upon sin. And the most remarkable display of judgment was seen upon His own dear Son, taking the sins of the world to pay the price of sin. And those who reject Him will take that judgment of God that was poured upon Christ, on our behalf, upon themselves for all of eternity, unable to satisfy its payment.

SIN

March 13

Compassion and Wrath

Justice and judgment are the habitation of thy throne: mercy and truth shall go before thy face. – Psalm 89:14

There are times where we come across opposites when dealing with the subject of God. At such times, we need to take a step back and realize that though they may seem contradictory in the eyes of man, they are not only in agreement but in tandem with the workings of God. The truth of the scriptures in dealing with the terror of the Lord, the wrath of God, the judgment upon sin, the finality of unrepentant mankind in Hell, and the lake of fire, are all areas that one might desire to overlook or dismiss as incompatible when they see the realities of the goodness of God, the love of God, the grace of God, the long-suffering, and the forgiveness of God. But in dealing with the eternal soul of man, one must be confronted with the truth that as we reach or desire to reach man's heart with love, of those who are blinded by the god of this world and are in enmity with their Maker, we are moved to reach out in compassion towards them. At the same time, we see the reality of the terror of the Lord and the fruit of those who reject this good and benevolent God to their peril and rightly reap what they truly deserve. Thus, compassion and terror both play a role in accurately seeing both ends of the gospel when reaching the heart of man.

THE GOSPEL

March 14

Purpose Driven Development

All things were made by him; and without him was not any thing made that was made.–John 1:3

In a desperate attempt to convince that life can come from non-living things, man has, in his darkened imagination, come up with spontaneous generation, which is supposed to have happened once "billions of years ago" and spawned what we see today. But yet there is a fundamental fact that all of evolution is missing; everything we see has a purpose; the question bears asking of how you start with something when not knowing what to build for since you have never seen it or know about what it needs to become in a future condition you don't know? And secondly, a language like the DNA is complicated that can only work within the parameters of the pre-defined syntax where it can interpret the given signals. Suppose there was no Creator who had given a purpose and a language to fulfill that purpose; no matter how blindly we can believe in blind chance, it becomes impossible to achieve an unknown end. In such a case, it is just as foolish to say that broken glass in our garbage can, given billions of years, will somehow become a sophisticated and intelligent dolphin. For something as simple as the human skin that needs to be elastic in its property for a mother to carry the baby as it grows in her womb, just that one fact of a defined purpose and instruction for what it needs to do is enough to drive an evolutionist insane, for the fool hath said in his heart, "There is no God".

THE GOSPEL

March 15

The Gospel of Confusion

For if the trumpet give an uncertain sound, who shall prepare himself to the battle?–1 Corinthians 14:8

The absolute necessity for anyone declaring the gospel to be sure of what they believe by what is conveyed to the congregation is of the utmost importance. Sounding a strange sound will confuse the hearers as to what to make of the doctrines preached in man's wisdom. Preachers have an uncanny way of adapting what they believe to what the audience would like to hear. To the one who preaches to just "believe" when questioned on repentance, there is an affirmation that they do believe in it, but in practice, they don't. To the one questioned on prayer, there is an affirmation that they believe in the critical need for prayer, but in practice, there is no seeking after God in a dedicated weekly all-night corporate prayer meeting. Such is the state of the Church where adding dead people to the pews and scratching itching ears has become the accepted norm of our Americanized Christianity. Those who suffer from it are the lost who assume they are saved and the saved who are malnourished to the point of death, trying to glean what they can from parched grounds. God will hold those who preach to the higher standard of preaching the truth in its purity, though it may cost them their congregation.

THE GOSPEL

The Nature of Lies March 16

Ye are of your father the devil, and the lusts of your father ye will do. He was a murderer from the beginning, and abode not in the truth, because there is no truth in him. When he speaketh a lie, he speaketh of his own: for he is a liar, and the father of it. –John 8:44

Satan deals with ambiguity, for he is the author of confusion, while God is the perfecter in clarity. We see it in the claims of man against the truth of God, which is evident by the confusion on the ambiguity portrayed in so-called "truth" and questioning the things of God. But underneath, there's no evidence of the facts of it when you start drilling down and trying to unravel the evidence. Satan relies on the initial input of error to take root while ignoring the contradiction to the truth that it brings in the long term. Adam's fall to the lie of Satan, "ye shall be as gods", was accepted and acted upon without clarified thinking or analyzing the truth of it and the long-term consequences of such an action. Such is the deception where man is entangled in addictions, gender therapy, religion, exploitation, scams, and so forth. The reality of Creation is seen in full force when one digs through the facts, open to truth, and the myriad of evidence that could not have come except from an all-wise Creator. Their perceived urgency to receive and act upon error, though the full weight of what is portrayed is not revealed yet, speaks to the nature of the father of lies, Satan.

THE GOSPEL

March 17

Divine Author

These were more noble than those in Thessalonica, in that they received the word with all readiness of mind, and searched the scriptures daily, whether those things were so. –Acts 17:11

It is not the text of the scriptures that we are to proclaim as the object of preaching, but the truth of the scriptures, the Spirit of the scriptures, the living voice behind the scriptures, and the God of the scriptures. Man shall not live by bread alone speaks of the carnal nature of man to take the scriptures and fit it into his method for justifying his sinful lusts; but when it is the word that proceedeth out of the mouth of God then we take it for who has said it and align our lives to conform to it, rather than fitting the word to my wants. The starting point to discern a cult is always to look at the teachings of their leader or movement, even though they may use the word of God, and begin with what saith the scriptures, and ensure we align with the scriptures and then look at the false teachings and see how they have made the scriptures to fit their way of thinking or practice. Thus, the Holy Spirit who wrote the book needs to illuminate the reader about the truth of God's word where we are willing to take it without question no matter how much we would like for it to conform to what we would like to do. It is the Spirit that brings life and not the letter of the Law.

THE GOSPEL

March 18

Restoration of Relationship

And all things are of God, who hath reconciled us to himself by Jesus Christ, and hath given to us the ministry of reconciliation;–2 Corinthians 5:18

When dealing with eternal matters, the foundation for such truths in the realm of spiritual needs must have the supernatural element, or nothing will prevail. The gospel does not begin with the fact that we are sinners and that we need a Savior. The gospel flows starting with the goodness of God who created us and gave us everything good, the desire of God that we obey Him not out of force but love, our response of rebellion against this good God, such rebellion that caused us to face the penalty of it because of our offense towards this good God by our sin, the utter inability of the lost man to reconcile himself to God because of how far man had fallen without hope, the voluntary act of God to love us and who came to pay the price of our sin, the hope of those who repent and believe the gospel who are convicted of their sin and God's perfection, the goodness of God to restore that broken communion with God and the witness of sonship by the Spirit. Salvation is about restoration, and Christ did not come to make us happy or give us Heaven or make us feel good; Christ came that we might know the One true God and that knowing Him we might be restored to that union of that lost relationship from the garden. Everything else flows because of the nature of God when He saves us and dwells inside of us.

THE GOSPEL

March 19

Sin and Sinners

For ye were sometimes darkness, but now are ye light in the Lord: walk as children of light:–Ephesians 5:8

Christ came to save us from our sin, and those redeemed by the blood of the Lamb can relate to the awfulness of sin in their own lives that Christ set them free from. But as we ponder on the horridness of sin, we realize that evil does not stand alone but lives and manifests itself in the heart of man and the acts perpetrated by mankind. We who were the children of the devil now stand against the evil one to warn the sinner of their plight and the path that they are headed to, we are to show the love of Christ as our Creator who gave the breath of life, to show the reality of the rebellion of man to become the enemy of God. We desire the Holy Spirit to bring them to the point of repentance. Yet, considering these, we realize that the sinner is cast into Hell and not just his sin. And thus, we cry out against sin but also against the sinner who calls evil good and good evil. The sinner is just as guilty before God along with the sin that has taken root in his heart. Man sins because he is a sinner who loves his sin and deserves the just wrath of Almighty God. And when a man looks at the death and sorrow around him, he is reminded of the just consequences of what he asked for in his rebellion against this good God who created Him.

THE GOSPEL

March 20

Christ, the Conquering King

Wherefore God also hath highly exalted him, and given him a name which is above every name: That at the name of Jesus every knee should bow, of things in heaven, and things in earth, and things under the earth;–Philippians 2:9,10

The gospel is the grace of God wrought in love for sinful men, a gospel brought to life by the illumination of the Holy Spirit. Yet when we pray for the gospel to take root in a lost soul, we come with a plea for the God of the gospel to move in the lives of those we love. God who is rich in mercy and love is not bound by the whims of man, and He is Lord of all who is high and lifted up in majesty and irradiant beauty. We who are unworthy creatures are the ones who need the grace of God where we come to Him in humility, pleading to show mercy and soften the heart of the hearers and convince them of the truth of the word. At times we see a concept portrayed of God pleading with man to come into his heart or sing songs of a God who is hoping that the sinner will accept His Son; the sentimental idea today of an impotent God waiting patiently for the man who subjects his Creator to his pleasure. A thousand tongues rise and cry with one voice, "NO", for He is the King of all the ages and as conquering King ravages the rebellion of man. We look to God and command men everywhere to repent and believe the gospel or reject Him to their peril.

THE GOSPEL

March 21
Everything has been Received

For who maketh thee to differ from another? and what hast thou that thou didst not receive? now if thou didst receive it, why dost thou glory, as if thou hadst not received it?– 1 Corinthians 4:7

One must realize the truth that all they have is that which has been given to them. Their life, health, intellect, food, shelter, finances, and such were not earned in the truest sense of receiving in illuminative impulse from within but has been given. In response to their ideas, one may find themselves rich, but it was made possible for them, where a million other such ideas failed in their inception. Thus, the man who thinks that he has built an empire like the pagan king Nebuchadnezzar did and was driven in insanity to live like an animal when restored gave worship and true acknowledgment to the God of heavens from whom he had received his kingdom, is a picture for us behold in our materialistic society. The worship of God with whom we have to do, for the true Christian, must cause us to come in humility, realizing that we have nothing off of ourselves since everything we have has been given to us from the kind hand of God. And what is the nature of pride? It is thinking we have something worth boasting about ourselves, but what do we have, other than that which has been received? Thus, works for salvation become an abomination in the sight of Almighty God, for what we bring are but putrefying sores and filthy rags instead of what God requires, perfection from within which we don't have.

THE GOSPEL

March 22

The Gift of Faith

No man can come to me, except the Father which hath sent me draw him: and I will raise him up at the last day. –John 6:44

In the realm of the supernatural, we are confronted with certain realities that cannot be explained with enough clarity but can be experienced by the outcome it produces. The human faith that has symbols of sitting in a chair and equating it to trusting in the chair or getting on an airplane is an inadequate and false alternative to that true saving faith that brings about regeneration and pleases God. In its finality, faith is a gift from God to the penitent sinner who hears the voice of God when hearing the word of God and realizes the truth of it and believes in its validity though it may cost him his own life in doing so. In such Divine transactions, it is not the evidence of coaxing one to believe but rather the outcome of their illumination that causes them to believe, and we say that faith has been imparted and then exercised on the part of the sinner to the Savior. Thus, faith does not stand alone, but rather it does something; it shows by their action that they have faith. And so, we need to look at faith in the reverse order in that grand hall of faith, of those men and women who did exploits which showed their faith as the impetus of their doing rather than the use of it to define faith itself.

THE GOSPEL

March 23
Examine Yourselves

But he that lacketh these things is blind, and cannot see afar off, and hath forgotten that he was purged from his old sins. Wherefore the rather, brethren, give diligence to make your calling and election sure: for if ye do these things, ye shall never fall:–2 Peter 1:9,10

Having certainty in an uncertain world is something many long for, and when dealing with man's eternal soul, it is a matter of the utmost importance. Upon death, those who have tried to find assurance for themselves in education, religion, philosophy, good works, even faith in an idol will find themselves facing condemnation before the Almighty God. When a man is drawn by the Spirit of God in the conviction of sin and turns to God in repentance, God acts on behalf of that man to save Him. It is an act that is carried in tandem with the part of God and the part of man. One who believes but has no desire to repent is in danger of intellectual assent; one who repents but does not believe is in danger of self-reformation. Has the Spirit borne witness that you are the child of God where you cry out Abba, Father? Has the hatred for sin manifested for the reason of offending a Holy God rather than the guilt from getting caught? Has God changed your desires to set you on a path of freedom from your sin? Have the scriptures borne witness by the Spirit of your standing before God? Has the word and prayer become precious in your longing after Christ? It is urgent that the call to examine oneself is done while there is still hope, for once we cross the threshold of death, those who have deceived themselves will find no remedy.

THE GOSPEL

March 24

Crucial Distinctions Required

And he was sad at that saying, and went away grieved: for he had great possessions.—Mark 10:22

The depravity of sin is such that it affords man an outlet for his nagging conscience while not allowing for true deliverance from sin. It will enable the sinner to slumber in the sleep of death by good works, religion, charity, and so on while robbing him of that essential faith on the Lord Jesus Christ. The nature of sin to blind Samson, who knew what was being asked, and the result of the Philistines trying to bind him is evidence enough that sin crouches close to the breast of men whispering lies of relief when none has arrived. The carnal man will gladly believe in Christ while keeping his sin with him for wanting Heaven. But the penitent man who comes in repentance will lay it all down and surrender to the command of the Master before believing on Christ's pardon. To be carnal is death, and Satan, who saw Christ crucified and rose from the dead, believes in the truth of who God is, yet he remains the devil, for he is in perpetual rebellion, not laying down his pride. Without repentance, there is no salvation, and repentance is not part of believing, for the Lord said to repent "and" believe the gospel. Judas repented but did not believe; the rich man believed enough to come to Christ but never repented of the earthly possessions that he desired to keep.

THE GOSPEL

March 25

Repent and Believe

I tell you, Nay: but, except ye repent, ye shall all likewise perish. –Luke 13:3

The ingrained desire and drive for sinful man to justify his sin and pass the blame to another are evidenced from Adam until today. The depravity of sin is highly deceptive in that it allows for a show of piety without the fruits of it. The Pharisees were the pinnacle of this where they loved to pray and claimed they believed and obeyed God but were, in fact, whitened sepulchers that covered the rotting flesh within. When a man is convicted of sin, the axe is laid to the root where his tendency to justify sin and nurture Agag while professing to offer sacrifice to Jehovah is stripped away. Thus, repentance deals with the nature of sin, him being made rightly aware of the heinousness of sin to turn from it, willing to forsake it, and "believe" deals with the nature of God. True repentance is always toward God and not primarily toward man, and believe is based on a Person, executed by the Spirit who regenerates, and not based on a decision that they have made. The self-reforming man repents but does not believe, as Judas did, allowing for his garnished home to be filled with devils, his end state being worse than the first. Believe, and the evidence of believing by the changed life is crucial for realizing the assurance that comes from God by His Spirit and is girded by the word of God.

THE GOSPEL

March 26

The Goodness and Severity of God

He that believeth on the Son hath everlasting life: and he that believeth not the Son shall not see life; but the wrath of God abideth on him.–John 3:36

The evidence of the goodness of God is seen all around us, in sustaining life, in His acts of kindness to the lost and to the saved in sending rain and healing to minds and bodies in times of distress, in sustenance, in providential care for His creatures both in mankind and nature, in keeping at bay the rise of evil and so much more. But the goodness of God culminated at the Cross, where the severity of God fell upon God's Son, and Christ took the judgment that was rightfully ours. The severity of God cannot be imagined or fully contemplated, such severity that the eternal fires of Hell and the lake of fire can never repay the sin debt that we owe to a Holy God. And such terrifying thoughts of the penalty of sin and the everlasting condemnation that rests upon fallen man was met with the love of God and His goodness to forgive us and call us justified, adopted into the family of God, joint-heirs with Jesus. For those who reject the severity of God that fell upon Christ for their salvation and choose to go on their own perceived merit, good works, or vain religion, will find at the last that the severity of God will fall on their naked souls that the blood of Jesus has not covered; but the wrath of Almighty God abideth on them forever, time without end.

THE GOSPEL

March 27

Original Intent

prepare to meet thy God–Amos 4:12b

The existence of man and all the world around us is predicated on the premise of the existence of God. For the finality of man and all of Creation, the source of truth comes from the One who made them after His good pleasure. Thus, the claim of God on His creatures is absolute and without room for deviation. The handiwork of His Creation demands a response, and an answer worthy of the Maker is to acknowledge and give due reverence based on His revealed purpose. Man was created for His pleasure, and the reasonable service is to give the due response in worship, adoration, praise, and submission to this great God who made us. His revelation of Himself through Jesus Christ, God in mortal covering, brings us to the double-claim of those who have been redeemed by the blood of the Lamb. The requirement of His children to worship Him and love Him becomes the greater purpose, for to whom much has been given shall much be required. Nothing can be sought as an alternative for mankind, for original intent must be met before the original purpose for man can be realized, to be authentic in fulfilling life's purpose and be able to meet death and life thereafter.

THE GOSPEL

March 28

A New Heart

A new heart also will I give you, and a new spirit will I put within you: and I will take away the stony heart out of your flesh, and I will give you an heart of flesh. –Ezekiel 36:26

The transaction of life in the new birth experience is more than agreeing to someone's persuasive ability. The confidence we have of the hope that lieth within us to be effectually conveyed and received is not in us but in the Spirit, who has been given to convict and convince of truth. The thrust of faith to believe in the God of the word behind the proclamation of truth, and our accountability to be ready always to give an answer to every man that asketh us a reason of the hope that is in us with meekness and fear, is our responsibility. The ability of God to birth as it were one who is dead and bring them to new life has in it the transaction of a new heart. Thus, the doubt of "if" they will believe when facing someone who has been given to this world and steeped in sin, whether in religion, sensuality, LGBTQ+, pride, atheism; or hiding behind the walls of philosophy, "science", piercings of the body and soul to satisfy their void, or any other vice that one is held in; is not one of doubt, but it rests upon the ability of God to give a new heart which brings new desires, confidence, and trust. It speaks of the nature of God to change a life from the inside out and the reality that truth will prevail. One who is thus changed will reflect the nature of their Creator who has called us to be holy, for He is holy.

THE GOSPEL

March 29

Defining Faith

But without faith it is impossible to please him: for he that cometh to God must believe that he is, and that he is a rewarder of them that diligently seek him.–Hebrews 11:6

Faith is not intellectual assent to facts; it is not an agreement to what is portrayed as truth, it is not trusting in an inanimate object that is equated for saving faith, it is not being convinced of truth by another mortal and relying based on the validity of them for their souls. True saving faith is confidence in the God of the word who has revealed Himself to them by the illumination of the Holy Spirit. Such revelation brings confidence in the things hoped for and the validity of the things not seen. Unbelief is the enemy of faith, for it tries to attribute the supernatural workings of God to natural causes of man and events of nature. Faith produces action not only to believe but also to keep on believing since the One upon whom it is acting is ever faithful until the end. Thus, the author of Hebrews speaks about faith that produced action where it performed the doing of, what the outcome was, in the various examples given in that great hall of faith. And the admonition to keep on believing by John when he reflects on that encouragement, that we may know that we have eternal life where it is closely tied with assurance and the call to hold fast until the end. A faith that is just hoping without the outflow of what it is meant to produce in good works and steadfastness upon the character of God is nothing but dead faith.

THE GOSPEL

March 30

Sin and the Gospel

For every one that doeth evil hateth the light, neither cometh to the light, lest his deeds should be reproved.–John 3:20

The fundamental nature of the gospel is in its dealing with sin and the price that Christ paid for redemption, the precious blood of Jesus Christ. The judgment that should have fallen upon us fell upon Christ, for all who will repent and believe in His work. Lifestyles that are contrary to the nature of God and His Creation, such as homosexuality, transgender, and so forth, are diametrically at odds with the gospel and can never be reconciled, no matter how much men in their sinful viewpoint tries to gloss over it. Calling someone "Christian" is not enough; God requires holiness and purity in the inner man on aligning oneself to what God requires of us in His word. Such blending of lines is seen everywhere because of man's rebellion against his Maker. Even in the area of diversity and inclusion, which are surface-level inclusion with people of contrasting views but requires adherence to agreement of thought to someone's narrative, or they are ostracized into a cancel culture. Furthermore, unconscious bias is about building a false narrative of what you don't otherwise have and bring you to the place of producing a pang of false guilt to create a victim mentality for feeding into the slogan of equity while building a downward spiral of deceit. Thus, the desire to form an egalitarian society denies the uniqueness of males and females in complementary roles at the altar of political correctness. And the desire for equal outcome supplants equality having a bias based on color by denying jobs based on one's ability in equal opportunity, thus becoming racial discrimination off itself.

THE GOSPEL

March 31

No Man Cared for my Soul

And judgment is turned away backward, and justice standeth afar off: for truth is fallen in the street, and equity cannot enter.
–Isaiah 59:14

We emphasize soul-winning and making sure people are going to Heaven, but in reality, we don't value the human soul. We are more concerned about people making an intellectual assent and become part of a statistic rather than to make sure that people are born of the Spirit of God, with a life that only the Holy Spirit can give. Human reasoning on a text of scripture is used for assurance instead of the assurance that comes from above by the Spirit. We don't value the human soul nor the purity of the Bride of Christ. We are not concerned that we may be plucking unripe fruits by leading someone into a decision without the evident working of the Holy Spirit, with the conviction of sin and bringing forth fruits meet for repentance; the true salvation where one becomes a new creature with new desires, new habits, new goals, and a new Lord. We justify the failure of our modern-day evangelism by giving excuses of being a babe in Christ, so we have to try to retrain them on how to live the Christian life, though they have no desire given by the Holy Ghost to do so. Religiously affiliated but lost.

THE GOSPEL

April

April 1

Original Claim

Male and female created he them; and blessed them, and called their name Adam, in the day when they were created.
—Genesis 5:2

As much as anyone tries to deny their true nature of who they are, sinners in need of a savior, the truth remains; the same is true of who they belong to. In his desire to suppress the truth in unrighteousness, the fallen man attempts many ways to try to thwart God's plan in vain. In evolution, he tries to deny the rightful Owner of all things which were made by Creation; in transgender ideologies, he tries to deny the fact of God-ordained gender at birth; in homosexual unions, he tries to deny the intent of God-honoring marriage, which is one man and one woman for life; in desiring power and demand social justice at the cost of true freedom, man denies the ordained law of God and becomes a law unto himself; in his desire for the love of money, man denies the law of labor and reward that has been given by the loving hand of God; in self-love and defying authority, man tries to overthrow basic tenants of God-ordained institutions of the home, church, and government. No matter how far man tries to go against God, one thing is for sure that God will always have the last word, and man will bow down in submission to the exalted King Jesus in that great and terrible day, for He has the original claim upon all of Creation.

THE GOSPEL

April 2

The Real Face of Sin

Good understanding giveth favour: but the way of transgressors is hard.—Proverbs 13:15

Would seeing the end of where a path will lead give us a cause for changing course at the onset of its beginning? While we are shown an ad of a happy and spirited social drinking party, drink takes money from his family, and leads to a drunkard's grave; while showing a cover page of a glossy magazine, lust drives men to forsake homes, divorce their wives and tears women down as a commodity for sale; while taking drugs looks appealing at the beginning, we see dysfunctional homes, the deadly downward spiral unto death that is passed on to many subsequent generations; while the love of money and pride is touted as the soul of America, we see suicides, ungodliness and inability of men to live useful lives in society; while sports and entertainment are heralded as the great fun of our day, we see the shallowness in the lives of Christians who give into it; while there is the hype of smoking and vaping, man chokes in his own blood with cancer and health problems; while following ones heart is portrayed as the way to happiness, if followed we see the reality that it is deceitful and desperately wicked as seen in genocides, sex crimes and bondage. While there is pleasure in sin for a season, the consequences of sin are up to God and far-reaching than one can ever imagine. "Be sure your sin will find you out" is just as true today as it was when uttered three thousand years ago.

THE GOSPEL

April 3

Conviction by Revelation

The entrance of thy words giveth light; it giveth understanding unto the simple.–Psalm 119:130

Truth has always been and always will be the elusive jewel of fallen humanity. And one who professes to have the truth needs to examine themselves regarding the source of how that truth came about in their lives to the point of conviction. There is the conviction that comes by indoctrination, at which point it is not a revelation of truth by the Truth-giver; instead, it is the revelation of ideas that are packaged as "truth" which follows the teachings that have been handed down, which is comprised of one person's opinion given to another, instead of absolute truth. There is a Giver of truth, God, and He owns the immutable right to absolute truth, and all else comes as error, for they all fall short of God's standard of truth, Himself. The truth that God gives is a revelation of truth that involves the supernatural. It makes men see things differently, such as Creation, life, death, purpose, gender, identity, politics, marriage, family, and many others. A conviction cannot be based on personal preference, bias, perception, teachings of man, and other sources, for they all have the innate nature of sin embedded in them. Conviction has to be from God who is perfect in all His ways, and His truth always prevails, and there is none other.

THE GOSPEL

April 4

Yea, Hath God Said?

For God doth know that in the day ye eat thereof, then your eyes shall be opened, and ye shall be as gods, knowing good and evil.
–Genesis 3:5

The first-ever question that Satan asked of mankind in his initial entry into the garden is still being asked today, six thousand years later. We see it evident in everything from someone practicing religion or denying it in atheism. This question echoes in an uncanny resemblance to that day when Satan tempted our first parents. The question becomes, has God created us in His image vs. we are self-made creatures by the process of evolution; where God gave life vs. man's quest for life in space and other planets; where we are appointed once to die vs. the lie of reincarnation; where Heaven and Hell are realities of the revealed truth vs. atheism that seeks no accountability; where God provided Christ as the only way to God vs. man's poor attempt in good works and religions; where Jesus is God in the flesh who rose bodily from the dead vs. the denying of His deity by various cults; where narrow is the way vs. the modernist and the universalist who deny it; where God created us as male and female vs. man's desire to transition his gender; where marriage is between one man and one woman vs. the lifestyle of homosexuality; where God's word is absolute truth vs. higher criticism and relativism in questioning God's word. The question remains, but the truth of God reigns supreme to shine His light into the darkness of a willing heart.

THE GOSPEL

April 5

Not Religion

All that ever came before me are thieves and robbers: but the sheep did not hear them.—John 10:8

The Bible tells us where we came from, why we are here and where we are going. It deals with the person of man, his spiritual condition, the accurate diagnosis of his condition, and how he can remedy it. To have the proper remedy, one must have the correct diagnosis, where they must have prior known the root cause. Though religions, philosophies, or man's poor attempt in evolution try to find purpose and meaning for life, the truth shouts from every blade of grass, tree, and cell of the glory of God that is echoed back to the void in the human heart of a Creator and the missing fullness in his life. In redemption, the restoration of that broken relationship to God is complete when humanity can once again be in communion with His Maker in perfect harmony. In its finality, Christ's work on Calvary is not about one religious' viewpoint. Instead, it is the foundational truth of man's purpose of existence. Religion tries to meet that need by man-made theories for life, death, and hope, but Jesus Christ reveals the way, the truth, and the life. And only the One who created us has the original claim to show us that way and is worthy of our worship, adoration, and obedience. Before the beginning was God and not religion.

THE GOSPEL

April 6

Point in Time Decision?

I have fought a good fight, I have finished my course, I have kept the faith:–2 Timothy 4:7

Standing at the precipice of death as a martyr, a new believer could have taken the beginning of his new life at regeneration and called it good and denied Christ, with the thought that eventually, he'll make it to Heaven anyway. If this attitude that is prevalent in American Christianity today were put to the fire of Nero's Garden, Christianity, as we know, would have never survived. A point in time decision that does not continue as a lifetime of change under a new Master is worth nothing, where when they die, they will find out that they have been deceived by a gospel that sends them to Hell. Prevalent today is the thought that "Jesus is good as my fire insurance from Hell, and let me now live as I please, and after I die, I will catch up with God in Heaven." Christianity is about ownership, and one who has exhibited no change at the point of decision is not saved; if believing did not change you where you had in you the Spirit's witness and started obeying the truth of the word of God, then you are not saved; not backslidden but lost. Salvation is about the Person of Christ where the heart of stone is changed to the heart of flesh that desires after holiness, reflecting the nature of their Redeemer.

THE GOSPEL

April 7

Repentance and Salvation

Testifying both to the Jews, and also to the Greeks, repentance toward God, and faith toward our Lord Jesus Christ.–Acts 20:21

"A man is not prepared to believe or to receive the gospel unless he is ready to repent of his sins and turn from them."–D. L. Moody. "Repentance is a godly sorrow for sin. Repentance is a forsaking of sin. Real repentance is putting your trust in Jesus Christ so you will not live like that anymore. Repentance is permanent ... repentance is something a lot bigger than a lot of people think. It is absolutely essential if you go to heaven"–Lester Roloff. "Repentance is a discovery of the evil of sin, a mourning that we have committed it, a resolution to forsake it. It is, in fact, a change of mind of a very deep and practical character, which makes the man love what once he hated, and hate what once he loved."–Charles Spurgeon. Someone once told me that the book of John does not have the word "repent", yet many have gotten saved from that book, in the same note the book of John does not have the word "faith", does it mean we don't need faith to get saved? Repentance is not good works; instead, it is the work of God that works in you which produces a spontaneous response of your abhorring of sin in your heart where you are willing to turn from it and forsake it. If your sin put Jesus on the cross and you are not willing to turn from it, what are you getting saved from? Repentance toward God is just as essential as faith toward our Lord Jesus Christ.

THE GOSPEL

April 8

Contrasting Truth

Follow peace with all men, and holiness, without which no man shall see the Lord:–Hebrews 12:14

Whenever one hears of a popular view of the gospel, it is the responsibility of every faithful follower of Christ to examine it under the scrutiny of the word of God. When the energy of the flesh is revealed under the guise of the "Holy Ghost," we look to the truth of when He is come He will reprove the world of sin; when the ease of the gospel is presented, that removes the need for repentance we look to the words of Christ, except ye repent, ye shall all likewise perish; when we hear of revival we look to the result of it if that moving produced the peaceable fruit of holiness; when we hear of a worship service that moves the flesh we look to the lives of those affected after the meeting on how it made them live holy lives for obeying Christ's command to be ye holy; when someone presents a feel-better religion we look to ask of the truth to, be sober, be vigilant, your adversary the devil; when we are told to accommodate sin for numbers we look to the way of the cross that points to the narrow way; when we are told to judge not we look to, come out from among them and be ye separate. We tread in fear desiring the closeness of Christ, for Satan can transform himself into an angel of light and preach half-truths that appease the flesh, give some false comfort to the spirit, and deprive man of that very true nature of the gospel that becometh like the Master.

THE GOSPEL

April 9

Fruits Meet for Repentance

For godly sorrow worketh repentance to salvation not to be repented of: but the sorrow of the world worketh death.
–2 Corinthians 7:10

There is a danger of accommodating truth to make it more palatable for getting a wider audience. The outcome of the gospel's message is the object of what it accomplished, salvation from sin to restore our relationship to God. Sin, at its core, is the repetition of that original sin that Lucifer committed, wanting to be as God. There is nothing more serious of a topic to deal with when dealing with the lost souls of men than the matter of the sinfulness of sin. Accommodation of compromise will lead to the desertion of truth. Promising Heaven to a man who has no desire to turn from his sin compromises that truth. To one who is in rebellion towards God, fruits meet for repentance show the work of the Holy Spirit by showing them the darkness of sin in light of the holiness of God, causing the sinner to cry out for mercy as his only plea. It is not "fruits meet for salvation" that one needs to produce, for salvation is not of works. Without conviction of sin by the Spirit, there is no repentance, and without repentance, there is no regeneration, and without regeneration, there is no salvation. To be superficially saved is to be eternally lost.

THE GOSPEL

April 10

Worthless Faith

work out your own salvation with fear and trembling.
–Philippians 2:12b

A change as big as God Himself when He saves us will change us. And it is not an intellectual change that is not discernible and moves on to more and more change over some time, where that change may inevitably come with getting old; regeneration brings immediate observable change where God removes the heart of stone and gives the heart of flesh and starts the lifelong process of conforming us to be like Christ. Faith that does not bring change is good for no one. For those saved by grace, there must be evidence of that grace that manifests itself in works. Knowing the utter inability of a person to save themselves, once saved, will shew forth works of the evidence of that true faith. One needs to be wary of someone who professes that they had a point in time faith when they were four years old but shows no evidence through their teenage or young adult stages of the result of their claim. It is not appropriate to reassure them of their "kindergarten" decision for believing; rather, they need to be brought to seek the Lord as one who has never been regenerated though they may have made some intellectual assent. With eternity in the balance, can we take this matter lightly of dead faith and not call them to repentance?

THE GOSPEL

April 11

The Narrow Way

Enter ye in at the strait gate: for wide is the gate, and broad is the way, that leadeth to destruction, and many there be which go in thereat:–Matthew 7:13

Has the price of the gospel changed? Has the way become broad that leads to life everlasting? Is the gospel just about what appeases the flesh to go to Heaven? A shallow gospel that preaches good at the cost of nothing deceives the hearer about the price of repentance and discipleship. It is easy to get someone to say a prayer and add them to the numbers. Satan does not care if someone believes in Jesus to go to Heaven as long as the Holy Spirit never regenerated them; Satan will get that soul at the last day, a soul that has been inoculated to the truth by error. If narrow is the way and few there be that find it, why is it that we boast of numbers, whereas the early church spoke of those who believed "continued stedfastly in the apostles' doctrine and fellowship, and in breaking of bread, and in prayers." How many of those that we boast as plucked from the depths of sin remain faithful? Of the twelve disciples who followed Christ, one was a devil. In today's Americanized Christianity, the numbers have been reversed; for every convert of the Holy Ghost, 11 false professions are counted as saved by this namesake gospel that makes light of the high call of salvation.

THE GOSPEL

April 12

Turn from Sin

And she shall bring forth a son, and thou shalt call his name Jesus: for he shall save his people from their sins.–Matthew 1:21

To have the notion that Christ died in my place, so I just believe in historical truth for saving my soul from Hell is to miss out on the most pivotal turning point in the sinner seeking the Lord. Conviction of sin is a work of the Spirit that brings the sinner to face his condition before God and that, even in the best of motives or interests, seeks his own way and justifies his sin. When the shroud of this deception of the heart is exposed in the light of the gospel, there is a call from God that says, leave all you have and come and follow me. At that moment, the sinner is confronted with the need for turning from and turning to. If he is to accept the call of God for the saving of his soul, he must turn. To be saved from has of itself the need of what we are saved from. If Jesus came to save us from our sin, and if sin put Him on that Cross, and if we have all gone astray desiring our own way, accepting Christ means hating what put Him on that tree, our sin. If one is not willing to turn from their sin, they are not ready to believe on the Lord Jesus Christ.

THE GOSPEL

April 13

Intellectual vs Supernatural

I am the door: by me if any man enter in, he shall be saved, and shall go in and out, and find pasture. – John 10:9

Confidence in the word of God is essential but plowing through and finding the God of the word is of greater importance. In one we know about God, in the other we know God; in one we may have our hope; in the other, we have life eternal through regeneration; in one, we read about Him, in the other, we hear His voice; the word profits with faith and faith without works is dead; in one we have the written witness, in the other, we have the most conclusive proof of the experiential witness; in one we can be misled by the reasoning of fallen men, in the other, we are confirmed by the seal of sonship; in one there maybe the ease of acceptance, in the other, there is the striving to entering in through the narrow way that leads to life; in one we can work it up in the energy of the flesh that leaves no lasting effects, in the other, it needs to come down from above; in one a person can be in sin and self-justify, in the other, they are faced with the reality of God and the conviction of sin that calls unto holiness. The work of the Spirit does not stay with the letter of the law. Instead, He leads us to experience the Person of the word. The intellectual may suffice for the temporal moment, but the supernatural is essential for eternity with God.

THE GOSPEL

April 14

Depravity of Man

How much more abominable and filthy is man, which drinketh iniquity like water?—Job 15:16

To fully realize the glory of Christ's sacrifice, one has to fathom the cost in some small way. Jesus came to save His people from their sin. Sin in our day has been reduced to manageable terms so man can coexist with it and call it as one's preference, personal right, disease, affair, gender choice, gay, and so on. In the eyes of God, the abhorrence of the utter vileness of sin has not diminished. Eternal damnation in the fires of Hell is because of sin, a person no matter how good they are or find themselves in an unfortunate situation, no matter how we see someone; God sees man as corrupted and utterly filthy from head to toe in the mire of sin, from birth until death by nature and choice, incapable of reconciling himself to God. Sin is any thought, action, or intent against God. And no religion or good works will ever be able to pay its wages; only the blood of Jesus Christ can cleanse us from all unrighteousness and make us declared as righteous before a Holy God, a God before whom the seraphims cannot look upon. Atrocities of man, murder, exploitation, injustice, inhumane experiments, wars, deception, and lies are just as wicked as an "innocent" whisper of "white" lies. In all, this man is woven into this fabric of sin where he cannot escape sin's condemnation unless he repents and turns to the One who died for His sin and is set free to love and serve Christ.

THE GOSPEL

April 15

Provision of the Law

What shall we say then? Is the law sin? God forbid. Nay, I had not known sin, but by the law: for I had not known lust, except the law had said, Thou shalt not covet.—Romans 7:7

By the law is the knowledge of sin. But the law of itself is not good enough to bring them to salvation. The law must be translated into truth by revelation. The hearer of the law may not be convinced of the truth of the law or even of the Giver of the law. But once the law pronounces judgment upon sin, the grace of God must reveal the validity of the law and the coming judgment by the Spirit, to bring the hearer to the conviction of sin. Without this crucial next step, the hearer may be convinced of the law, but it won't penetrate enough to produce that true work of repentance and regeneration. As the law plows man's heart, it is made ready for the seed of the word of God to take root and is watered by the showers of the mercy of truth by the Spirit through preaching, witnessing, praying, and so forth. The final breakthrough happens when the cry of sin has become an overwhelming burden in the sinner's heart, and he realizes the danger of facing a Holy God, cries out for mercy, and is born-again by the Spirit of God. The role of the Spirit is paramount in the final step since that is His exclusive work, and we are not to take that step for the sinner. We roll the stone, as it were at Lazarus's grave, that the sinner might hear the voice of God. While some plants and some water, it is God who gives the increase.

THE GOSPEL

April 16

Conviction of Sin

For he shall grow up before him as a tender plant, and as a root out of a dry ground: he hath no form nor comeliness; and when we shall see him, there is no beauty that we should desire him.
–Isaiah 53:2

The single act of disobedience in the garden plunged all humanity into sin; every disease, crime, hate, divorce, genocide, natural disaster, evil, war, etc., came when a man tried to play God. Man is not inherently good; he is infinitely evil and dead in trespasses and sins. Conviction of sin is an exclusive work of the Holy Spirit. We can convince someone of wrongdoing and cause them to make an intellectual assent. Only the Holy Spirit can bring the sinner under the awful realization of the holiness of God and the utter heinousness of sin. The one who wrote the word is the only one who can bring it to life. A sinner who doesn't see himself as God sees him is not convicted of sin; instead, he is just toying with the prospect of what he can gain by becoming a Christian. True conviction brings the sinner to the place where he is not just acknowledging his guilt before God but is also deeply sorrowful for his offense toward God. Oswald Chambers states, "There is nothing attractive about the gospel to the natural man; the only man who finds the gospel attractive is the man who is convicted of sin."

THE GOSPEL

April 17

Saving Faith vs Natural Faith

Who also hath made us able ministers of the new testament; not of the letter, but of the spirit: for the letter killeth, but the spirit giveth life. – 2 Corinthians 3:6

In a sincere attempt to make the gospel more easily receivable, men have humanized the supernatural workings of God to human reasoning and logical terms. In the genuine workings of God, there is always the supernatural element that is evident when dealing with the fallen heart of the man who is dead in trespasses and sins. To redefine believing as sitting on a chair or getting on an airplane is falling short of that true faith that produces the good fruit of salvation. It is the danger of requiring natural human faith to receive supernatural truths. Just the affirmation of the word is not enough to produce this kind of faith; instead, it is produced when God convicts of sin and reveals by the Spirit of man's standing before God. Thus, the conscience is made alive, and man hears the God of the word, and to those contrite of heart, saving faith comes when desiring that way of escape, to call upon Him and to fall on His mercy. Without the supernatural element, we will be left with the superficial, which will make him twofold more the child of Hell. "But as many as received him, to them gave he power to become the sons of God, even to them that believe on his name: Which were born, not of blood, nor of the will of the flesh, nor of the will of man, but of God."

THE GOSPEL

April 18

Regeneration, the Turning Point

And many that believed came, and confessed, and shewed their deeds. Many of them also which used curious arts brought their books together, and burned them before all men: and they counted the price of them, and found it fifty thousand pieces of silver.—Acts 19:18,19

The universalist belief that all will be saved is just as phony as a three-dollar bill. Did all get saved when Noah went into the ark, and God shut the door? Did all get saved when God rained brimstone and fire from heaven upon Sodom and Gomorrah for the sin's finality in homosexuality? Did all get saved when the judgment of God fell upon Babylon? Will all be saved when God said, "whosoever was not found written in the book of life was cast into the lake of fire"? The fundamental problem with the universalist is their utter lack of truth about the heinousness of sin, the holiness of God, and the blood sacrifice that was paid through Jesus Christ. To love God with all your heart and to love your neighbor as yourself is impossible without having a right relationship-by-adoption with God, for we have all gone our own way and have become the enemy of God, our good works are as filthy rags before a Holy God who is the judge of all the earth; and regeneration by the Spirit restores us to that right relationship with God; to love God with all our heart, to love our neighbor as ourselves and to care enough to weep for them knowing their eternal damnation, to take the news of the gospel with humility that they may know the One true God, to be set free from sin, as we have been.

THE GOSPEL

April 19

Is Salvation Free for Nothing?

And he that taketh not his cross, and followeth after me, is not worthy of me. – Matthew 10:38

The cost of following Christ is not something to be trifled with. What does believe on the Lord Jesus Christ entail? Salvation is not in a decision, prayer, or scripture verse, but in a Person and by a Person. While regeneration is the act of being made right with God, it brings a changed life that realizes the lifelong disposition of our standing before God, which calls for a life of discipleship. A salvation that offers forgiveness without repentance cheapens God's grace and leads to the deception of what the Roman Catholics do in selling indulgences. And one who considers the cost of that act of faith realizes that it is a life of obedience to Christ, carrying our cross daily, forsaking of sin and the world's ways, and be willing to be loyal to Christ at all costs. It is not for going to Heaven but to live the Christ-life on earth until we die and go to Heaven. Though the act of justification is not of works, the process of sanctification is filled with works. And one who has no change or desire to follow Christ is, in reality, showing that their salvation was a mental assent to facts, and they are still lost in their sin, though they may have believed on Jesus to save them. "Shalt be saved" is an active realization of the promise that it will happen and not that it has already happened, to keep calling upon Him until He saves them by His Spirit and bears witness in their hearts of their sonship before God.

THE GOSPEL

April 20

Truth, Fallen in the Streets

For precept must be upon precept, precept upon precept; line upon line, line upon line; here a little, and there a little:—Isaiah 28:10

You don't interpret truth in isolation. God in His mercy has given us a myriad of ways to discern, walk and obey what He has graciously revealed to humanity. His truths never change, for He never changes, from eternity to eternity. The reality of who He is, a Holy God; the evidence of what He has done, a loving God; the beauty of what He has given, the God of Creation; the necessity of what He requires, judgment upon sin; the perfection of His oversight, in Divine Providence; the requirement of what He expects of His children, obedience in love. In a time where man wrestles with what he sees as the "truth" of who God is and what He accepts, including perverted lifestyles that God calls as an abomination, God's grand declaration of "I change not" echoes to every generation from Creation to the end of time. And that echo will be heard in the corridors of Heaven and felt in the fires of Hell, of a God who is the same yesterday, today, and forever. The same declaration of Christ "In the beginning God," who created the heaven, and the earth will be the same Christ before whom sinful man will bow in terror when they are judged and cast into the lake of fire, to be consumed in torments but never die for all of eternity. Oh, that men might turn from their fallen and polluted views of God before it is too late.

THE GOSPEL

April 21

Finding Fault

And they said, Go to, let us build us a city and a tower, whose top may reach unto heaven; and let us make us a name, lest we be scattered abroad upon the face of the whole earth.—Genesis 11:4

In our zeal to prove our doctrine and reject a contradicting viewpoint, one can be tempted to question the writings of religion and find fault in its text and so forth. While that is warranted on certain levels, for the writings show the author and the validity of their teachings compared to their lives, whether they are built on truth or the imagination of man's fallen heart, that of itself is not the final determinant of truth. The "scriptures are truth" is based on the divinity of its saying but furthermore on the message of its content, to restore man to his Creator, to have peace with God, and to deal with the root cause of sin and its consequences now and in eternity. It shows the validity of God reaching down to man in grace rather than what every other religion portrays, a feeble and failing attempt of humanity to reach God in good works. While the response of man's baser desires is seen as not producing good but evil, the ability to produce good out of the corrupt inborn nature of man is impossible, good that is acceptable in the sight of a Holy God. Thus, all the books of religion, cults, and philosophies put together speak of the attempt of man, but the Spirit who inspired the word of the living God portrays the glorious truth of God reaching down to man; the man who cannot save himself, no matter how hard he tries.

THE GOSPEL

April 22

Why Repentance?

Seek ye the Lord while he may be found, call ye upon him while he is near: Let the wicked forsake his way, and the unrighteous man his thoughts: and let him return unto the Lord, and he will have mercy upon him; and to our God, for he will abundantly pardon. –Isaiah 55:6,7

The battle of the sexes is not about inclusion or tolerance; instead, it is about the original sin when Satan tempted Adam and Eve with the lie that they shall be as gods. From that was thrust the impetus to open Pandora's box, with sins against others and sins against self. Our compassion for those in sin must be seeded with tears generated by the Holy Spirit for those who are bound in its grip. With humility and love, we look at sin through the eyes of Christ at a man or a woman who is caught up in thinking that there is no other way, whether it be pride, homosexuality, transgender, adultery, or lying. Though we don't discriminate the person who is made in the image of God, we do bring forth the truth of God who will have all men to be saved, and to come unto the knowledge of the truth. A salvation that has no call to repent mocks what Christ died for, to save us from our sin. A heathen will gladly keep Jesus as one of his many gods, but Christ reigns supreme as the only way for all of humanity, Jews or Gentiles. Conviction of sin shows the heinousness of sin in light of the holiness of God, which will cause the sinner to see it as God sees it. To proclaim freedom, victory, and a way of escape to be set free from sin to serve Christ, our loving Creator.

THE GOSPEL

April 23

God's Sovereignty and Man's Responsibility

Then spake Solomon, The Lord said that he would dwell in the thick darkness. – 1 Kings 8:12

Truths from an infinite God are like the facets of a diamond. They shine with unmatched brilliance no matter which way you see them. To conclude one facet is the whole diamond would be illogical; to fit all facets into a single dimension would be impossible. It comes from an infinite God, which may cause us to see truths that seem to contradict each other. In such times we utter "God forbid" and move on. Seeing and accepting, as God has said, is more important than trying to fit it into a manageable spectrum of colors. When we come to the topic of God's Sovereignty and man's responsibility, we look at both in tandem from the same lens. Though we don't see it as reconciling in human terms, we come to realize that they cannot be forged in the intellect of human wisdom. Instead, they are given from the mind of God where truth rejoiceth one with another. If truth causes us to go and sow in tears calling all men to repent and believe the gospel, and we leave the matters that belong to God in His bosom, then we have the proper response. We do what we are commanded to do by the Spirit in submission to a Sovereign God, and our part is not ambiguous.

THE GOSPEL

April 24

The Lord Jesus Christ

And why call ye me, Lord, Lord, and do not the things which I say?–Luke 6:46

In an age where the truths of repentance that Christ has preached, followed by the faithful in all generations, are shunned in our modern feel-good religion called "Christianity," the need to reevaluate our "only believe" peddling of the gospel should be seriously considered. Though the church today lacks power and is unable to keep her "converts" interested in the things of God, she seems to be content to pick and choose text that fits her method for making the gospel acceptable in the eyes of degenerate men. The Lordship of Christ implies the act of surrendering to the call of the Master and turning from anything that hinders that call to follow Him, the hindrance of sin. Thus, repentance is part of our acknowledgment of Christ's ownership upon us when we come to Him by faith for salvation or in our times of being the prodigal and returning to our Father. The grand call of "Believe on the Lord Jesus Christ and thou shalt be saved" of itself implies the emphasis on the Lord of the gospel in repentance though not explicitly mentioned by that term, before believing. The thread of repentance is woven all over the scriptures, for the essence of the gospel is that He shall save His people from their sin. And if one does not repent from their sin, they have no part in the purpose of why Christ came into this world.

THE GOSPEL

April 25

The Offense of the Cross

And I, brethren, if I yet preach circumcision, why do I yet suffer persecution? then is the offence of the cross ceased. – Galatians 5:11

The cross was a cruel instrument of death, and when Christ told those who come to Him to take up his cross and follow Him, He makes the grand invitation to be partakers of His glory through the sufferings of mortal flesh. To die to the things of this world gladly for the world to come. Preaching a half-baked gospel of forgiveness without the cross to the sinner for the judgment of sin, and after becoming a Christian to leave out the cross for the victorious Christian life by their death on the cross to what the world has to offer; such half-baked gospel brings damnation and is not the true gospel of Christ. Those deceived into a false gospel are still lost no matter how sincere they are or how much we make the gospel acceptable using the correct phrases. The gospel not only liberates the sinner from the penalty of sin but also requires the call for the redeemed to follow Christ in the newness of life. Life can only flourish in the absence of death, and our old man through dead with Christ, his influences, and desires through this body of flesh must be put to death daily and be crucified with Christ: nevertheless, I live; yet not I, but Christ liveth in me. Any gospel that cheapens the cost of the call will attract goats and give them coats of sheep, but it will never change their heart or the judgment of the tares that will be theirs on the last day.

THE GOSPEL

April 26

The Inner Person

For God so loved the world, that he gave his only begotten Son, that whosoever believeth in him should not perish, but have everlasting life. –John 3:16

Deep down within the heart of every man, woman, boy or girl is a person. Before they are anything on the outside, they are a person who is unique on the inside, a person with an eternal soul. A soul bound by the grips of sin because of the fall and waging war to resist its Creator, God. And no matter how we see someone on the outside, whether Caucasian, African, Hispanic, Asian, man, woman, transgender, atheist, religious or extremist, we must see the individual as a "person" before Almighty God. And it is this battle for the soul that we are here to wage war against. Though the outward appearance may be different, God's call is to the inner person, the call to turn from their sin and turn to the Savior who loves them and holds original claim upon them through Creation. Our love should look beyond the external and into the spiritual to seek God for His truth and love in reaching the soul of that individual. Do I care, or am I ready to condemn based on what I see or what they do? Though we don't condone or call evil as good, we start with all individuals as a person who has a soul that has an eternal worth before God who loved them and died for them; that they might know the only true God and experience freedom from their bondage of sin.

THE GOSPEL

April 27

Who is a Christian?

And this is life eternal, that they might know thee the only true God, and Jesus Christ, whom thou hast sent.–John 17:3

With the blurring of lines of what a Christ-bearer means to the ever-changing culture of our day, it is imperative that the true meaning of this term is revisited to bring some small semblance of clarity and meaning to the original intent of the word. A Christian is one who the Holy Spirit has regenerated and in whom the Spirit has borne that inner witness of sonship. And it is evident by the life which reflects the change that has taken place in carrying the nature of his Master. It is a transaction that is by grace through faith and not of works. In its finality, it is the revelation of Christ's finished work on the cross, the conviction of the awfulness of one's sin and his standing before a Holy God, this conviction that causes one to turn from their sin to the hope that is through Jesus Christ for freedom from sin; the Spirit orchestrating as He pleaseth. Anything short of that is a superficial facade to name the name of Christ but to be eternally lost. It is not in intellectual assent, Christian heritage, good works, baptism, the supreme pontiff, or being part of a church that one is justified before God, a Christian.

THE GOSPEL

Guide me, O Thou great Jehovah
William Williams

Guide me, O my great Redeemer,
pilgrim through this barren land;
I am weak, but you are mighty;
hold me with your powerful hand.
Bread of heaven, bread of heaven,
   feed me now and evermore,
   feed me now and evermore.

Open now the crystal fountain,
   where the healing waters flow.
Let the fire and cloudy pillar
lead me all my journey through.
Strong Deliverer, strong Deliverer,
   ever be my strength and shield,
   ever be my strength and shield.

When I tread the verge of Jordan,
   bid my anxious fears subside.
Death of death, and hell's Destruction,
   land me safe on Canaan's side.
Songs of praises, songs of praises
   I will ever sing to you,
   I will ever sing to you.

Public Domain

April 28
The Lordship of Christ

If any man come to me, and hate not his father, and mother, and wife, and children, and brethren, and sisters, yea, and his own life also, he cannot be my disciple.–Luke 14:26

Following Christ is about allegiance to Him and acknowledging Him as Lord. Christ must reign supreme; to deny Him would be to deny the faith and be Anathema. When faced with certain death, these early Christians, all they had to do was call Caesar as "Lord" to get their freedom and their family back. There was not a moment of confusion as to what that meant, for "Christ is Lord" meant that no one else was; and at the cost of watching their children and wife torn apart by beasts or crucified on crosses they chose to say, "my allegiance is to Christ and none other," thus proclaiming that Christ was Lord alone. It was not the shallow cliché of "once saved always saved" attitude and not consider the ramifications of obeying Caesar. It was about their lifelong loyalty to follow Christ at all costs. There can never be two King's; it was either Christ or Caesar, Christ or riches, Christ or food, Christ and death, or Nero and temporal-life. Those willing to be baptized realized the consequences of such an act, where baptism would cost them their lives when they have identified themselves with Christ. In such circumstances was Peter's call by the Holy Spirit to repent and be baptized. The outcome of those who truly believed would show their allegiance by their baptism amidst the threat of death. The mark of the beast is about allegiance before anything else.

DISCIPLESHIP

April 29

The Call to Discipleship

The next day John seeth Jesus coming unto him, and saith, Behold the Lamb of God, which taketh away the sin of the world. –John 1:29

In the mystery of sanctification, we see the radiant beauty of God's Sovereignty and man's responsibility in the lifelong process of conforming us into the image of our Lord and Savior, Jesus Christ. We see God's part such as [God] able to keep you from falling, and to present you faultless; neither shall any man pluck them out of my hand; faithful is he that calleth you, who also will do it. And then we see our responsibility before God, to stand fast in the faith; let us hold fast the profession of our faith without wavering; be thou faithful unto death; he that endureth to the end shall be saved; endure hardness, as a good soldier of Jesus Christ; work out your own salvation; warnings of the punishment of the branch that was natural; sinning wilfully; the just shall live by faith: but if any man draw back, my soul shall have no pleasure in him; the call to put on the whole armour of God, that ye may be able to stand against the wiles of the devil. While God preserves us unto the end, the call to persevere is very real, to work out our own salvation with fear and trembling.

DISCIPLESHIP

April 30

Freedom in Christ

(For the weapons of our warfare are not carnal, but mighty through God to the pulling down of strong holds;)
–2 Corinthians 10:4

While there is the reality of living the victorious Christian life on a day-to-day basis, the truth of being freed from the bondage of religion, rituals, snares are something that one can have contention about. From the foundation of living a separated life because of the imparted holiness of God by the seed of Christ that was placed when we were born of the Spirit of God, we look to enjoying God's gift of life to the fullest on what He intended it to be. Freedom from sin, from man's opinions, from the fear of man, from being bound into one way of thinking in personal holiness as taught by a particular persuasion, and many others. Our direction should be God, and His word, which is the core foundation for Christian living, and anything that causes us to deviate from that should be rejected lest it brings us into bondage. Desiring the fullness of the Spirit and walking in it, the life of prayer, are critical cornerstones for enjoying the reality of Christ and His love relationship with us as we serve Him in truth and get to know Him. Being a servant of Jesus Christ is the greatest freedom one can have, for we have responded to His original claim upon us and gladly surrendered to the original intent for what we were made for.

DISCIPLESHIP

May

May 1

The Cultural Impact

To the weak became I as weak, that I might gain the weak: I am made all things to all men, that I might by all means save some.–1 Corinthians 9:22

The teachings of Christ are not about making everybody fit into one cultural mindset. Unless a culture that Christianity goes to is contradictory to the word of God because of certain symbols and practices of that culture, which is against Christ, unless that is the case, one can have the uniqueness of a culture in a people group represented well within the bounds of one becoming a Christian and thriving in it. A Christianity that tries to impose a particular mindset or perspective upon a culture that is not given in the word of God is not biblical and is a hindrance to the cause of Christ. In a land where one may wear a unique cultural dress unless contradicting the principles of modesty or pagan religious affinity, one has no reason to change to adapt to another, such as the Western dress code. When ministering in India, Amy Carmichael wore the traditional dress of a saree in South India to help adapt to that culture. She became all things unto all people while not compromising on the word of God. Christ calls us to be set apart as Christians irrespective of where we are, and it is beyond ones adapting of particular cultural traits which are unique to that part of the world. Instead, it is about being given to godliness and holiness as becometh saints.

DISCIPLESHIP

May 2

The Proclamation of Adoption

Having predestinated us unto the adoption of children by Jesus Christ to himself, according to the good pleasure of his will, To the praise of the glory of his grace, wherein he hath made us accepted in the beloved.–Ephesians 1:5,6

Our reality of who we are in Christ needs to permeate every area of our lives daily. As long as we live in this body of flesh, we are to put it to death daily and live unto God in the newness of life. In Christ, we have His victory that was complete on the Cross. We are seated together in heavenly places in Christ Jesus far above the principalities of darkness. We are joint heirs of His riches and co-laborers with God and God's husbandmen. Such truths ought to grip our perspective of who we are in Christ and free us from our narrow view of who we were in sin before we were redeemed of the Lord. The victorious Christian life is the culmination of our position in Jesus Christ, where His victory is ours by faith, claimed because of our position of sonship in Him. The truth of the holiness of God and the sinfulness of sin ought to resonate in our hearts that we seek those things that are above and not the things of this world. To be dead to sin and live in total freedom is not a pipedream of a Christian, but rather it is the daily reality in this process of sanctification and its growing pains. Our surrender to God begins with this recognition of who we are as a child of the King and not what we were as a child of the devil.

DISCIPLESHIP

May 3

Truth and Trust

And we know that all things work together for good to them that love God, to them who are the called according to his purpose. For I am persuaded, that neither death, nor life, nor angels, nor principalities, nor powers, nor things present, nor things to come, Nor height, nor depth, nor any other creature, shall be able to separate us from the love of God, which is in Christ Jesus our Lord.
—Romans 8:28,38,39

When dealing with the heartache of someone who has been deeply hurt because of broken trust, it is easy to quote scripture and desire for them to move along; but God who created us and knows the innermost pain of our heart desires for us to separate truth from trust in those crucial moments. The truth of God is to be received with implicit trust and without reservation if it is from God; since God is trustworthy and has displayed His faithfulness in Creation and sustenance of life itself. We are to be pliable to hear, believe, and follow God with all our hearts, soul, and mind. Trust in God always follows revealed truth, for God is always good and perfect in all His ways, and there is no shadow of turning in Him. Trust, on the other hand, when dealing with fellowmen, is always earned and never demanded. Try the spirits, whether they be of God, is a command we must pay careful attention to. To lack trust in God for the failure of fellowmen is to fall into the snare of evaluating God by the corrupted standards of man. The judge of all the earth will do right; looking unto Jesus will give us the proper perspective of obeying God rather than man when human trust is broken, and God alone remains.

DISCIPLESHIP

May 4

Christ In You

Fear thou not; for I am with thee: be not dismayed; for I am thy God: I will strengthen thee; yea, I will help thee; yea, I will uphold thee with the right hand of my righteousness.
–Isaiah 41:10

The most significant reality of Christianity is not found in God answering prayers, healing of the body, some miracle that happened, or so forth. Moses standing before God when interceding for Israel spoke the awe-inspiring truth of God being in their midst; the Omnipotent God, the eternal One, the omniscient Creator of all life, the God of the Universe, the God who is alive and Omnipresent; in the new covenant, this same God dwells in the hearts of His people as God Almighty, having His abode in the heart of man. This reality of God dwelling in the heart of a man whom the Holy Spirit has regenerated sets us apart from any other so-called religions or philosophies of this world. This is what separates truth from error, and the incredible privilege of knowing God in such a fashion should be our greatest desire on earth. All other areas such as answers to prayers, miracles, healing, and so forth are all peripheral, which the god of this world can counterfeit. God living inside of man and having that witness of the Holy Spirit is crucial to understanding a Christian's true core of his innermost being. Since the reality of God-in-us is much greater than God-with-us, shouldn't that show in the life of the one claiming the name of Christ?

DISCIPLESHIP

May 5

Judge Not?

Beloved, when I gave all diligence to write unto you of the common salvation, it was needful for me to write unto you, and exhort you that ye should earnestly contend for the faith which was once delivered unto the saints. –Jude 1:3

The standard of judgment is Christ, and His command for His church is to earnestly contend for the faith which was once delivered unto the saints. And to contend means the connotation of contending for truth against error. It is not only the exposing of error but also the proclamation of the truth. Judgment must always be based on righteous judgment; that there is One who is righteous of whose truth we are to uphold. Jesus warned against the self-righteous judgment in the case of a hypocrite but rather to judge according to the truth. Judging others for their false teachings, the doctrine of devils, calling evil good, wolves that are in sheep's clothing, and so forth does two things, it protects the true sheep to be aware of the dangers, and it prevents the compromise of truth that is to be passed to the next generation while staying true to the current generation. Being unequally yoked is not about the clash of personalities or preferences; it is about who one is indwelt by. It is about the antithesis of the Spirit of God, who will always be against the spirit of this world. Error never stands alone; it needs a medium to rest upon so it can spread like leaven, and it never remains without corrupting everything it touches. Truth stands alone, for it does not need an ally to prove itself, for it comes from the giver of truth, God. To weed out compromise and follow church discipline though painful it might be, will have the benediction of God and His enablement to preserve the purity of the gospel.

DISCIPLESHIP

May 6

The Sacredness of Marriage

Marriage is honourable in all, and the bed undefiled: but whoremongers and adulterers God will judge.–Hebrews 13:4

In the ancient Jewish culture, we see the initiation of the intent by the father for his son; the groom getting betrothed (legally bound) to the girl he desires to marry; the bride being faithful to her future husband while the groom prepares a place in his father's house; the bringing of the mohar, the price that was given for the redemption of the bride; the finality of the act in marriage when the bride is brought back to his father's house; the eventuality of the marriage itself that is for life; a love relationship based on commitment more than emotions. All these are beautiful pictures of Christ and His Bride, the redeemed of the Lord; we who did not desire Him or deserve Him but crucified Him. The high price of salvation is portrayed by the innocent blood which was shed to buy us back from the god of this world in paying the price of sin. Such sacred pictures are too pure to be polluted or misinterpreted. And the act of marriage that has always been given as one man to one woman in the Old and New Testament takes new significance when we realize the beauty and purity of Christ and His Bride.

DISCIPLESHIP

May 7

Revelation and the End Times

He that hath an ear, let him hear what the Spirit saith unto the churches; To him that overcometh will I give to eat of the hidden manna, and will give him a white stone, and in the stone a new name written, which no man knoweth saving he that receiveth it.
–Revelation 2:17

The instinct to survive is one of the fundamental drives of mankind. With this comes the drive to escape suffering at all costs, which opens the door of making it easy for men to interpret scriptures to their benefit. While treading on last days' eschatology and the reality of American Christianity with its lack of experiencing persecution, escaping persecution using the Rapture as the next event seems enticing. While parts of the world have been going through intense persecution, and in some places, it has been so severe that escaping the great tribulation does not seem attractive anymore. Looking at Revelation as a topic for staying faithful to Christ and preparing for persecution, as something that will come, should be the proper perspective we should have when dealing with this topic. The cycle of evil that is repetitive in every generation on the way it manifests itself and the need for God's people to stand, even unto death until the Lord's return, is the central theme of Revelation. The need for self-evaluation in examining oneself against the letter to the seven churches of Asia Minor should help keep our focus on Christ irrespective of the generation and circumstances we find ourselves in. The book of Revelation was just as relevant for the First Century Christians as it is today.

DISCIPLESHIP

May 8
Impatient Requests

The soul of the sluggard desireth, and hath nothing: but the soul of the diligent shall be made fat.—Proverbs 13:4

Our generation's pattern of looking for quick answers to deep-rooted questions speaks to the shallowness of their asking. One who is desirous of truth must seek it as a pearl of great price, willing to sell all that he has to acquire it and as a treasure worth striving for, though it may cost his own life and opinions in the process. God, who is infinite, gives out of the abundance of His heart truths that are so spellbinding that they are hard to contain and express in a few words of philosophical didactics. Truth always has a price that you have to pay, and once received, must be obeyed being mixed with faith. Though truth reaches the lofty peaks of one's intellectual fringes beyond understanding, it can be easily received by those who are pure in heart, for they shall see God. Wisdom uttereth her voice in the streets for all who will come with a penitent heart and receive of her, but it is those who are proud that God will resist, and they will go back grieved having great possessions of this world but bankrupt in the eyes of God. The revelation of truth as an illumination of the Spirit will not be granted unless one is willing to receive it desiring to obey, though it may contradict what they believe or how they have perceived it.

DISCIPLESHIP

May 9

Dead to Sin

For sin shall not have dominion over you: for ye are not under the law, but under grace.—Romans 6:14

In baptism, a vivid picture is portrayed regarding the victorious Christian life. To be immersed is to be buried with Christ where the old man has been put to death with no more power to overcome the regenerated man, which reminds us that when Christ died, I died with Him, and my "old man" of sin was put to death and buried with Him, never to have dominion over me anymore. When we resist the flesh, we must realize our position in Christ where when we rise from the waters, we have been raised to walk in newness of life, and we were raised to be seated in heavenly places in Christ Jesus. In being tempted, we realize that giving into sin is not a necessity but a choice to stoop down from heavenly places to desire the bondage of Egypt. This reality needs to be a constant reminder of what Christ died for when He took our sins upon Himself. If Christ did not take our sins upon Himself, He would have never died since He was sinless, and it is the wages of sin that brought death. But as an innocent lamb of God, Christ paid the price for our sin, without any sin that was inherited from Adam since Jesus had no earthly father, being born of a virgin. And since life is in the blood, His blood was shed upon the mercy seat as a sinless, spotless Lamb who gave Himself for us that we might be raised to walk in victory; to be dead to sin which shall no longer have dominion over us.

DISCIPLESHIP

May 10

Truth vs Life

Who through faith subdued kingdoms, wrought righteousness, obtained promises, stopped the mouths of lions. Women received their dead raised to life again: and others were tortured, not accepting deliverance; that they might obtain a better resurrection:–Hebrews 11:33,35

The drive to live is one of the greatest motivators at the core of the human response. When faced with a threatening situation, the instinctive physiological response to fight or flight can be overwhelming. All through the centuries standing for truth has been tested against the desire to live. It was either the preservation of truth or the preservation of life. To preserve life was to compromise and deny the faith; to preserve truth was to die a martyr. We are creatures of comfort, and if we get too comfortable with this world, then preservation of life becomes the greater factor for denying the faith, for where your treasure is, there will your heart be also. But when God calls us to preserve truth at the expense of our lives, it goes against the natural response to those facing certain death. God's truth always prevails; at times, it finds itself shining brightly in the valley of death, for by it, the Church is once again revived by the blood of the martyrs, and the wheat is separated from the tares.

DISCIPLESHIP

May 11

Restitution

And I will give them one heart, and I will put a new spirit within you; and I will take the stony heart out of their flesh, and will give them an heart of flesh:–Ezekiel 11:19

The essence of the gospel is freedom from sin and to be reconciled with a Holy God. When thus reconciled and the offense towards God is covered under the blood, the offense towards men is brought to light. Restitution is an immediate outflow when the Holy Spirit convicts you of your standing before men. Whether a young Christian or seasoned believer, restitution is getting right with fellow men in desiring purity of heart. A salvation that does not bring a changed life and the outflow of an inward change is not the true salvation wrought by God. If you have an offense against your brother Jesus said to leave the gift at the altar and make amends before seeking God. Thus, when one is changed from the inside out, they are made to see the reality of their sin as to how it affects not only God but also its effect on fellowmen. The demonstration of Christianity is not in its teachings but rather in its action of loving God with all our hearts, soul, and might and loving others as ourselves. While the response to those from whom we desire restitution cannot be predicted, the act requires sincerity of heart to humble ourselves and be willing to receive their just or unjust reward in seeking forgiveness, leaving the consequences to God.

DISCIPLESHIP

May 12

Vanity Fair

For all that is in the world, the lust of the flesh, and the lust of the eyes, and the pride of life, is not of the Father, but is of the world.—1 John 2:16

The need to be in the world and not of the world has the command of our Lord to call us to consider what we may have given in to what the world has to offer in the context of good fun. Evaluation of self and the need for one to recognize the siren call of what pleases the flesh in fame, popularity, and the worship of self-esteem, are all areas that can be influenced by the weights that so easily beset us. The worship of self in the desire to look young at the cost of all, the want of money through corporate progress at the altar of compromise, the acceptance of the world by blending with the ways of the world, and so forth can set us on a path that we never intended to tread in. The world will take notice of the pure in heart and berate them violently. And the worst of all will come from so-called carnal Christians who neither desire the life of separation nor allow for others to follow the path of their Savior but are as thorns and snares to hinder the way of the one who loves His Lord, and their desire is for the sheep to stumble. Those who hinder are they that God will spew out of His mouth.

DISCIPLESHIP

May 13

The Patience of Satan

Be sober, be vigilant; because your adversary the devil, as a roaring lion, walketh about, seeking whom he may devour:–1 Peter 5:8

When dealing with temptation, there are times where we come across an area where we are vulnerable to fall when Satan entices us to sin. At such times when seeing that temptation for what it is, sinning against a Holy God, we resist the devil who flees from us. While we know the necessity of being sober and vigilant, there at times, we skip over the seed that Satan sows in our lives and do not deal with it in asking for the Spirit to search us and to cleanse us by destroying the seeds. But, if we fail to do so though we may not see any effects of that seed for a while, there will come a time where those seeds will sprout if forgotten. Before we know it, it will overwhelm us and cause us to sin. At such times it is not for us to wonder how we fell; instead, it should cause us to realize the patience of Satan to silently sow those seeds on our soil, hoping to blind us in leaving some of them unnoticed or ignored. As they take root, he continues to water it and let it grow to the point of a great forest, which makes it multiple times more demanding to uproot than when Satan first placed it.

DISCIPLESHIP

May 14
The Simple Life

The thing that hath been, it is that which shall be; and that which is done is that which shall be done: and there is no new thing under the sun. –Ecclesiastes 1:9

What does God think of me? The image of the man representing himself has the danger of seeing everything in light of what others perceive of him by the praises or accolades given to him. To be known of men and unknown of God is one of the greatest tragedies one can live their lives in. When I stand before God, nothing else matters but the burning question, what does God think of me? For we brought nothing into this world, and it is certain we can carry nothing out. Anything mankind had done in the field of technology, science, or any human advancement since Creation has been received freely and built on what has already been. Artificial Intelligence is the enrichment of raw materials derived from the progression of electrical impulses that makes 1's and 0's. His pursuit of going to Mars uses what is available to find a way to harness the planet and find new ways of applying it; and echoes with Solomon that there is no new thing under the sun. Oh, to be free from the pleasure of riches, sophistication, and walk-in humility with a pure conscience before God; to live a simple life, to seek neither power nor possession or pride but to behold the face of Jesus day by day where worldly gains are counted as heavenly losses.

DISCIPLESHIP

May 15

The Conquering of Sin

And to know the love of Christ, which passeth knowledge, that ye might be filled with all the fulness of God. Now unto him that is able to do exceeding abundantly above all that we ask or think, according to the power that worketh in us,–Ephesians 3:19,20

The destruction of the gods of Egypt in the ten plagues and the serpent, and the final judgment upon Pharaoh and his horsemen to be drowned in the sea, speaks of God's war against sin and His complete victory over sin. For the Christian who has been redeemed from Egypt by the mighty hand of Almighty God and set free from the power of sin has the assurance for those saved to live in complete victory over sin. The reality that sin in the life of a believer is not a necessity is refreshing and exhilarates oneself to live from the dominion of sin to experience freedom through Christ. The picture of the Israelites who were no longer under the dominion of Pharaoh, though at times they longed to go back, portrays the fact that while the siren call of sin may evoke desires of the flesh in us to long after it, the ability of God to guide us far away from the direct enslavement of sin which has been broken at Calvary shows us that we should not serve sin. Thus, the Apostle John's grand declaration that "Whosoever is born of God doth not commit sin; for his seed remaineth in him: and he cannot sin, because he is born of God." rings true to the feeble believer who trembles at the thought of his habitual sin which had enslaved him before he came to the Savior.

DISCIPLESHIP

May 16

Doulos of Jesus Christ

I beseech you therefore, brethren, by the mercies of God, that ye present your bodies a living sacrifice, holy, acceptable unto God, which is your reasonable service. –Romans 12:1

The effectiveness of an individual who has been bought with a price to be adopted into the family of God is not about how much they can use their talents or ability to impress the people for God. God's call for every believer is to be a doulos of Jesus Christ. The word doulos means "slave," and it is a word that has been translated at times as "servant" in the King James Version. In its implication, a doulos has lost all his rights for the express purpose of serving another. This position does not speak of oppression but to willingly lose our rights for the One who bought us with His blood in a privilege that is most joyous. To serve God is to lose our talents, desires, wants, ability and let the mantle of God cover us and use us as He pleaseth. And when He exalts a vessel unto honor, there is no recognition of the vessel of what it has done; instead, the vessel realizes the position of being a slave and representing the Master in whatever way the Master has chosen to use them. Thus, in its finality, the vessel's usefulness is based on its reliance upon God to shew forth His glory by being a doulos of Jesus Christ, where the vessel has no pride of what it can do for the Master but how much it can die to self for the glory of another.

DISCIPLESHIP

May 17

Accountability Under Grace

For unto whomsoever much is given, of him shall be much required: and to whom men have committed much, of him they will ask the more.–Luke 12:48b

Throughout the scriptures, we see God's handiwork in His dealings with His Creation. From Adam to the giving of the law to the Prophets and the final revelation of fulfillment in Christ, from the Epistles to the end-time revelation; through all this, though the Canon of Scriptures is now closed, we see a panorama of the progressive revelation of God in them. Though we will never know in perfection God's dealing with man in our mortal flesh, we can look to an all-wise God and see the handiwork of His hands. As more was revealed, more was required. Where under the law obedience was required, under grace, it was brought to a higher standard. Where adultery in action was forbidden in the law with externals, in Christ, it begins with the heart. Thus, Christ dealt with the core issue that was the finality of what the law was intended to reveal, but under grace, it was brought even more into the open. One who desires to take the Old Testament for fulfilling their sinful desires such as divorce under the law of Moses must realize that they are not held under the law but under grace where the accountability is much higher for much has been given. To reduce the deity of Christ in such matters for making provision for the flesh is to commit spiritual suicide and end up with neither truth nor grace, but they will be held in bondage to their delusions.

DISCIPLESHIP

May 18

Reaction vs Truth

And when he had called the people unto him with his disciples also, he said unto them, Whosoever will come after me, let him deny himself, and take up his cross, and follow me. – Mark 8:34

The cross of Jesus Christ ought to be our most excellent comfort against what we see in the potential for the world, flesh, and the devil to overpower us in our walk and service for God. Our daily desire should be to have Christ keep us near the cross, to put to death anything that rises against Him violently. In being vessels of clay, the temptation to be heard and see a response to a preached message can overshadow the necessity of truth to go forward. In such times one may be desirous of seeing a reaction from the audience in an appeal or to try to use rhetoric and graphic descriptions to move the audience. But the simplicity found in Christ desires truth to go forward as a mighty flood, and the reaction becomes secondary and according to the working of the Holy Spirit in imparting truth and grace in the ears of the hearer. Our greatest desire as a vessel should be to be crucified with Christ from the affections of this world, not desiring the praise of men, to see the pure, untouched truth of God revealed in the heart of the hearers where men hear the voice of God and not the exhortation of man. God uses lowly vessels, but it is sobering to realize that the earthen vessels are only used as they are made fit for the Master's use.

DISCIPLESHIP

May 19

Response to Government

For we wrestle not against flesh and blood, but against principalities, against powers, against the rulers of the darkness of this world, against spiritual wickedness in high places.—Ephesians 6:12

I don't want the Lord to come in the context of getting out of here; once He comes, it's all over; instead, I want to see the Lord work here and now. The three God-ordained institutions are the home, government, and the church in that order. Anything that subverts the authorities that God has kept on our behalf for our good is resisting the ordinance of God. No one has the authority to subvert God's institution, no matter which political party they belong to. Above all, there is the law of God that supersedes the law of man, and when in contradiction, we ought to obey God rather than men, not by insurrection and desiring the works of the flesh; but by seeking the face of God, preaching the word by the Spirit, contending for the faith, exposing evil, reaching out to others in love and leaving the rest to God. No matter who rules the White House, we don't follow man but God, we don't surrender to the popular culture of inclusion that calls for the acceptance and promotion of sin, but instead, we follow Christ alone who said, "He that is not with me is against me." Christ is Lord over all, and He [as God] demands total allegiance exclusively to Him. And there is only one true God, the God of the Bible known by the names of Jehovah, Jesus Christ, and the Holy Spirit, the Godhead.

DISCIPLESHIP

May 20

Living by Faith

It is of the Lord's mercies that we are not consumed, because his compassions fail not. They are new every morning: great is thy faithfulness. The Lord is my portion, saith my soul; therefore will I hope in him.–Lamentations 3:22-24

Man shall not live by bread alone. If you live for bread, one who controls the food controls you; if you live for money, those who control money controls you; if you live for religion, those who control religion controls you; if you live for man's laws, those who control the law controls you; if you live by fear, those who control the media controls you; if you live by feelings, one who controls your circumstances controls you; if you live for this world, those who control society controls you; if you live by trusting in man, then politics will control you; if you live for self then the god of this world controls you. But, if it is by every word that proceedeth out of the mouth of God, then God who created you in love and truth controls you where you have been set free from anything this world can bind you with. Instead of bread, God provides sustenance; instead of the money, God meets our every need; instead of religion, God has given a relationship; instead of man's laws, God has given His eternal, unchanging laws; instead of fear, God gives hope; instead of feeling, God gives victory; instead of the world, God gives His word to conquer the world by the power of the Spirit; instead of confidence in man, God gives us His faithfulness that never fails.

DISCIPLESHIP

May 21

Privileged to Serve

But thou, when thou prayest, enter into thy closet, and when thou hast shut thy door, pray to thy Father which is in secret; and thy Father which seeth in secret shall reward thee openly.
–Matthew 6:6

Everything we have has been received, and in the realm of service, one may be tempted when they see someone who shares a testimony to cause us to desire the need for recognizing us when we have invested our lives for that cause. When this does not come to fruition, we feel slighted when recognition has not been given. But we must come to the place of acknowledging that God who of His own desire chooses the vessel, molds them, empowers them, uses them as it pleases Him. We are humbled and deeply grateful that we would even be a part of this panorama when serving Him, with or without recognition. If our lives were given to God and none knew of it, that would be enough since we are here for God and not for desiring men's acceptance or praise. The impact of Lydia, Eubulus, Tychicus may never be known, but while they are just names on a page, their record is in Heaven. To please God should be our greatest goal, and directing man's focus to be upon God should be our utmost goal. Anything that hinders that lofty goal should be avoided, for God will not share His glory with another.

DISCIPLESHIP

May 22

God in a Box

But will God in very deed dwell with men on the earth? behold, heaven and the heaven of heavens cannot contain thee; how much less this house which I have built!–2 Chronicles 6:18

One of the great dangers of well-intended people in desiring to give the audience a better view of the hidden things of God, such as the doctrine of Trinity, has portrayed such truths utilizing entertainment through animation or movies. In so doing, we tend to limit the mystery of God through those senses of hearing or seeing, and we find ourselves relating to what we heard and saw whenever we encounter eternal truths. When we read about Christ, a picture of someone's portrayal in a movie comes to mind, and an event such as a miracle becomes nothing more than an animated sequence. Such limiting of the eternal aspects of God, while may help convey certain truths, can also be the cause of great danger to remove the awe and the wonder of the transcendent nature of God that He has revealed to us in His word. God desires to open our understanding and go deeper as we learn of Him, but it can cause a human mind to fall back into a movie as the fullness of that truth. Such skewed views can apply in many areas where incomprehensible attributes of God can be made into something that can be packaged in a box with a bow, given to be unraveled at the audience's desire. Profound supernatural truths that we try to explain using natural means can immediately cause that truth to become intellectual, sterile, and commonplace.

DISCIPLESHIP

May 23

Approachable vs Agreeable

Sanctify them through thy truth: thy word is truth. –John 17:17

One must always be a conduit for spreading the grace of God, the love of God, the justice of God, the wrath of God, and so forth. But in so doing, it must be done with the Spirit of Christ and not in the spirit of Adam. The Spirit of Christ is peaceable with all men, for it knows the foundational issue of man that he is dead in trespasses and sins, the god of this world has blinded him where he hates the light and those who proclaim it, and that except he repents he shall likewise perish. So, with the undergirding of love, the man of God preaches truth while being approachable. Being agreeable, on the other hand, even on areas that seem peripheral while disagreeing on the fundamentals of the faith will immediately mean compromise. Agreeing that man needs help while holding hands with a modernist, who denies the deity of Jesus Christ, is not only foolish but an abomination in the sight of a Holy God. An agreement must be on the common ground of the truth of the word of God and not on the opinions of men, no matter how sincere they are or how much of a platform it can give for the propagation of truth as one may see it. A compromised truth ceases to be the truth, for it carries with it the leaven of error.

DISCIPLESHIP

May 24

Relevant for every Generation

For ever, O Lord, thy word is settled in heaven. Thy faithfulness is unto all generations: thou hast established the earth, and it abideth. They continue this day according to thine ordinances: for all are thy servants. –Psalm 119:89-91

The ability of the scriptures to identify the real problem of man and prescribe the proper remedy speaks of the nature of the Author of the Bible. While fallen humanity can only try to stop the symptoms such as racism, hatred, injustice, and so forth, only God who created man can adequately diagnose the real need of man, salvation from sin. In the interest of man's self-glorying seed of sin, man tries to elevate his belief over another by stating that education, laws, good works, being kind, and so forth can of themselves cure man's greatest need. Still, they are only dealing with surface-level issues, and death cannot cure death. While man can only produce death, only God, the Creator of life, can create that turning point of regeneration where new life is imparted into those dead in trespasses and sins, and life begins. Such is the nature of the remedy, for a good doctor does not cure the symptoms but looks to dig deeper into the root cause of the matter. Thus, the scriptures are relevant in every generation, for man's fundamental need is not the betterment of himself; instead, it is in the creative act of God in changing him to what God created him to be in the first place, and until then, the symptoms will persist in one form or another.

DISCIPLESHIP

May 25

Who is my Neighbor?

Which now of these three, thinkest thou, was neighbour unto him that fell among the thieves? And he said, He that shewed mercy on him. Then said Jesus unto him, Go, and do thou likewise.
–Luke 10:36,37

In a world that has the desire to create objects of lust, abuse of power, and lures with the god of mammon to destroy a soul, what is to be our response? Seeing others as objects of love that God desires to redeem, as one who is made in the image of God, is crucial for realizing the worth of a soul. The Samaritan who showed compassion needs to evoke this question of who our neighbor is in our generation. Instead of shying away from those whom the world has put on gaudy display and eventually discards them, those who are tired of trying what the world has to offer but who realize that they are emptier than when they started; our eyes must look upon these who are ravaged by their sin. Whether it be a prostitute, those in prison, street gangs, religion, and cults, given to drugs and alcohol, trying to find fulfillment in LGBTQ+, promiscuous sex, or any other vice of sin that leads to destruction, we need to see them, as we travel to the Celestial City to be with our Lord, as our neighbor who is lying wounded and bleeding on the side of the road. And we stop and bind up their wounds in love; we carry them on our transport and meet their real need so that our Lord may have many in His banquet at the table. We go into the highways and hedges and compel them to come in, by the power of the Spirit and the effectual working of the Word that whosoever will may come.

DISCIPLESHIP

May 26

God's Desire

> *The steps of a good man are ordered by the Lord: and he delighteth in his way.* –Psalm 37:23

Doing God's will is not about opposing our will. The regenerated man who is desirous of God Himself will, in turn, do God's desire and, in so doing, will fulfill God's will. There is a temptation to think that because of the amount of work I put in seeking after God, such as fasting, prayer, weeping, etc., we weigh it against what God needs to do for us as an entitlement. It becomes a work that we do in comparison to the work we ask of God to do. Many get discouraged when God does not seem to answer though we have asked, wept, and fasted for something we are asking for. When we align ourselves to God's desire, the work we do in seeking God is meant for purifying our asking and our vessel for His giving and filling. And there is always the grave danger of quitting before God's complete work is done. We desire God by wanting Himself, for His will to be done on earth as it is in heaven, by obeying His word, having faith that pleases God, and submitting to the Lordship of Christ, realizing the truth that He owns everything that we are, have and do. It is not about just doing God's will; it is about fulfilling God's desire which means we need to be walking in fellowship with Him. When we repent and return to our first love to God, then God's desire can genuinely become ours.

DISCIPLESHIP

May 27

The Receiving of Truth

He that goeth forth and weepeth, bearing precious seed, shall doubtless come again with rejoicing, bringing his sheaves with him.—Psalm 126:6

In a desire to justify the behavior of self, in the guise of sincerity, one may question the truth of the deity of Christ or the commands of Christ or the Lordship of Christ. To pry open the scriptures, beyond what the scriptures intended to reveal, for justifying one's pride speaks to the deceitfulness of sin. The declaration of John the Baptist to "Behold the Lamb of God, which taketh away the sin of the world" speaks of the laying down of the evidence for Christ but leaving the following of Christ to those who are convinced of Him. The purpose of contending has to come to the point of presenting the truths, reasoning, and such. Still, after the truths have been laid out where the Spirit has made manifest the witness to the truth, we must step back and let the listener take the step of believing and obeying, lest they trample them under their feet and turn again and rend us. We come to the place where we stand at the precipice of the revelation of God and realize that faith is not convincing the other that it is true; instead, it is because God convinces them that it is the truth. While we sow in tears, we realize that it is God who gives the increase.

DISCIPLESHIP

May 28

Grafted into Christ

I am the vine, ye are the branches: He that abideth in me, and I in him, the same bringeth forth much fruit: for without me ye can do nothing.—John 15:5

Many of the astounding truths of the gospel and what it means to a believer can be lost when we hastily read through the scriptures with little consideration to the supernatural element of the Author in His infinite depths of revelation that He has given us. The position of the lost who in Adam is dead in sin, to be bound to sin's sway for the destruction of the flesh, searing of the conscience, living in bondage, and so forth, are seen when we realize the reality of the Adamic nature in us. When God saved us, we have been plucked as it were from the burning and plunged into the eternal stream of God through Jesus Christ. In Him dwells all fullness. The perfection of His life, His victory over sin and death, His ability to respond with all knowledge and wisdom, His command over demons, His penetrating power over the heart of man, His display of perfect love and wrath, and so forth were made ours when we were plunged into Christ. Our position was taken from Adam and placed into Christ, where the apostle was able to say that we are dead to sin through Christ, that we should not serve sin. Because of this engrafting and being taken away from the dead branch of Adam, we continue to purge ourselves from the pollution of this world that has its pull on our body of flesh, who is crucified with Christ daily.

DISCIPLESHIP

May 29

It is Finished

And you, that were sometime alienated and enemies in your mind by wicked works, yet now hath he reconciled. In the body of his flesh through death, to present you holy and unblameable and unreproveable in his sight:–Colossians 1:21,22

Oh, deplorable, despicable, and utterly wretched sin; that steals the love of God, His glory, the purity of His fellowship, the sanctity of life, polluting everything that is Godward. Jesus Christ is the author and finisher of our faith and our victory. Christ's grand declaration of "It is finished" has put to death the law of sin and death, and in salvation, His victory had become ours when He saved us and gave us a new heart and imparted His life into us, with the Holy Spirit living inside of us. But the presence of sin in us can only be made to respond when we allow sin to influence us from without. For the death on the cross has effectively put to death the end of sin, of the old man, in us. In this body of flesh, it is brought to a place of influence when we allow it to be left alive like king Agag. But keeping Christ as our victory, we bring every thought under scrutiny to the obedience of Christ and into captivity those that are of sin. The impetus for sin that will make it alive should be put to death before it can perform its intended desire in us; what glorious truth we have been given to enjoy our Creator in perfect fellowship, putting to death daily this body of sin and live unto the glory and praise of the Father and the enjoyment of their communion, our God who is three in one.

DISCIPLESHIP

May 30

Forsaking All

And Jesus said unto him, No man, having put his hand to the plough, and looking back, is fit for the kingdom of God.—Luke 9:62

The cost of discipleship in the realm of following Christ is something every true child of God needs to consider before desiring a deeper walk with Christ. The call to forsake all stands tall and beckons those who come by faith to put everything they hold dear to death. This call to "forsake all" is not just the world, the flesh, and the devil but rather the greater temptation of desiring good things at the expense of the best and the temptation to ask amiss. We are called to forsake recognition among God's people, the praise of other Christians, acceptance in the realm of a godly audience, and a myriad of others. Paul's desire to consider everything as dung for the knowledge of Christ Jesus precedes his declaration of wanting to know Him at all costs. Anything that hinders our desire to ascend the mountain with God to reach greater heights of our knowledge and intimacy with Christ, anything that interferes it must be put to death even at the cost of walking alone and a path that is unknown to the rest of Christendom. Grand glimpses that God gave to Moses of Himself were done in the secret peaks of Mount Sinai when he was alone with God. And Christ's clarion call to forsake all stands as a testament for those humble hearts who will take up its baton to desire God at all costs.

DISCIPLESHIP

May 31

God's Treasures

Labour not for the meat which perisheth, but for that meat which endureth unto everlasting life, which the Son of man shall give unto you: for him hath God the Father sealed. –John 6:27

In the carnal mind and the world we live in, having provision for our lives seems as natural and normal as the air we breathe. This mindset can bleed into our call to follow Christ's way of life, where God's provision is always equated to material benefits. In response to the truth of God owning the cattle on a thousand hills, we can feed our desire to be rich and keep our flesh entertained to the thought of riches, though we spiritualize it as from God. But the scriptures paint a very different picture of those who were destitute and wanderers in sheepskins and goatskins having no earthly homes or provision, being accounted into the hall of faith. We think of the example of Lazarus, who was a beggar and eating the crumbs off the rich man's table and covered in sores. But God's who is eternal, as much as He desires to provide for the temporal needs of His children, desires treasures in accordance with His nature which is eternal. The fruits and the gifts of the Spirit which are given for the glory of God speak of the genuine desire that one needs to have for following hard after God in search of eternal riches, culminating in desiring God Himself for who He is and not for what He can give. If all we had was God, and there was no Heaven or Hell, would that be enough to love God with all our hearts, soul, and mind?

DISCIPLESHIP

June

June 1

The Greater Responsibility

Let no man deceive you with vain words: for because of these things cometh the wrath of God upon the children of disobedience. Be not ye therefore partakers with them. For ye were sometimes darkness, but now are ye light in the Lord: walk as children of light:
–Ephesians 5:6-8

One needs to consider specific areas of caution with all diligence lest they are found wanting on the last day. Such is this matter of one who is regenerated by the Spirit of God and the responsibility that rests upon them in their newfound freedom to serve Christ. In Adam, we died, and we became slaves to sin, enslaved in our will, with Satan as our master; in the act of regeneration, our will is freed, given new desires to live and enjoy what was lost in Eden with God our Creator. The various passages of scriptures such as, shall not inherit, wrath upon the children of disobedience, drawing back from their calling, the branch rejected due to unbelief, and so forth are all written to believers with warnings associated with them to those who partake of it. In the mystery of God's ability to be able to bring us to the very end and present us faultless before the Father and the responsibility of the man who is called to stand and not partake of the unclean works of darkness has the great need for being sober and vigilant lest we are frivolous in our obedience toward God for what He has done. We have the greater personal accountability before God, for whom much has been given, much shall be required. We ought to pay careful attention and live circumspectly lest we don't find ourselves as we expected or were led to believe when we die.

DISCIPLESHIP

June 2

Righteous Anger

Then Peter said unto her, How is it that ye have agreed together to tempt the Spirit of the Lord? behold, the feet of them which have buried thy husband are at the door, and shall carry thee out. Then fell she down straightway at his feet, and yielded up the ghost: and the young men came in, and found her dead, and, carrying her forth, buried her by her husband.—Acts 5:9,10

The human emotion of anger in response to events or actions that one may see such as defiling of the glory of God, the perversion of taking the blessings that have been received from the kind hand of God and abusing it to the satisfying of one's lust, the attribution of God's character for man's sinful behavior and lifestyles, the deception of Satan, and so forth can result in this emotion surfacing from within. Yet the command to "Be ye angry, and sin not" speaks of being angry but not letting anger control us, which will lead to a fleshly response. Paul's stirring at Athens, Christ's zealous cleansing of the Temple, God's anger toward the wicked every day, Peter's rebuke of Ananias and Sapphira, which resulted in their death, and so forth speaks of the reality that while our spirit is stirred when wickedness is seen around us, realizing the grief, it brings to God, the truth of "Vengeance is mine; I will repay" causes us to not respond in anger. While standing on Mount Carmel and mocking the prophets of Baal, Elijah looked to God for the vindication of His name where the fire fell and consumed the sacrifice. The impossibility of having this proper response of being swift to hear, slow to speak, and slow to wrath should drive us to our knees and cause us to realize that the only way this is possible is by being filled with the Spirit of God.

DISCIPLESHIP

June 3

Walking with God

And it came to pass, that a whole year they assembled themselves with the church, and taught much people. And the disciples were called Christians first in Antioch.–Acts 11:26b

One naming the name of Christ realizes the incredible privilege they have to walk with the One who said, "Let there be light." Christ-life is not a sporadic theme based on a particular day of the week or program. It is a lifelong continuation of a steady, purposeful, and daily walk with God. The beginning of that relationship through regeneration by the Holy Spirit is crucial to enable that first step. Those who claim His name but show in action by being a one-day-a-week on a Sunday morning "Christian" are deceiving themselves by living like the devil the rest of the week. Such hypocrisy can only point to the truth that they were never really born of the Spirit of God. Instead, they made a "decision" that neither affected them nor their eternity. If salvation did not change you, it is wise to acknowledge that you were never really made a child of God but are still in the gall of iniquity. In Antioch, they were called Christians by unbelievers by what they saw in the lives of those professing to follow Christ. It would be wise not to call ourselves a Christian until we prove it where unbelievers call us one, seeing our Christlikeness and reflecting what God has shown in His word. Let us never forget that we are called to a life that reflects on the holiness of God and the unblameable character of Christ.

DISCIPLESHIP

June 4

God Molding Man

yea, I have spoken it, I will also bring it to pass; I have purposed it, I will also do it.–Isaiah 46:11b

The reality of God's intricate involvement in sustaining His Creation daily, to uphold all things in their place, speaks of the Omnipotence of God. The ability of God to bring about what He intended to pass is seen where God, as promised to Abraham, brought forth the blessed Savior of the world, Jesus Christ, by sustaining the lineage in prophecy from Abraham to Mary and his earthly corporeal father, Joseph. The promise of God and the ability to keep it in absolute Sovereignty speaks of God keeping four thousand years of history to bring forth His Son at the appointed time. Evangelical Christianity has made the grave error of seeing Christ's victory at Calvary as an end and the gospel as being up to them to convince those being dealt with to get them to believe the event of Scripture and its historical significance and pray a prayer. On the contrary, God actively works in drawing, convicting, regenerating, giving a new heart and a new Spirit indwelling in man, assurance, and so forth. As we work, our Father works in and through us for His purpose and glory. And those who do not show evidence of that pull against sin by the Spirit must be carefully evaluated and instructed to allow the deep plowing needed for the harvest. Shallow views of God will produce a spurious number of false converts, bringing down the glory of God.

DISCIPLESHIP

June 5
Spirit and in Truth

Enter into his gates with thanksgiving, and into his courts with praise: be thankful unto him, and bless his name. For the Lord is good; his mercy is everlasting; and his truth endureth to all generations.–Psalm 100:4,5

The grand declaration of Christ to the Samaritan woman who had desired earthly objects of love and was left unfulfilled, Christ declaring "God is a Spirit: and they that worship him must worship him in spirit and in truth" speaks of the dynamic nature of worship and the need for every individual and Church to evaluate what worship means to them. Worship is not about singing Hymns, worship bands, atmospheric moods to evoke emotions, and such. While worship can affect feelings, it never begins with emotion. It has two crucial elements, truth, of who God is, and spirit, of man's regenerated spirit that has been made alive to commune with his Creator. When the truth of a song impacts the heart of the hearer in his spirit, the spontaneous response to that truth and the inner witness of the Spirit to his spirit makes the worshipper respond to His God with reverence, adoration, and love to the One who is being spoken of. Thus, worship is always directed to the One who deserves it, God. Any act that takes away the focus of the worshipper from God, be it the song, worship leader, emotional rollercoasters, or such, may give an emotional and temporal feeling of happiness but will take away the true worship that God requires. And so shall it be in Heaven when we join the voice of all the ages to worship God in spirit and in truth.

DISCIPLESHIP

June 6

The Journey of Knowing God

Humble yourselves in the sight of the Lord, and he shall lift you up. –James 4:10

To begin and continue the ascent to a lofty mountain requires volition, planning, and perseverance. The tide against the Christian who desires such an undertaking will find himself confronted by the world and the devil. In addition, to thwart one from this lofty goal, there is the ever-present element of the flesh, where pride of the endeavor or the desire to have an elevated view of self due to their knowledge of God is real. This journey of knowing God must not be undertaken for the doing of it, but instead, it must begin with humility. The humility that realizes that we have nothing of ourselves, but all we have is what we have received. And any knowledge of God that we embrace is from the kind hand of God that He has chosen to reveal to us, who loved us before we loved Him. Such awe must inspire one to fall in love with His God and desire to know Him even more. And so, the journey begins and culminates in death when he is brought face to face with His God. Draw nigh to God is the call for man to lose confidence in his ability and depend on God's ability for that sacred communion with God, where knowing God becomes the end goal for fulfilling the original intent of a man who was made for the pleasure of His Creator.

DISCIPLESHIP

June 7
Soldier of Jesus Christ

No man that warreth entangleth himself with the affairs of this life; that he may please him who hath chosen him to be a soldier.—2 Timothy 2:4

There seems to have been a monumental shift in the calling of the Christian church. The call of a Christian is to die to self, to be in absolute surrender to another. In so doing, he is to be a soldier of Jesus Christ. A soldier has a few crucial qualities that seem to have been lost in our day and age. A soldier has no rights; he obeys orders without question; he is prepared for one thing, to battle; he realizes that he does not dialogue with the enemy but finds the enemy's weakness to kill him, for the alternative will be the death of himself. He has pledged his allegiance to one Master, the Lord Jesus Christ, and he is not afraid to die or to see blood on the battlefield. The Israelites were God's arm of justice against sin when they utterly destroyed the heathen and their gods or, in the case of Elijah, in mocking the prophets of Baal. Today's sentimental Christianity has prepared God's people to be cooperators, compromisers, and "all about love" while ignoring the truth. Though we realize the necessity of love that rejoiceth not in iniquity, we also recognize the need for truth, and the same God of the Old and New Testament is the same God we worship today, who just as much hates sin and calls us to contend for the faith which was once delivered unto the saints.

DISCIPLESHIP

June 8

A Changed Heart

Therefore if any man be in Christ, he is a new creature: old things are passed away; behold, all things are become new.
–2 Corinthians 5:17

God's salvation is about something much more than what can be displayed externally. Some works of the flesh can be done without the Spirit. One can "believe" in Jesus and not be regenerated; one can make changes in their lives in their dress, music and not be saved; one can pray sincerely, read the Bible from cover-to-cover and agree with its truths and not be saved; one can be sincere in following Christ and not be saved; one can pray the sinner's prayer and not be saved; one can be faithful to Church, pass out tracts, give to missions and not be saved; one can have visions, dreams, and spiritual experiences and not be saved; one can be sincere in their good works and help others and not be saved; one can be religious and not be saved. The rich man had morality but went back lost with great sorrow; the Pharisees were righteous in the eyes of men, said prayers, tithed, and fasted but did not know God. So, who then can be saved? Salvation is a work of the Spirit in the heart of the repentant sinner who has been convicted of their sin and flees to Christ for mercy upon seeing the holiness of God and the sinfulness of sin. With men this is impossible; but with God all things are possible.

DISCIPLESHIP

June 9

Though He Slay Me

It is enough for the disciple that he be as his master, and the servant as his lord. –Matthew 10:25a

The tendency of the human desire to expect something in return is a well-known trait of sociological behavior. To come to the place of desiring God at the cost of receiving nothing is something the natural man fights against. To be able to rejoice in the God of our salvation no matter what prayers have been uttered or what longings we have that we desire to be fulfilled may sound morbid, but maturity in Christ requires the lonely path of moving from dying to self to living for another, the Lord Jesus Christ, having been convinced of the loveliness of Christ. When God brings us to the place of absolute surrender, the excellency of the knowledge of Christ, the riches of having known His salvation, the joyous privilege of knowing this Being of splendorous beauty and glory is all there is to desire after. This lifelong journey of knowing Him comes with it the place of where when one gets closer and closer to Him, they become less and less aware of their wants and desires and lose themselves in God, where at the end, they can say, "Though he slay me, yet will I trust in him."

DISCIPLESHIP

June 10
The Cross before Me

Lay not up for yourselves treasures upon earth, where moth and rust doth corrupt, and where thieves break through and steal: But lay up for yourselves treasures in heaven, where neither moth nor rust doth corrupt, and where thieves do not break through nor steal:–Matthew 6:19,20

The desire of the flesh to make sure it has some influence in the life of a Christian is evident when we see the number of decisions that are made under the guise of God's will but has as its outcome in making some provision for the flesh, speaks of the deep roots the flesh has on our hearts. The cross symbolizes death, and whenever a person was put on the cross, they never came down until they died. In effect, that famous song "the world behind me, the cross before me" speaks of embracing the cross by putting to death everything the world has to offer. It is an intentional submission to Christ for desiring His riches in the place of what the flesh wants from this world which is nothing but pleasure in sin for a season. The conscious consideration and intentionally taking up of our cross, to carry it as it were, knowing the realization of its weight on our back, the jeering of the world as we pass by it, the injustice of an innocent man put to death, the loss of one's right, the receiving of whips from the ridicule of those whom we may have trusted or loved, are all in the nature of this path that we choose. But the desire to be with Christ, identify ourselves as His follower, desire that imperishable crown, the joys of walking with Him, and so forth not only motivate us but humbles us for the privilege that is ours to follow Him at all costs.

DISCIPLESHIP

June 11

As Little Children

And said, Verily I say unto you, Except ye be converted, and become as little children, ye shall not enter into the kingdom of heaven. –Matthew 18:3

Depending on God's righteousness for we have none of our own, realizing the helplessness of one's own ability in grasping or being able to convey the truths regarding the holiness of God and the heinousness of sin; looking to God's enablement instead of our perceived strength in doing what He has called us to do, depending on God's provision for living the Christian life rather than relying on our strength by being crucified with Christ that He might live through us. Becoming as a little child is an act of the Holy Spirit that begins at regeneration where the pride that you inherited through Adam, because of sin, is crushed under the law of God, and you are clothed with the meekness of the Lamb. We become as a little child looking into the hand of our Father, which art in Heaven. And this is a lifelong process that begins at the new birth, continues in sanctification, and finds its rest in glorification upon our death. No matter where God takes one, whether in the depth of intellectual prowess or in a deeper walk with God to learn the hard things of God, we need to have a daily desire and longing to be as a little child who implicitly trusts his Father for provision, protection, love, sustenance, strength, and the most sacred bond of paternal trust.

DISCIPLESHIP

June 12

Killing Agag

That the righteousness of the law might be fulfilled in us, who walk not after the flesh, but after the Spirit. –Romans 8:4

The subtlety of the flesh to hide under the cloak of sincerity and mercy speaks of the dark deceptions that we are faced with, even when we think that we have put our flesh to death. Keeping Agag as a prisoner will allow him to be an influencer in our lives though he may be behind bars. Agag may stay silent at times, but his presence will seduce us into thinking that we are right with God. The act of using the choicest of sheep from the Philistines to sacrifice unto the Lord speaks of the justification one makes when preserving them. In such cases exposing him and rejecting even "good" methods, as painful as it may be, is the only remedy for taking the next step. What follows will be to recognize in a spirit of humility that God is our source of all things, desiring the spirit of repentance from God that exposes sin for what it is, rebellion against God and idolatry, bringing the Agag's of our lives into the open and hacking him to death, not just maiming him, and taking up our cross and following Christ. Such drastic measures cannot be done by the source of our problems, the flesh, but must be done by the power of the Spirit, which indwells in us and empowers us for service by His fullness. Walking in the Spirit is a daily intentional walk of self-examination, repentance toward God, surrender, and doing what we are called to do.

DISCIPLESHIP

June 13

Ownership

He that spared not his own Son, but delivered him up for us all, how shall he not with him also freely give us all things?
–Romans 8:32

To realize the truth that God gave me life and everything that I can look back to or look forward to as my goals, dreams, and so on, all these rest on the fact that I would not have been born unless God gave that first impulse of life. Coming to grips with that original claim that God has on me because of being alive should cause me to be willing to forsake all for His sake, to give back to Him willingly for what He gave to me. Furthermore, when we rebelled against this good God and sinned against Him and became His enemy, God gave His only begotten Son of His own volition to redeem a doomed and damned race from eternal death. To reflect on the sacrifice God paid for saving us should cause us to see the gift of life and the regenerated life to realize the double claim upon us and solidify our ownership to Him, making it perpetual. Oh, the love of God to create mankind and to love us even further to die for His creatures speaks of the unsearchable riches that we have in Christ that are past finding out. Is it too hard for us to give our all to Him? We are here because of Him, from our conception, to have been born-again by the Spirit of God.

DISCIPLESHIP

June 14
Mercy and Truth

Let not mercy and truth forsake thee: bind them about thy neck; write them upon the table of thine heart:—Proverbs 3:3

In a day where "Christians" find any possible way to compromise truth to go after their version of the "truth," the great need to align ourselves to who God is and how He has revealed to us in His word is even more crucial. In the name of mercy and forgiveness, we have people in leadership divorce and remarry and continue their position as Pastor. However, the scriptures forbid it, as their choices have disqualified them for those types of leadership positions. Mercy does not override truth, and our lack of the proper view of the holiness of God shows in our attitude towards sin and God's truth. While we are to be abundant in mercy, we need to make sure that truth does not fall in the streets and that Christ's name does not become a reproach among the heathen around us. The greater accountability of those in leadership who, in one sense, portray what a true Bride of Christ looks like cannot afford in any way to reduce the proper perspective we are to bring to a lost and dying world so that they can see the truth of the nature of God represented by His people. The amount of good that one does cannot be accounted for burnt offerings and sacrifices, for rebellion is as the sin of witchcraft, and the same God who judged Saul for his disobedience is the same God we serve today, or at least we claim we do.

DISCIPLESHIP

June 15
Still Small Voice

Be still, and know that I am God: I will be exalted among the heathen, I will be exalted in the earth.—Psalm 46:10

In an age of clamor and noise, the great temptation to be part of it in our knowledge of the Holy and define progress as the ability to know much can hide us from our true sense of what God desires us to be. Elijah trembled when he saw God's power amidst the wind, earthquake, and fire but quietened and hid his face when he heard God in the stillness of the aftermath of such display of power. Yet in our hearts, the times we are called to experience God may not be in the claptrap of peaks in an emotional worship service; instead, it is in the closet, of time standing still and being alone with God. The solemn moments of Moses meeting God were when Moses lay on his face to the ground prostrate when meeting God that God spoke. The voice of God can only be heard to our spiritual ears that have been tuned to recognize His voice. The noise of entertainment, religious talk, opinions of men about God, the humdrum of busyness in ministry can all become a distraction when we ignore the time to open His word and sit still in worship and ponder, to gaze and know that He is God. In times of stillness, when God speaks, we learn to obey, grow, be content, surrender our deepest fears and follow our loving Shepherd into pastures green no matter what the rest of Christendom chooses to talk and be busy about.

DISCIPLESHIP

June 16

Victorious Christian Life

But thanks be to God, which giveth us the victory through our Lord Jesus Christ.—1 Corinthians 15:57

Hearing about salvation as a means to go to Heaven is not appealing to an addict; he goes "there" every time he gets "high." What he needs is salvation from sin and victory over sin; if our gospel cannot produce that, something is very wrong. The salvation that brings no enduring change is good for no one. It will be found wanting, with something given to ease the conscience and give a false assurance of Heaven. The scriptures do not teach "sinless perfection" or the impossibility of sinning, but it does teach that it is "possible not to sin." In 1 John 2:1, it does not say "when any man sin," instead it says "if any man sin" as in something that is not a norm. "This I say then, Walk in the Spirit, and ye shall not fulfil the lust of the flesh."–Galatians 5:16. "Awake to righteousness, and sin not;"–1 Corinthians 15:34a. "For he that is dead is freed from sin."–Romans 6:7. Jesus said in John 8:11, "... go and sin no more". True Christianity is not a sinning religion.

DISCIPLESHIP

June 17

Humility and the Crucified Life

But he giveth more grace. Wherefore he saith, God resisteth the proud, but giveth grace unto the humble.—James 4:6

The humble man will be lifted up, and the proud will be abased. Humility is a matter of giving up all our rights to the One who has redeemed us by His blood. When a man joined the Roman army, he was altogether dead to his way of life, personal preferences, or comforts; instead, he has made a binding oath to live for the cause of another. When we realize that God owns us, we come to recognize the reality that everything I have belongs to Him, and we have lost all our rights. The word in the New Testament for a servant in this context is Doulos (ex. Romans 6:16), which means a slave. As we submit willingly to our loving Master, we realize that just as Jesus submitted to His heavenly Father even unto death, we submit to Christ. The Christian toying with the idea of living for the world and wanting to serve Christ will get neither. When a man was crucified, he immediately lost all his rights. Christ's clarion call is to take up our cross daily and follow Him.

DISCIPLESHIP

June 18

Saved unto Righteousness

But as he which hath called you is holy, so be ye holy in all manner of conversation; Because it is written, Be ye holy; for I am holy.—1 Peter 1:15,16

The essence of salvation is based on the object of what we are saved from and saved to. Salvation is primarily to be saved from sin unto Christ's righteousness. The beauty of the gospel is in its purpose and not in its presentation or its ability to satisfy men's carnal desires. When the Spirit works in the heart of man, He brings the wrath of God upon sin to the penitent soul, who realizes that there is no hope. In recognizing the sinfulness of sin when he flees from sin to the savior, then the gospel becomes that hope to the drowning man. The logic of the gospel of itself is not enough for salvation, and it is the Holy Spirit who brings the truth of the work of Christ to a darkened heart and gives light to the sinner to see hope through the eye of faith. A gospel that does not produce the nature of the Person saving them will be found as a counterfeit. In its finality, salvation is not in the text of Scripture; instead, it is in the Person of Scripture, the God of the word.

DISCIPLESHIP

June 19

Getting Right with God

Search me, O God, and know my heart: try me, and know my thoughts: And see if there be any wicked way in me, and lead me in the way everlasting. –Psalm 139:23,24

Today, there seems to be a notion for the believer to the effect that claiming a verse of itself can make us get right with God. There is a missing aspect of the work of the Holy Spirit, who not only convicts of sin but also assures us of the cleansing when we with sincerity plead with a heart-cry towards God in repentance. The word is crucial in revealing to us the mercy of God and the hope of the work of Christ, but it is the Spirit of God who brings that sweet assurance that He has performed the work of cleansing and restored our fellowship with our heavenly Father. One can claim a verse and move on to ease their conscience, but without the renewing of the Holy Spirit, they find themselves back in their sin desirous of its pleasures in a greater measure. The man who has genuinely repented is the one who realizes the sinfulness of sin, is desirous of turning from sin to the Savior with a longing for victory and holiness. God creating a clean heart and renewing a right spirit within us is more than reciting a verse and mentally agreeing with it.

DISCIPLESHIP

June 20

End Goal, Disciples

And the things that thou hast heard of me among many witnesses, the same commit thou to faithful men, who shall be able to teach others also.—2 Timothy 2:2

Christ's command throughout the ages is to make disciples. The moment of faith during regeneration is just the starting point. Christianity is a lifetime of many steps pertaining to holiness unto the Lord in the process of sanctification. If all our desire is about getting them to believe in Jesus, agree on facts, and make consent to ease their conscience, then we have accomplished nothing. It is not any better than any other religion that gives temporary relief to the sinner and casts them into Hell in its finality. If there is no conviction of sin or the sinner crying out for mercy when faced with the holiness of God or bringing forth fruits meet for repentance that evidences the work of the Spirit's plowing of the heart or the inward witness of sonship or a life that displays the results of that effectual calling; if we don't see any of these, then all we are doing is playing a game called religion. The lack of nights of prayer, teachings on the fullness of the Spirit, the visible and invisible effects of regeneration, the gospel for all tongues and nations that whosoever will may come, when we lack in these areas all we have done is to have a form of godliness, but denying the power thereof. The primary reason why Christ came was not to take us to Heaven but to save us from our sins and to know the One true God. Anything that deviates a sinner from this sole purpose is a cheap imitation of the gospel.

DISCIPLESHIP

June 21

The Missing Jewel of Prayer

For this child I prayed; and the Lord hath given me my petition which I asked of him:—1 Samuel 1:27

The life of prayer exhibits the power of a Church or a Christian. Christ's life was a life that was dominated by prayer. His zeal was not that His house should be called a house of singing or preaching or fellowshipping; it was to be called a house of prayer of all nations. Prayers embedded with heartfelt cries toward God can change the course of a nation and a Church headed for destruction. Prayer first changes the person within before it changes the events that are external to the individual. God's desire is the purity of the inner man before He deals with the outer circumstances. Prayer shows dependence upon God for His Holy Spirit and His working in our midst, knowing that we can do nothing without Him. When we lack prayer, our motive speaks for itself that we know what to do, and we don't need God. Thus, America suffers from the powerlessness of the Church, and the Church has become a place for breeding goats and starving the sheep. One of the most strenuous tasks that require blood and sweat is to disciple a goat who thinks they are a sheep.

PRAYER

June 22

Prayer and Submission

And when all the children of Israel saw how the fire came down, and the glory of the Lord upon the house, they bowed themselves with their faces to the ground upon the pavement, and worshipped, and praised the Lord, saying, For he is good; for his mercy endureth for ever.–2 Chronicles 7:3

Prayer in a demanding society has a danger of exercising arrogance when approaching the throne of grace. It almost has a sense of entitlement for our wants where it bleeds into our interaction with God. Though we are God's child by the relationship, we are still God's subjects. In the time of the king's, his subjects would come in a humble submission requesting by supplication and not by demand. I don't come to my earthly father demanding my way or things that I may need. Proper respect, being right with him and asking for his favor, and desiring his will, for he knows best, is the same attitude I need to have when approaching the God of eternity. In a culture where getting something is almost as easy as swiping a credit card, approaching the holy of holies in the tabernacle was a whole another matter. There is preparation, supplication, confession, cleansing, remembering God's covenant promises, and finally entering into the holy of holies to make our requests known unto God in fear and trembling. And even in that final place, the realization of the Being we are dealing with, a most Holy God before whom the heavens are not clean in His sight, should cause us to pause and take serious thought when we come together to pray.

PRAYER

June 23

Faith that Overcomes

Ye have not chosen me, but I have chosen you, and ordained you, that ye should go and bring forth fruit, and that your fruit should remain: that whatsoever ye shall ask of the Father in my name, he may give it you.–John 15:16

Mustard seed faith is not about a point in time faith. It is about the perseverance of faith predated by a life of faith. Just as a mustard seed takes time to grow and become that great tree while growing amid drought, storms, and danger, faith is that seed that grows over time in patience and persistence to produce that great tree where the fowls of the air can lodge in its branches. It is a life in union with Christ, filled with the Spirit, and living a life that is set apart and pure before God. The point in time faith may give us a temporary victory, but it can also cause us to see the storms around us and cause us to sink. But the faith that is as a mustard seed has the foundation that is rooted in the bedrock of Christ and stands in a calm composure by the rivers of living waters which bringeth forth God's fruits in God's season. The deeper life of Christ that matures this faith can look at the face of death and say, "I have fought a good fight, I have finished my course, I have kept the faith:" and this is the faith that moves mountains, overcomes the world, laughs at doubts and is pleasing to God.

PRAYER

June 24

Answers to Prayer

A double minded man is unstable in all his ways.–James 1:8

We see in vast numbers of those who claim to seek after God but give up after a while for their reason given that God did not answer, and as a result, they conclude that there is no God. A solemn truth has to be taken to heart when seeking God, that God is not subject to our wants; instead, we are subject to God's pleasure. It does not matter how much I ask though I feel it may be sincere. It does matter if I am aligned with God on what His will and desires are. Though our asking may be genuine and proper, our motives still flow from a deceitful and desperately wicked heart. If we, in love, toward God ask desiring His will, then His will becomes our will, and we are aligned to God in our asking. We soon discover that His will is not hidden, for they are recorded in the pages of His book. If He cares for the sparrows and the grass that soon withers away, could we not trust Him to know what's best for us and in absolute surrender submit to His pleasure and ask wanting His will to be done on earth as it is done in heaven? And looking unto Jesus produces that faith which pleases God so we can ask believing. Asking and receiving is a matter of alignment in desiring our asking to align with God's will.

PRAYER

June 25

Praying Through

But let him ask in faith, nothing wavering. For he that wavereth is like a wave of the sea driven with the wind and tossed. —James 1:6

There comes the point in one's life where one's persistence in prayer determines their maturity in God. But a prayer that expects results as the only goal to be attained can cause one to be discouraged and give up. Instead, a prayer that desires God as the goal and flowing from God the desire of one's asking in faith, that prayer is willing to wait, plead and die praying while knowing with confidence that God answers prayers even unto the next generation. Abraham raised his knife to slay Isaac, knowing that God was able to raise him from the dead, Job in his darkest hour, uttered, "Though he slay me, yet will I trust in him." These kinds of prayers and obedience come from a life that is bred by the Spirit, one that has built its confidence in God Himself and has made bare the things of this earth that grow strangely dim. Prayers that storm the gates of Heaven and gives God no rest are those that have heart-wrenching cries toward God, abandons all hope except in God, takes God at His word, and pushes through till they can really pray and see God move mountains. Praying through against all odds are kept as a memorial by God, which is stored in Heaven for eternity. They hush the hosts of Heaven and lays waste the forces of evil.

PRAYER

June 26

God's Work and Man's Responsibility

According to the grace of God which is given unto me, as a wise masterbuilder, I have laid the foundation, and another buildeth thereon. But let every man take heed how he buildeth thereupon. – 1 Corinthians 3:10

From a human perspective, we see things that are hard to accomplish as impossible but attainable. It produces a general sense of the magnitude of the work involved but the eventual ability to finish it. We are confronted with something radically different with statements like being born again, given a new heart, opening blind eyes, and deaf ears in the Christian realm. In that context, you're not faced with something hard to attain but something impossible in its truest sense. God's call is for us to realize the impossibility of the task and look upwards to the possibility of God. The call for preaching, witnessing, and seeing God move is predicated upon three key pillars of prayer, the Holy Spirit, and the word of God in that general order. Man's responsibility to have personal and corporate prayer desiring the Holy Ghost to work and make alive the word of God is paramount for true Christianity to thrive or have any impact on the world. While facing the world, the flesh, the devil, and preaching life to those dead in trespasses and sins, nothing else will do.

PRAYER

June 27

Fasting

For if ye live after the flesh, ye shall die: but if ye through the Spirit do mortify the deeds of the body, ye shall live. –Romans 8:13

Bringing one's body under subjection is crucial and part of the Christian's growth for any serious follower of Christ. To deprive oneself of their basic necessities should not cause us to do it as a habit for the sake of doing it, though it is good to do it in remembrance. The need for depriving comes from the desperation of desiring God and wanting a deeper relationship with Christ. In this process of maturing, fasting drives one to forsake earthly things for heavenly rewards. There is a battle between the flesh and the regenerated man. In desperation for God to have the preeminence, to see the miraculous, seeking after God in fasting and tears are conditions that will be met with the dew of heaven. To be earthly-minded is to miss out on eternal treasures, and when we stand on the cusp of death, what we lived for in comfort will not be the one that we will take pleasure in, but rather what we gave up for cherishing the One we are going to see face to face shortly thereafter, this will be the thought that will be burning in our minds. While there is still time, let us utter in solemn worship with Johnathan Edwards, "Lord, stamp eternity on my eyeballs."

PRAYER

June 28

Alignment

Be ye followers of me, even as I also am of Christ.
–1 Corinthians 11:1

You don't begin prayer by looking at the need, you begin prayer by looking at God, and as you get to know God, you can bring it to the One who can meet that need when it arises. Truth from God is like an ever-flowing stream of pure water. It does not matter how much I partake of it; it always remains and is sufficient to give us more than we can ask or think. Any man's declaration of truth is judged based on how close he is to that stream, as he desires to be filled with the Spirit and pour out to others as God has poured out into him. And no man or denomination has exclusive rights to that stream of truth. Following Christ is our supreme goal from whom truth flows, letting God be true but every man a liar. When a man falters or falls, we are always responsible for being aligned with that stream of truth, and my accountability is to God before it is to fellowmen. And when a move of God is sent in an awakening, no denomination or a group of people can claim that it was because of them, but rather stand in awe and worship a God who in wrath remembered mercy to a people called as the remnant that sought after God with their whole heart, to remove the reproach that is on the name of Jesus.

PRAYER

June 29

Unknown Expectations

but the people that do know their God shall be strong, and do exploits. –Daniel 11:32b

After His bodily resurrection, the disciples of Christ were told to wait. Here was a time where the known world was ruled with a rod of iron by the Romans, the intellectuals of Greece ruled with their great philosophy and lofty ideals of their day, the Pharisee and the Sanhedrin ruled with absolute authority the religious tenor of the Jewish system, and man worshipped the creature more than the Creator and the imaginations of his fallen heart in the gods of Rome. Yet with all this, the disciples waited, not knowing what to expect. Christianity, as we know it today, did not exist, the Bible as we have it was not written in its entirety, the worldwide influence of Christendom was unheard of. The strength of that early Church was not in its radical teachings but rather in the supernatural power of the Holy Ghost. They went and turned the world upside down. Unless we rediscover that power of Pentecost, their nights of prevailing prayer and the anointed preaching of the word of God, unless we travail for that and move into that realm of the supernatural, the current facade of Americanized Christianity will continue to deteriorate, and the world will continue to ask, "Where is thy God?"

PRAYER

Costly Prayers   **June 30**

And she was in bitterness of soul, and prayed unto the Lord, and wept sore. – 1 Samuel 1:10

There is an unwritten law that is to be given careful thought to. It is this, the depth of sacrifice that one makes is proportionate to the amount of the selfless cause of desiring the favor of another will be. Hannah was supposed that she was drunk because of her agony of soul needing an answer from God; Rachel came not caring for how she looked or what she had but came with one cry for bearing a child lest she die. Such prayers are costly and may send one to an early grave but have God's benediction to declare them as being a prince having power with God and men and having prevailed. Such prayers may cost a halted thigh but are carried swiftly to the bosom of God and are the delight of angels. Coming to God like the woman with the alabaster box, broken and poured out at the feet of Jesus desiring to see His face are precious in the eyes of God. It is the Spirit who teaches us to pray. Giving orders to God on what He should do is to send prayers directed at heaven that never reach the ear of God. They are worthless and, in its finality, a waste of time and, in all honesty, powerless. And powerless prayers are the blush of heaven and the amusement of devils.

PRAYER

July

July 1

Corporate Prayer Meeting

And being let go, they went to their own company, and reported all that the chief priests and elders had said unto them. And when they heard that, they lifted up their voice to God with one accord, and said, Lord, thou art God, which hast made heaven, and earth, and the sea, and all that in them is:–Acts 4:23,24

The echoes throughout Holy Writ bring us again and again to the same conclusion. [Jesus] It is written, My house shall be called the house of prayer; After they prayed, the place where they were meeting was shaken. And they were all filled with the Holy Spirit and spoke the word of God boldly; [Disciples] Lord, teach us to pray. The early church thrived on prayer and the fullness of the Holy Spirit, while the church today is shrinking on government mandates and false professions. The early church multiplied amongst persecution and privations, while today's church has become impotent with prosperity and politics. A Chinese Christian who toured churches in America said, "I am amazed at how much the church in America can accomplish without the Holy Spirit." Having a dedicated time of weekly corporate prayer may be inconvenient to our schedules and our flesh. Still, without one, we are the laughingstock of devils with our programs and financial prosperity, which are nothing more than the bankruptcy of a church under the pretense of "God's blessing."

PRAYER

July 2

A Humble Plea

And David said, What have I now done? Is there not a cause?
—1 Samuel 17:29

See the need, hear the cry, learn to pray. We have a great need in front of us; the need for the vindication of God's name that is a reproach in our land, the need for the manifest presence of God in our services, the need for the fear of God prevailing once again in our midst, the need for Christians experiencing the fullness of the Spirit and living the victorious Christian life, the need for a revived life of prayer. Do we hear the cry of the lost who are dying without God, the cry of the powerlessness of our own lives to set people free from their bondage of sin by the Spirit, the cry of families that are broken in the clutches of sin, the cry of the church that is powerless to stop the tide of sin, the cry of our youth who have lost interest in the living God? When we set our heart to seek God and to know the heart of God. When we, with spiritual eyes, see what God sees and feel what God feels, it can then bring us to the place where we can pray effectively for what He desires to answer. Can God trust us to be honest in recognizing the truth that we claim to worship the God of the Bible, but His manifest presence is not there? He will only come where He is desired and not where His name is invoked.

PRAYER

July 3

Prayers of Abomination

Up, sanctify the people, and say, Sanctify yourselves against to morrow: for thus saith the Lord God of Israel, There is an accursed thing in the midst of thee, O Israel: thou canst not stand before thine enemies, until ye take away the accursed thing from among you.–Joshua 7:13

In a desperate attempt to maintain religion and somehow "protect" God, the church has come to the place of claiming truths which they think happen by assumption in areas such as prayer, presence, and the friendship of God. Yet, we are faced with the stark reality that God does not care about maintaining our assumptions; instead, He is interested in us being honest before Him. "If I regard iniquity in my heart, the Lord will not hear me; Every one that is proud in heart is an abomination to the Lord; But they rebelled, and vexed his holy Spirit: therefore he was turned to be their enemy, and he fought against them." The greatest danger we face today is not the devil, politics, or the media. The greatest threat we face in America is God becoming our enemy. [The Lord] will not fail thee, nor forsake thee is a conditional promise that was first given to Moses, which was predicated upon Israel keeping His commandments. And unless the Achan's of our lives are put to death, God will not hear us, and we will continue to see the destruction of America because of our sin. Desiring God to turn us unto Himself and forsaking known sin in repentance with brokenness and tears is the proper way to seek God for the healing of our land.

PRAYER

July 4

Call Unto Me

Whoso keepeth the commandment shall feel no evil thing: and a wise man's heart discerneth both time and judgment.
–Ecclesiastes 8:5

One can have a temptation when going to God with our petitions to claim God's promises in almost an arrogant way of expecting God to answer because we have kept our part of the bargain. True prayer is always uttered with humility realizing the need to discern the situation before bringing it to God. The prayers for rain during the season of famine in the time of Elijah would have been unanswered. It was not that God's promise was not true; it was praying without discerning the times; praying for healing when the sickness is because of God's judgment would be futile. When we realize that we deserve nothing, and God in His infinite mercy has saved us by His blood, with a payment for sin that we can't pay, when we realize this, then our prayers as His child are really to be prayers of desiring mercy, for we don't deserve anything that has been received from the kind hand of God. Though we go boldly because of our position of sonship, and we are not consumed approaching the holy of holies, we go with humility and reverence seeking the face of a Holy God. We pray, pleading God's promises even in the darkest of times when seeking for a heaven-sent awakening that He might in wrath remember mercy.

PRAYER

July 5

The Way of Blessing

For the time is come that judgment must begin at the house of God: and if it first begin at us, what shall the end be of them that obey not the gospel of God?–1 Peter 4:17

When Abraham's servant met Rebekah by the providence of God in response to his master's desire for Isaac, he realized that his "being in the way" of God led him to experience the blessing of God's moving. When we place ourselves by the Spirit in the way where the streams of God flow when it gushes forth in revival blessing, we can be part of the recipients of God's fulfillment of His promise to pour water upon him that is thirsty and floods upon the dry ground. If we don't have corporate times of focused agonizing prayer for God to come, lack honesty in calling our churches as nothing more than a social club with a religious veneer, being content in not seeing the church experience seasons of people being born of the Spirit of God and being faithful in the beauty of holiness, be happy to bring down the high view of God by calling sin as "normal" in the life of a believer and give into secret sins, if we don't desire conviction of sin and repentance before providing hope to the sinner; if we thus operate then we are not in a place of "being in the way," but instead we will be as the foolish virgins who being absent when the bridegroom came faced a God who knew them not.

PRAYER

July 6

Progression of Prayer

For they have healed the hurt of the daughter of my people slightly, saying, Peace, peace; when there is no peace.–Jeremiah 8:11

The prayer that is seen among men, which is prayed for the praise of men, will have no heavenly reward or reach the throne of God. Such prayers are an abomination to God, and God is angry with our prayers in such cases. The ornate display of the Pharisee while had the veneer of godliness and standards lacked in God's requirements of brokenness and tears that the Publican had, who went home justified, while the Pharisee went to Hell. Our prayers for revival must be preceded by praying for holiness, our prayers for power must be preceded by praying for contrition of heart, our prayers for healing of our land must be preceded by the humbling of self and turning from our wicked ways, our prayers for desiring Christ to be glorified must be preceded by prayers for the denial of self and putting our flesh to death, our prayers for the manifest presence of God must be preceded by being willing to acknowledge the lack of it in our services before the people. God's requirement for hearing and answering prayers has not changed, and He is not planning to cheapen His grace of prayer to meet our sloppy, lazy, and self-satisfied Christianity. The progression of prayer always begins with the reality of one's need before going to the One who can meet that need.

PRAYER

July 7

Prayer and Holy Hands

The sacrifices of God are a broken spirit: a broken and a contrite heart, O God, thou wilt not despise.–Psalm 51:17

Certain presuppositions are assumed when called out concerning seeking God's face in the grand topic of prayer. The necessity of holy hands has with it the understanding of our personal responsibility to be in the right relationship to God by salvation, proper communion with God in purity, having clean hands toward our fellow beings, and finally, the need to understand the mind of God to ask according to His will. Many vital elements are at work in the intrinsic nature of why God chose to send revival to a community and answer prayer for those asking for it. There is God's desire on what He intends to do, God's will on what He has revealed to us in His word, God's vessel that has been consecrated and prepared for the Master's use, God's enablement in asking for the impossible by the moving of His Spirit, God's Sovereign purpose for the furtherance of His kingdom that spans beyond the present generation, and finally God's promises that have been made effectual for claiming the validity of it for what it has been revealed thereto. Though the promises of God off themselves are trustworthy and yea from the mouth of God, they are only made effectual by the Holy Spirit. Blindly claiming the promises of God cannot in any way bind God to the whims of the man in his asking.

PRAYER

July 8
Obedience Proves your Asking

They profess that they know God; but in works they deny him, being abominable, and disobedient, and unto every good work reprobate.—Titus 1:16

It is one thing to pray for revival and another to pray and then obey. The wisdom of the virgins was displayed by their obedience to have their lamps ready and filled with oil, and they revealed their desire by how they prepared while waiting for their Master. By their action, they proved their wisdom. Praying for revival is not enough; doing what God desires of you by your obedience is the greater proof. The Spirit came because they obeyed and waited in the upper room, and under Peter's preaching, those who believed obeyed by their action to seal their testimony by baptism during a time when it was an act unto persecution. To have our house in order, for Him to come, doing it daily and consistently while praying for Him to come is needed at this hour. Praying is a poor excuse when obeying what you know, as revealed in the scriptures, is required. A revival that comes from above is a Sovereign work of God, but we know that God delights to hear and answer prayers from His children, but until He comes, we get prepared for it by obeying and making ready the paths for the coming of the Lord.

PRAYER

July 9

Examining our Motives

But ye shall receive power, after that the Holy Ghost is come upon you: and ye shall be witnesses unto me both in Jerusalem, and in all Judaea, and in Samaria, and unto the uttermost part of the earth.–Acts 1:8

Anointing or the Baptism of the Holy Spirit is how God opens access for the Christian to the heart of fallen man and the heart of God in penetrating the veil. Why reach the heart of man? Is it that God might receive the reward of His suffering? Why reach the heart of God? Is it so that God's will be done on earth as it is done in heaven? In seeking after God, these are sobering questions that we need to consider for examining our motives. Is God in our midst? Is He really among us? Have we considered the tragedy of Samson that he wist not that the Lord was departed from him? What if we stand before God and all we have after a lifetime of service for God, Church buildings, much activity in the realm of evangelism, professions that did not have the witness of God, only to find out that our labor of love was wood, hay, and stubble, and God was never present? Would we do something different? The call of Christ for His disciples to tarry for the enduement of power is just as valid today for seeking that more profound work of grace that men like Evan Roberts, John Hyde, Charles G. Finney, A. W. Tozer, Frances Havergal, W. P. Nicholson, and a host of others who sought after it, experienced it and were mightily used of God.

HOLINESS

July 10

To Whom Much is Given

Come, and let us return unto the Lord: for he hath torn, and he will heal us; he hath smitten, and he will bind us up.–Hosea 6:1

Resolving the root issue is crucial in meeting a need rather than staying with the fruit and fixing it for the here and now. The destruction of Nineveh was averted when the people believed Jonah and sought-after God, and in return, the destruction of their souls was averted when they repented and turned to God. Why do we need a Spiritual Awakening? God desires repentance and restoration, for He does not take pleasure in the death of the wicked; but that the wicked turn from his way and live. A Nation to whom much has been given, much will be required, and if we as God's people don't stand in the gap and seek the Lord for mercy, the destruction that will come upon America will be required of us. The purpose of an Awakening is not for having a better political party, better laws, freedoms, or even better-living conditions. It is that the world might know that there is a God in heaven who created us and loves us, that all may come to know the one true God who died for them before it is eternally too late. So that God's final judgment may be averted, and America does not follow the fate of Rome, Babylon, and Ancient Egypt.

HOLINESS

July 11
Justifying Selfish Motives

But he, willing to justify himself, said unto Jesus, And who is my neighbour?–Luke 10:29

Since the fall, man has always been trying to take excesses and uses them to accommodate what he covets and fulfills in his flesh while justifying it by pointing to folks in the Bible. There is a way that God has called us to, and then there are areas of man's failure which bring leanness into their soul. Since Creation, it was the command of God of one man to one woman as the only proper grounds for marriage. Still, the fallen man desiring to justify areas such as polygamy takes these excesses of David or Solomon and uses them to justify his lust. Instead of David and his many wives, how about we desire the love David had by the many Psalms that has blessed millions around the world for many generations; instead of Moses and his Ethiopian wife, how about the intercessory prayer of Moses pleading on behalf of Israel that we are to emulate? While God has set the standard for what is right, in the permissive will of God, man has found mercy where he has failed, though it brought with it the dreadful consequences of their actions. Some outright sinful acts against the explicit command of God brought judgment like Sodom, while others show the hardness of man's heart to sow unto the wind and reap the whirlwind.

HOLINESS

July 12

The Eternal Journey

Brethren, I count not myself to have apprehended: but this one thing I do, forgetting those things which are behind, and reaching forth unto those things which are before, I press toward the mark for the prize of the high calling of God in Christ Jesus.
–Philippians 3:13,14

Christianity is not about point-in-time accomplishments. It is a lifelong journey of perpetual moving of God in the lives of His people. Thus, there is nothing for the disciple to get the glory but God. For it is not by might, nor by power, but it is by God's Spirit. Seeking after God does not end with the result of meeting a goal; though there are seasons of the nearness of God, it is a lifelong commitment to follow hard after God desirous to know Him. And even with the little things that we get awestruck at times, such as the intricacies of Creation or something that overwhelms us in its beauty, how much more of God who created all things and gave us richly to enjoy. Thus, Heaven will be a place of perpetual enjoyment of God, for He is infinite, and we will never exhaust His beauty or the ecstasy of His presence. When we desire God Himself solely for who He is, then as He makes Himself known, it will be as the dew of heaven which is poured out into small vessels of clay that will constantly overflow, unable to contain the fragrance and the gushing forth of the streams of living waters. There is nothing more spectacular than the Being of God in all the Universe.

HOLINESS

July 13
Pharisee and Subtle Sins

The heart is deceitful above all things, and desperately wicked: who can know it?–Jeremiah 17:9

For the Christian, what he sees on the outside that offends God is much easier to recognize and deal with than what goes on inside himself. The depravity of man's heart displayed in pornography, lying, stealing, anger, and so forth can be easily identified and dealt with. The sins of the Pharisees, which are of greater danger and harder to detect, and more challenging to resist, are manifested very differently. A high view of self while looking at the lost as beneath themselves, especially against someone whom they feel does not look the norm; prejudice with better-than-thou attitude; false humility; self-conceit because one fasts or abstains from worldly pleasures or maintains separation on the externals such as music and dress; one's attitude of self-ego because they are right and others are wrong; despise someone who is struggling in some area that they are victorious in; pride because of race, color, social status; and many others. This body of death and the wretchedness of the subtlety of the flesh to snare us is a solemn reminder of the danger of falling into silent sins of the flesh that may never be displayed but can be secretly nurtured in our interaction with others. Resisting the enemy within must be given greater vigilance than the enemy without.

HOLINESS

July 14
Personal Holiness

For I say, through the grace given unto me, to every man that is among you, not to think of himself more highly than he ought to think; but to think soberly, according as God hath dealt to every man the measure of faith. –Romans 12:3

The sin of Lucifer was, desiring to receive the glory that was due unto God alone, to dethrone God and be as the most High. And that seed of sin which causes us to see ourselves more highly than we ought to think and desire glory that is only due unto God puts us in the same tangent of why Lucifer fought heaven for. Cultivating personal holiness by the Spirit before God is one of the cornerstones for the Christian. To walk perfectly before our God; to uphold His holiness by our living; to be crucified with Christ and be dead to sin; to be set apart; to be dead to self in word, thought, and deed; to have a fear of the Lord evident in our actions before fellowmen; to represent the Christ-life on earth; to uphold truth, mercy, and judgment. Such lofty desires are enough to crush a sane man to dust. Yet, the victory is there in purposeful and continual abandonment of self to the sufficiency of the sacrifice of Christ for the cleansing, to live under the fountain of His triumph. Though Christ died for our sins and paid a high price for redemption, salvation comes at the cost of discipleship, where a sham Christianity of having a form of godliness but denying the power thereof will be cast away as chaff for the burning.

HOLINESS

Dealing with Pride

July 15

And he said O Lord God of my master Abraham, I pray thee, send me good speed this day, and shew kindness unto my master Abraham. – Genesis 24:12

The desire of Abraham's servant was not about who he was but what Abraham meant to him, everything. The servant had one goal, to fulfill Abraham's desire and seek the glorification of his master by completing the task that was put forth before him in finding a bride for Isaac. The darkness of pride in a man's heart is the most depraved enemy one faces in their service for their Master. To lift our eyes off ourselves and be able to seek God with a pure heart is of tremendous worth. By rejecting the desire for the approval or praise of men and dismiss the censorship of others or the thought of what others think of oneself, are all demons that a serious disciple of Christ needs to contend with daily. To be dead to sin by the death of Christ who overcame pride and all else and avail it as our victory can be experienced when we realize that we died with Him, to identify ourselves with the truth that His resurrection is our resurrection in the new man while the old man is buried with Christ; the reality of this thought needs to be much pondered upon and brought to bear fruit by the Holy Spirit. Living with the intense reality of what God's desire is and be consumed with wanting the glorification of Christ alone, at the expense of all else, is the key to live a life of victory with a pure conscience in our service toward Him.

HOLINESS

July 16
The Self Problem

And when they found them not, they drew Jason and certain brethren unto the rulers of the city, crying, These that have turned the world upside down are come hither also;–Acts 17:6

There are two main areas that a serious follower of Christ needs to be constantly desperate for, one in a genuine longing for God to fulfill His desire on earth completely, and two for the singular focus for God to be glorified. The greatest hindrance to both is not necessarily external, but the hidden enemy called self, this body of flesh. Those men and women who were waiting in the upper room, before they could go and proclaim the truth of the Messiah to a world that had just put Him to death, had no New Testament, no money, no social standing, no religious affiliation, no guns and glory, no college degree, no church buildings, no newsletters, no Bible commentaries, were unlearned and unknown. Yet the most significant hindrance of self was put to death when the Holy Ghost baptized them with power that they might see God's desire fulfilled, God, glorified and move as He pleased in that early Acts of the Holy Spirit. And it was not a one-time baptism at Pentecost to declare the risen Christ, but we read of many such fillings throughout the book of Acts. When self, our old Adamic nature ingrained in our flesh, is put out of the way, then God's desire and glory can be fully manifested in our midst. The wages of sin is death, but the cause of sin is self. In salvation, the soul is saved from sin; the old man is put to death with Christ; in service, our self needs to be saved from self.

HOLINESS

Weights and Hindrances

July 17

And he fenced it, and gathered out the stones thereof, and planted it with the choicest vine, and built a tower in the midst of it, and also made a winepress therein: and he looked that it should bring forth grapes, and it brought forth wild grapes.–Isaiah 5:2

To move forward, one must cast away anything that hinders that act. The tendency of sports and entertainment to become an idol is that it introduces the desire for being worldly-minded, creates a hindrance for spiritual matters of utmost importance such as the burden of revival, it creates a lack of sacrifice needed for attaining the treasure of the deeper life with Christ, it produces a shallow Christianity that erodes faith and stifles growth, it dampens the Spirit in allowing injurious conversations and enables us to get used to the dark, it turns us aside with our stewardship of time, it presents God in entertainable terms in par with any other type of amusement, it sets a tone for trying to serve God while having one foot on what the world has to offer, and if given enough time and energy, it will eventually put out the fires of God's desire and cast doubt on the promises of God in one's life and will lead to barrenness. While every man or woman needs to realize where they are in their walk with God and the hindrances that vie for their attention, knowing the danger of what it can eventually become needs to be considered with all seriousness. In its finality, more than what it does to our walk with God, we have to evaluate what it does to our high view of God that we ought to have; One who is high and lifted up.

HOLINESS

July 18

Much shall be Required

Wherefore take unto you the whole armour of God, that ye may be able to withstand in the evil day, and having done all, to stand.–Ephesians 6:13

God's sobering declaration of "Draw nigh to God" should cause those who desire to get closer to God to give serious consideration to its implication. It is something that speaks of the unbelievable opportunity for those who have been regenerated to get to know more profoundly this Being of infinite beauty and majesty. But to have this treasure in earthen vessels and be given such privilege should cause one to, in a sober way, consider the gravity of this benefit. There is a price to pay for knowing God, and there is a deep knowledge of God in experiential witness that one can learn of Him by the Spirit through the word. Though such encounters with God in unique ways are remarkable, the price for obtaining it or disobedience to it is also great. For Jacob, it was wrestling with God all night and the hollow of his thigh in the sinew that shrank; for Moses, it was fasting and prayer, or in not entering the promised land; for Elijah, it was to stand alone against the four hundred and fifty prophets of Baal; for Paul, it was the thorn in the flesh. No matter the cost, the beauty of the nearness of Christ is for our good and is of supreme worth. To guard our hearts against any perpetrator with all seriousness, lest anything come in our way of knowing God, should be undertaken with paramount importance.

HOLINESS

July 19

Three Altars

Then he answered and spake unto me, saying, This is the word of the Lord unto Zerubbabel, saying, Not by might, nor by power, but by my spirit, saith the Lord of hosts. –Zechariah 4:6

One must consider the seriousness of the Christian life when one looks at the bloody sacrifices that were part of worship in the Old Testament. As we follow Christ, you must realize the three altars you need to evaluate in your life constantly. First, we have the altar for sin, where anything that has become an idol is put to death. It could be sports, hobbies, entertainment, job, family, health, and so forth. Agag must be put to death, for our flesh loves to have an ally. Second, we have the altar of consecration where we present our bodies as a living sacrifice that is holy and acceptable unto God. A most holy offering to God in dying to self and living a life of victory for service. Finally, we have the costliest altar of burning coals around the throne of God. One who has been baptized by the Spirit and burns with the fire of God to produce light and heat from God to a world that is dark and cold with the grip of death. Just as an individual piece of coal loses its burning when taken out from the fire, this altar is a constant reminder of the need to stay close to God in purposeful intent and being constantly filled with the Spirit. The world is tired of theories of lofty mountaintops but is instead looking for Truth in demonstration of the Spirit and power, and nothing short of God can satisfy that need.

HOLINESS

July 20
Humility, the Beauty of Holiness

That no flesh should glory in his presence.—1 Corinthians 1:29

What a tremendous worth of great magnitude when we have our inner-man and outward piety reflect humility in a Christian's life. A quality that is treasured by God and must be desired by every follower of Christ. Yet this jewel is as fragile as the dew on the grass, where it falls to the ground when touched. The seed of Adam that is in the breast of every man has its beginning in pride in his response to the desire to be as gods, and thus humility is one of the most delicate treasures to be kept in earthen vessels. To reflect on the simplicity of Christ, God becoming a man and washing the feet of His disciples, the tremendous responsibility of holding the revelation of God in truth, the holiness of God that reflects on the corruption of man in every area that he can think of; should drive us to the place of walking humbly before our God. The contrast of the antithetical nature of God and man, reflected in the holiness of God against the pride of man, should move us to keep short accounts with God daily. The discipline to desire the Spirit to produce in us the humility of the sheep in following his Shepherd in meekness, relying on the goodness of his Master, and not caring about one's own ability to impress the world around them is a perfect picture of humility, which is as a sweet-smelling savor in the eyes of God.

HOLINESS

July 21

The Battle for the Mind

The hearing ear, and the seeing eye, the Lord hath made even both of them.—Proverbs 20:12

The one critical area of weakness that Satan uses to infiltrate a person is the mind. If it's captured, a beachhead is established where the enemy can move further by affecting perspectives, influencing behavior, and performing sinful actions on the part of those giving into it. Thus, the significant influence of media, the internet, advertisements, and so forth are geared towards getting loyalty to what is conveyed, beginning with the mind. For the Christian, their victory also starts with the mind, to reckon or consider themselves dead unto sin. Since Christ died on the cross and we died with Him, our old man was crucified with Christ. When we reckon that old man to be dead, since Christ overcame death by His bodily resurrection, we can live in complete victory and freedom when we constantly put to death this entry point of the mind that relates to the old man. When we realize that sin cannot have dominion over me, for Christ overcame it, and I, as a servant of the new Master, can live in victory under the shadow of His protection. And this is a daily reckoning, for the flesh lusteth against the Spirit, for they are contrary one to the other. When we deny the false narrative of Satan that we "have to" give in to sin, then we can live in complete freedom for which we already have access through Jesus Christ, and we don't fight for victory, but from victory.

HOLINESS

July 22
Purity at all Cost

Blessed are the pure in heart: for they shall see God.–Matthew 5:8

Protecting something of value always has inherently the danger of the item getting lost or compromised. Furthermore, in matters of eternal worth, it's crucial to the inestimable value of truth given at such a high price. Suppose the purity of the scriptures with its truths such as faith, repentance, regeneration, Lordship, etc., offends those it is preached to. In that case, it is better to offend the listeners rather than compromise and preach a false gospel. Having a proper view of God will allow one to have an accurate view of their responsibility before God to preach the truth as it is written. To fear man is to preach error, and to fear God is to preach truth irrespective of the human consequences one may face. How we represent God in the eyes of the people should cause us to approach that sacred topic with fear and trembling, realizing the consequences that are so great as to affect for generations to come on their view of God. No denomination has a corner on truth, and our responsibility to stay close to the stream of living waters is tested by its effect on our dedication to the purity of upholding truth at all costs.

HOLINESS

July 23

About You vs About God

But I will sacrifice unto thee with the voice of thanksgiving; I will pay that that I have vowed. Salvation is of the Lord.—Jonah 2:9

In any religious system and its tenants, the end goal comes to these two pillars of conviction. If the practice drives the need for self to be vindicated, this speaks of beginning and ending with the man in mind; on the contrary, if there is a system of belief that has the core desire as beginning and ending with God since man changes with the times and seasons, then that is the genuine system of truth for man has no truth from within himself. With religions and even those who profess no adherence to a system of religion as what is pertained in a set of beliefs, of which atheism is one of them, nevertheless, we see that all of them are based on works of what man can do to reach God or have peace with God. It could even be in following Orthodox Christianity of works for the desire of Heaven. But true faith rests on Christ realizing that it is not about what I can attain but what God can give by His grace and not of works. When one can see sin as an offense toward God more than an excuse for self or avoidance to a future punishment or remorse for getting caught, if one has the proper perspective of their offense toward God, then we can be assured that God is at work in drawing the sinner unto Himself. For the true believer, it is in Christ we live, and move, and have our being.

HOLINESS

Sacred Music July 24

And it came to pass, when the evil spirit from God was upon Saul, that David took an harp, and played with his hand: so Saul was refreshed, and was well, and the evil spirit departed from him.
−1 Samuel 16:23

Having a proper view of God can give us the ability to have a proper perspective of self. For the heart desirous to please God, anything that pleases the flesh will be considered a hindrance in having an audience with God. An encounter with a Holy God will cause one to reflect on the holiness of God and the continual change that God brings in conforming us to the image of our Lord and Savior, Jesus Christ. With this in mind, one needs to consider the matter of music, if it pleases God or pleases the flesh, does it touch my emotions and not the heart by leaving me cold after the emotions have run out. Music is not amoral, for it defines the response of man on what it brings focus upon. In considering our purpose to glorify God, and to enjoy Him forever, having lyrics and songs that bring us to view the nature of God and arouses our response in the spirit to enjoy Him is crucial for discerning the spirit of the song and the accompanying music. Alignment to the word of God and to the Spirit of God in understanding the consequences of handling holy things in our worship toward God should cause us to evaluate every song that is sung, irrespective of who sings it or promotes it. Any song or style that builds a bridge to error or desensitizes us to the nature of God ought to be vehemently rejected based on the greater goal of our worship of God.

HOLINESS

July 25

Enjoying God

There is no fear in love; but perfect love casteth out fear: because fear hath torment. He that feareth is not made perfect in love.–1 John 4:18

To come to grips with the original intent for us as God's Creation is to be in the place of the love relationship we were created for. To be in submission to God who as our Creator and benevolent Master loves us with a perfect love, to be in the place of absolute surrender as we realize our complete dependence upon our Kinsman who has redeemed us, to be as it were, having our ear pierced with the aul in the express desire to be His slave for eternity knowing the good heart and care of our Lord. To enjoy the pleasures of His bestowment upon us in this life and for the life that is to come, to please Him by the love that we have which has been shed abroad in our hearts, to live for the interest of another, to know and be secure in the protection of our great King knowing that He rules all things with absolute Sovereignty. To be responsible to fellowmen in loving them and showing forth His salvation out of compassion, to receive in the abundance of joy the needs that are met or the trials that we face knowing that He is our great reward. The finality of such communion culminates in the knowledge and reality of who God is, where He is everything He says He is, and more than what we can ask or think while living in a world where there is no comparison for Him. God's grand declaration at Sinai of "I AM THAT I AM" captures it well.

WORSHIP

July 26
The Love Factor

Behold, what manner of love the Father hath bestowed upon us, that we should be called the sons of God: therefore the world knoweth us not, because it knew him not. – 1 John 3:1

The ability of Satan to pervert all that is good and given by God is seen in this area of love that God has provided for the good of man concerning Himself and to his fellowmen. But we see it perverted to the extreme by Satan's deception and our sin. The love of brotherly kindness and friendly affection, Phileo, has been perverted with sexual exploration, obsession, and justifying inordinate relationships; the selfless and unconditional love in the interest of another, Agape, has been perverted with validating adult to child perversions and obsessive behaviors; the love of family bonds with its desire for the betterment of the other, Storge, has been perverted to incest and exploitation of a sibling for fulfilling personal lust; the love of romance within the confines of marriage for enjoying each other between one man and one woman in sexual purity, Eros, has been perverted with pornography, premarital sex, prostitution and so forth. Thus, we see that everything good and pleasant that has been given from the kind hand of God, even in this gift of love for one toward another, has been idolized, made into objects of lust, and exploited. But God reigns supreme as the Author of true love which desires the good of the other, which He exemplified on the Cross at Calvary for all the world to see.

WORSHIP

July 27
Desiring Holiness

Give unto the Lord the glory due unto his name: bring an offering, and come before him: worship the Lord in the beauty of holiness.—1 Chronicles 16:29

To the man who has genuinely fallen in love with his future bride, nothing can seem too hard or be as asking too much. A life that shows their commitment and devotion to cherish that relationship until and after the vows of marriage have been taken. Holiness has a threefold purpose; one is being desirous to know God where holiness is the prerequisite for making any progress in the area of knowing God; second, the heart that is overflowing with love and gratitude to the point of being instantly aware of any sinful thought which can hinder that fellowship with our Maker; and finally, to continually enjoy the communion with God even in times of darkness to be able to say with Job, "Though he slay me, yet will I trust in him." Such passions of love for Christ and enjoying Him are steeped in the desire to live a holy life. To such a person, holiness is not for others to see or for receiving the praise of men; it is not the showing forth of externals which has no inner bearing of their relationship to God; it is not a one-time event that portrays a submissive life at the point of regeneration. Instead, it is a daily walk with God that reflects on the nature of God by the inner longing to be like their Savior. It is an ever-present inclination to ensure that my walk with Christ is reflected by my enjoyment of Christ and being a partaker of His holiness.

WORSHIP

July 28
The Knowledge of God

But let him that glorieth glory in this, that he understandeth and knoweth me, that I am the Lord which exercise lovingkindness, judgment, and righteousness, in the earth: for in these things I delight, saith the Lord. –Jeremiah 9:24

For the true believer in Christ, the key to knowing God rests on the need for us to see everything in life such as victory, defeat, sorrow, joy, trials, trying of our faith, and such in light of how it can bring us to a richer and closer knowledge and fellowship with God, to focus on the One who, in Sovereign Omniscience, knows all things and in Omnipotence controls all things and in Omnipresence sees all things. Our smallness to His greatness. While Moses's perspective was the backside of the desert, God was molding His man to stand before kings and pull-down kingdoms. Can the rain boast of its clouds? Can the leaf boast of its color? Who gave thee thy life-giving strength? Who gave thee thy color but God? Oh, vain man, why boasteth thou? What strength didst thou have to bring thyself to birth into this world? What power didst thou have to ensure the sanity of thy understanding? For thy knowledge of God is but because of God, thou deserveth death and Hell, but God gave thee life, thou deserveth wrath but God shewed mercy upon thee, thou didst not desire the revelation of God but God chose thee of His own Sovereign free grace and love, for it was not of thy works but according to His mercy that He gave Himself for thee, fall down and worship thy God, Behold your God.

WORSHIP

July 29

The Curse of Words

Thanks be unto God for his unspeakable gift.—2 Corinthians 9:15

Here we find ourselves facing the dilemma of words to put to sentences depths too precious to contain within them. All we have are words, and plain words cannot explain the beauty and majesty of God, this glorious Being who lives beyond what words can describe or put together. Yet we come in reverential worship and fear to approach the God who created us for Himself and showed the man of Eden the ivory palaces that were meant to be his resting place with God. And oh, how we have fallen to such depravity from our original love that was God, depths that have taken the form of death and the stench of the dunghill, to follow after what this world had to offer; fame, prosperity, "love." And the best of what the world has are nothing but smelly husks consumed amongst human waste. Such is the mercy and beauty of God who came to save us from our sin, where man cries night and day longing to reason with himself that he is in a good place, not realizing his original claim and treasures that he was endowed with, which he has sinned away, and desired the filth of corruption. Oh, that men might know the love and beauty of Christ, that they might learn to worship Him who lives in the high throne of eternity, who sees everything in Omniscient knowledge without any effort. God of wonders who is clothed in majesty and fearful glory, before who fallen man stands clothed in the nakedness of his sin.

WORSHIP

July 30
The Facets of Christian Living

Wherefore seeing we also are compassed about with so great a cloud of witnesses, let us lay aside every weight, and the sin which doth so easily beset us, and let us run with patience the race that is set before us,–Hebrews 12:1

At times we come to portions of scriptures or how God used men and women of the past in various areas such as prayer, missions, etc., and it can overwhelm us to the point of exhaustion and frustration on where to begin and what to give importance to. Seeing the life of Christ is the perfect example of God's desire for us. Christ knew the Father, and we ought to know God; Christ did great miracles, and we are to be strong and do exploits against the enemy; Christ taught profound doctrinal truths, and we ought to study to shew thyself approved unto God; Christ loved little children and we ought to have compassion for those who are overlooked in life; Christ set free those who were blind to the truth and we ought to preach the gospel to every creature that they may know the One true God; Christ obeyed His Father even unto death and we ought to obey with joy and run with patience the race that is set before us; Christ overcame temptation in the power of the Spirit and we ought to be filled with the Spirit and live the victorious Christian life; Christ communed with the Father and we ought to give time to prayer and seek the face of Almighty God for all our needs. And so, we see Christian living as a diamond that shimmers with its many facets shining forth the beauty of Christ for adorning His crown.

WORSHIP

Search Me, O God
J. Edwin Orr

Search me, O God, and know my heart today;
Try me, O Savior, know my thoughts, I pray.
See if there be some wicked way in me;
Cleanse me from ev'ry sin and set me free.

I praise thee, Lord, for cleansing me from sin;
Fulfill thy Word, and make me pure within.
Fill me with fire where once I burned with shame;
Grant my desire to magnify thy name.

Lord, take my life and make it wholly thine;
Fill my poor heart with thy great love divine.
Take all my will, my passion, self, and pride;
I now surrender; Lord, in me abide.

Public Domain

July 31

Revival

Repent ye therefore, and be converted, that your sins may be blotted out, when the times of refreshing shall come from the presence of the Lord.—Acts 3:19

The word "revival" in today's Christianity evokes the preplanned method of meeting for a week and making decisions. It is something we can schedule, control, and soon forgotten. The shallowness in our generation is not about talking or praying for "revival" in one sense; it is in the application of what we term as revival, which suits our status quo and our prevalent word games of "grace." Revival is life from above, which can be to those awakened by regeneration, Elijah and the widow's child, or restoration for the prodigal when he came to himself. In historic revivals that I read of; while seeking God and obeying His Word, the times of refreshing come where it is generally never scheduled, the community is suddenly made aware of the manifest presence of God, time is forgotten as God is in the midst, there are spontaneous bursts of worship followed by a torrent of witnessing, conviction, salvation and many acts which are beyond the control of the people but under the perfect control of the Holy Spirit in Divine disorder, sin is arrested in the community, there is no exaltation of human personality or ability. Our generation has not seen one, and we have been made to be comfortable living without it.

REVIVAL

August

August 1

The Inconveniences of an Awakening

O Lord, I have heard thy speech, and was afraid: O Lord, revive thy work in the midst of the years, in the midst of the years make known; in wrath remember mercy. –Habakkuk 3:2

There is almost a desire for revival for the sake of the name or the fantasized results of what we think will happen. We have the ideology that revival will be painless, giving Christians the much-needed voice they "hope" to get in the secular world. But genuine revival has many inconveniences. If we imagine a time where God moves us to fast, pray, weep, and lose sleep for days and weeks for the coming revival, would that be appealing to the flesh? There was always a cost associated with genuine historic revival such as prayer, travail, tears, repentance, brokenness, forsaking worldliness, entertainment, sports, etc. Revival is a work of God that hinders the flesh. There may be persecutions, arrests, and martyrdom; are we ready for that? Yes, there may be restoration, healing, and ecstasy of love to our Maker, but we cannot predict the outcomes. The intensity of the revival, the labor, and burdens, the ask will be great for God to come. Before we say Lord send us revival, we need to ask if I sincerely want one and am I willing to pay the price for it. Do you really want revival?

REVIVAL

August 2
Unpredictable Moving's of God

Wilt thou not revive us again: that thy people may rejoice in thee?–Psalm 85:6, Oh that thou wouldest rend the heavens, that thou wouldest come down, that the mountains might flow down at thy presence–Isaiah 64:1

We see again and again in the scriptures the unpredictability of the early Church when anointed men led them in Spirit and power. In Acts 5, we see Ananais and Sapphira struck dead for lying to the Holy Ghost. In Acts 13, we see Elymas go blind for subverting the gospel and phrases such as "great fear came upon them" or "the rest durst no man join himself to them." We see similarities in the Old Testament with Elijah, Samson, and other instances where the moving of God was sudden and unpredictable. Today everything that happens in our Churches is predictable. We know what to do, when to sing, when to stand, when to leave, and we don't expect an unpredictable invasion from God. We are creatures of comfort and habit, and anything that disrupts our "routine" we shy away from. In historic revivals, unpredictability was one of the common themes that you often see with the moving of God. We need God to send us a Divine disorder and break us away from the rut we find ourselves in.

REVIVAL

August 3

The Gift of Tears

weeping may endure for a night, but joy cometh in the morning.
–Psalm 30:5b

It is a sorrowful thing to be in a place of dryness in heart and spirit. There is joy in the expression of tears that the Holy Ghost has produced. It may have been to weep for a nation that is perishing without hope, or a Church that has lost its way, or a loved one who has gone astray, or a lost soul who is close to death's door. Tears given by God should be precious in our sight, and we should be desirous of them. They that sow in tears shall reap in joy; the tears of the faithful are as a swell smelling savor to a Holy God, the One who stores them in a bottle. In a day where men have pleasure in being stoic, God's call is brokenness and tears. W. C. Burns plowed through the dry ground in China with prayers and tears where Johnathan Goforth reaped those marvelous moving's of God many years later. May God grant us the gift of tears, not just tears of repentance but also the heart filled with the Spirit where we can weep for the things that do matter, the eternal purposes of God. Dry-eyed prayers never moved a nation or the heart of God. It is not the tears of joy but the joy of tears to be able to weep for the moving of God.

REVIVAL

August 4
Spiritual Stronghold

O God, thou hast cast us off, thou hast scattered us, thou hast been displeased; O turn thyself to us again.–Psalm 60:1

The other day when walking in a large store, I was struck with the forceful impression of this truth that America has been plunged under a spiritual stronghold. We have the massive influx of sin that has been made to be accepted as good, we have the stronghold of darkness in our churches with apathy and indifference, we have the stronghold of falsehood that has captured the next generation with evolution and vain philosophy, we have the stronghold of temporal things with sports and entertainment, we have the stronghold of Americanized Christianity with predictable services and methods, we have the stronghold of fear with social and political correctness, we have the stronghold of bondage with the invasion of cults and religion, we have the stronghold of paralysis within God's institution of the home, government and the church with defiance. The times of the past of following a cookie-cutter method is not enough to break through these strongholds; the time is now for the church to rise up and repent in dust and ashes, not to sing but weep, not to talk but groan, and seek God with prayer and fasting before we reach the point of no return.

REVIVAL

August 5

Two Kingdoms

Strive to enter in at the strait gate: for many, I say unto you, will seek to enter in, and shall not be able.–Luke 13:24

It is not about a nation's strength in military might, or about the power of education, or financial prosperity, or about an egalitarian society. It is about the kingdom of darkness against the kingdom of light. Just as Satan rules the kingdom of darkness, the kingdom of light is governed by the only true God, the God of the Bible; Jehovah, Jesus Christ, and the Holy Spirit; the Godhead. If a nation, irrespective of who they are, obeys God, they will be blessed; if disobeyed, they will be judged, for God is the rightful Owner of His Creation, and the consequences cannot be predicted. They may be given over to sin, sickness, or destruction of morality or the blindness to the reality of their plight unto destruction. The goal of Satan is the destruction of the soul of man, be it through false teachings or religion. The veneer of religion or politics and rulers are just minions in the kingdom of darkness who fight against the kingdom of light and its followers. Those who fear God, be it in authority or civil society, are called in every generation to stand against the kingdom of darkness in love, truth, and holiness, portraying their King, the Lord Jesus Christ. He will rule one day and reign over the whole world in righteousness and truth, as it was meant to be. Until then, the struggle continues.

REVIVAL

August 6

Organizing "Revival"?

If my people, which are called by my name, shall humble themselves, and pray, and seek my face, and turn from their wicked ways; then will I hear from heaven, and will forgive their sin, and will heal their land. –2 Chronicles 7:14

When we talk about God coming in the midst of His people, that is not something we can trifle with. In revivals such as in 1904, the Hebrides or other moving's of God; the Divine manifestation was so powerful that people coming near the movement could sense the presence of God miles away not being told of it, and it changed the whole community to bankrupt saloons and close-out ill-repute places for years to come. Sadly, we have a shallow form of theology that is neither revival nor a moving of God as seen in the historical context. Revival cannot come because of organizing it or because of a denomination. One cannot plan it as an event in a Church's calendar and schedule it to happen in a set week. Having special meetings focused on revival could be profitable if the expectation is that we need to continue until God comes, even after the week is over. The Holy Spirit of God cannot be told when to or when not to come at the whim of man's schedule. And these meetings lose all remembrance among the people a week after it is done. The outcome of such a shallow attitude to holy things can give a false sense of God working in our midst and cause the people to expect no more than a hyped-up fervor for that duration that leaves the community untouched.

REVIVAL

August 7

The Making of a Prophet

Now Moses kept the flock of Jethro his father in law, the priest of Midian: and he led the flock to the backside of the desert, and came to the mountain of God, even to Horeb. –Exodus 3:1

Prophets who are taught of God are bred in the wilderness by the school of loneliness. There is a daily life of repentance which the vessel undergoes as the prophet is purged and made to reflect the purity of Christ. The closer one gets to God; the more one repents living in this tabernacle of flesh. This is not the repentance from sin, which is from daily living, but rather repentance for producing fruit unto holiness. As metal gets hotter, it burns brighter in the furnace, so is the prophet whom the coals have touched from the altar that God uses to cleanse and purge the dross before being sent to confront the kings and rulers of their day. What we need today is for God to raise up prophets who declare "thus saith the Lord" and move God's people from compromised Christianity to either accept or face the consequences of rejecting a benevolent God. A prophet is strange, unreasonable, and unpredictable according to the people around him by their standards. A prophet is short-lived, for the world will not put up with him, and at the forefront of those who reject his message will be the lukewarm Church that has distanced herself from the burning vessel and his pleas.

REVIVAL

August 8
How Desperate are We?

And he said, I beseech thee, shew me thy glory. –Exodus 33:18

In the spectrum of the workings of God, we see on the one end God meeting man where man has confined himself to what he has learned or has been taught by other men. On the other end, we see God raising men where men have been broken and made into purified vessels in the fire of desperation. The former may be content with seeing a few mercy-drops amidst the prevalence of errors; the latter desires an outpouring of rain that purges and purifies the Church. Though God works on both sides of the spectrum and everything in-between, the one who is desperate for the workings of God must come to the place of desiring more than mercy drops and seek God for the difficult asking of their vessel to be broken and crushed so that God can make a vessel of His own choice and desire. In the final analysis, for the truth to be preserved, every generation needs to see a revival that changes the moral climate of their community. Anything less than that just speaks to the reality of our dependence on what we know rather than what God has for us.

REVIVAL

August 9
Fruit that Remains

Examine yourselves, whether ye be in the faith; prove your own selves. Know ye not your own selves, how that Jesus Christ is in you, except ye be reprobates?–2 Corinthians 13:5

There is a teaching today that despises the workings of God in the change that it produces following regeneration. A new creature who has been born of God has in himself the seed of God, and one born of the Spirit of God will, in its response, produce change. And act as big as God demands that their fruit should remain as God has promised in the scriptures. Any movement that minimizes the change that God brings when someone claims to be a Christian must be rejected as an inconsistent message contrary to God's word. The times where Christianity meant change seem to have been forgotten. The times where being a believer meant that the home would be different because of their profession seems to be a foreign concept. Yet, in the shallowness of this message and to possibly justify one's own lack of assurance, this belief of the lack of change has been embraced with zeal but without knowledge. In its summary, one is technically converted but spiritually lost. This is evident by the multitudes who lack the assurance of salvation and show it by their lives, which are contrary to the Creator because they were never really born again by the Spirit of God.

REVIVAL

August 10

The Workings of God

And he gave them their request; but sent leanness into their soul.
–Psalm 106:15

Finite man is infinitely limited to what he can see or deduce from desiring to learn from an infinite God. God's immutable will speaks of "what is." The sun follows its course upon heaven and earth, the laws of sin and death, etc., are ordained and in motion which cannot be changed. God's perfect will is born out of love from the heart of God for that which is beneficial to man. In the garden of Eden, God's perfect will was to have perfect fellowship with man. And if that had persisted, it would have continued in that perfection forever. Such perfect will of God speaks of "what can be." In the unclear portions allotted to man is God's permissive will, which is allowed within God's Sovereignty. In man's rebellion towards God, we see God's response of a sacrifice to make the way of escape. Within this construct, we see God's permissive will that speaks of "what God has allowed," which determines the result based on man's responsibility. In all this, God is Sovereign. To the Christian, He works all things together for good, and to the lost, His justice is satisfied in the finality of sin, which is death and Hell. We tremble at the fate of man, one who is lost and has spurned the grace of God, a God who is rich in mercy and not willing that any should perish but that all should come to repentance.

REVIVAL

August 11

Baptism of Fire

I indeed baptize you with water unto repentance. but he that cometh after me is mightier than I, whose shoes I am not worthy to bear: he shall baptize you with the Holy Ghost, and with fire:
–Matthew 3:11

In events that have significance, fire seems to be one of the natural elements that cause great attraction in its natural state. Considering what John declared of Christ regarding this baptism, fire plays a crucial role in the preparation and the ongoing continuation of the life of Christ in the soul of man. Fire has significant importance that one needs to consider if they are willing to be used by God. Fire in its ability to melt any object in extreme temperatures cleanses and separates the dross in the process of purification. Fire reveals where it was once darkness and had stayed hidden in the deep recess of one's heart. Fire attracts in equal relation to the amount of source it relies upon to cause the greater burn. Fire sears the desires of sin that were pleasurable to indulge in and brings death to the lusts thereof. Fire spreads like an unstoppable force when set aflame upon the dry ground. God desires men of fire, and they are those who have come to the altar, offered themselves as a living sacrifice, holy and acceptable unto God, carrying in their bosom the fire of God. These are those who have stayed on the altar amidst the crucible of the potter's flame that hardens the clay and has been made ready for the Master's use.

REVIVAL

August 12

God Against Us

Then shall they call upon me, but I will not answer; they shall seek me early, but they shall not find me: For that they hated knowledge, and did not choose the fear of the Lord:–Proverbs 1:28,29

It is a fearful position for a person to be in the place where he has scorned the grace of God to the utmost that the Spirit of God takes His flight away from him. To no more call, to no more convict, to no longer impress the truths of Scripture; to become an enemy of God with no recourse. A point of the searing of the conscience and a place of judgment where God is against that individual with no remedy. The warnings are clear of God resisting the proud, God fighting against Israel because of their sin, God giving Ephraim over to his idols, Saul to his rebellion, Samson to his Delilah, and Judah to Babylon. It is a greater fear to think about the reality of God who can not only be against an individual but the One who can be against His church. A church that has wandered far enough and has preached a watered-down truth to the point where He has withdrawn His Spirit from her in being a candlestick. It was this warning that John wrote about in the book of Revelation. The God of the Bible not only judges sin but also to whom much has been given; much shall be required. The purity of the Bride is of far greater importance than how busy we are in the name of Christ.

REVIVAL

August 13

Altar unto God

The Lord is nigh unto them that are of a broken heart; and saveth such as be of a contrite spirit.—Psalm 34:18

The repetition of Abraham's life was not that he had Ishmael and Isaac. Abraham's life was persisted by the many times he built an altar unto God. An altar represents the purpose of considering it, the effort to build it, the covenant to keep it, and make the sacrifice to seal it. An altar meant death, signifying that there was something you died to when you came to that altar. An altar has no meaning if you are not willing to sacrifice. It would have been foolish for an Israelite to bring a lamb to the altar and take it back; it meant separation and death to the lamb and life to the one bringing it. God desires altars in our lives not to repeat what we once promised but never did, but in a moment of solemn worship to perform the doing of it. Without sacrificing and putting to death the things that hinder our walk with God, one cannot experience the beauty of Christ. God only accepts the best, for He is worthy of it. The destitute who brings his most prized possession, the image of God that he is stamped with, to its rightful owner, God, and in complete surrender lays it at the feet of Jesus is giving a worthy offering in the eyes of God. Thus, the publican was justified while the Pharisee was rejected.

REVIVAL

August 14

The Time Factor

And the Lord said, My spirit shall not always strive with man, for that he also is flesh: yet his days shall be an hundred and twenty years.—Genesis 6:3

There seems to be this strange amnesia within the Church today, where she appears to have forgotten her past. God never works on man's schedule according to his conveniences. A revival that is wrought by God is inconvenient to man. It disrupts his status quo and exposes things that he wishes stayed in secret. Yet God desires to cleanse us and draw us unto Himself to experience Him as we would when we see Him face to face. Anything less than that is just an impatient clatter of trinkets. The revivals of the past had months and even years of agonizing prayer and crying out to God before God purified them and sent His gracious move from Heaven. Any move of God is costly and more than a cheap jukebox that plays to our wants. We expect God to work as an emergency switch. We pray before a crisis or a special effort and expect God to come down all blazing from Heaven. Such conditioning of the people has led to a watered-down Christianity, with Christians having no desire or longing for knowing the deep things of God and knowing God. It has no depth and, in its final verdict, bankrupt.

REVIVAL

August 15

The Mercy of God

The heavens declare the glory of God; and the firmament sheweth his handywork. –Psalm 19:1

Whenever we see the judgment of God, there is always a pattern of mercy before the fullness of sin causes the judgment of God to fall. We see it frequently repeated in history like Babylon, Assyria, Rome, and other nations, and those that repented like Nineveh who were spared. But when a man in his arrogance rejects God and persists in the path of sin, mercy will end, and judgment will begin. In the event of Babel, it was an act of mercy to slow man's rise of pride and self-destruction when God judged their speech. In many areas that we see today where man feels astounded or comes to something unfamiliar like Quantum Inference, man is at a loss as to what it is. It is a way for man to realize that he is not God, and it is an act of mercy on the part of God to allow him to see the majesty of God in it, repent, and turn to Him for salvation. The man who desires to be proficient in such areas needs to begin with Jesus Christ, the Creator of true science, as many scientists in the past did, such as Newton, Pasteur, Galileo, Pascal, and a host of others; to know the true meaning of the word "unknown variables."

REVIVAL

August 16

Are you Thirsty?

For I will pour water upon him that is thirsty, and floods upon the dry ground: I will pour my spirit upon thy seed, and my blessing upon thine offspring:–Isaiah 44:3

Precious are the times when the purpose of God intersects with the need of man. There is a clear contrast seen in the scriptures of those who came thirsty, and they were filled in comparison to those who came filled with their knowledge, such as the Pharisee with their phylactery and intellect of the word of God and were sent empty. The primary qualification for God to use you depends on how thirsty you are. One who is thirsty and realizing their desperate need sees the need to be holy before Him, and those who are thirsty are the ones who can be emptied and be filled. And without this filling or the anointing of the Holy Spirit, true Christianity can never be realized. This separate work of grace is not necessarily because they are clean vessels, but to thirsty vessels that have been broken and set apart for the Master's use. Those persistent in doing whatever it takes to meet their need are they who can be molded, made pure, and poured into. The testimonies of Rahab the harlot, Hannah with her barrenness, Ruth the Moabite, and the woman with the alabaster box speaks loudly of God's desire to satisfy those who are yearning to be filled. Such has been the pattern repeated over the centuries past and will continue to be required of this generation.

REVIVAL

August 17

The Dilemma of Extremes

But God hath revealed them unto us by his Spirit: for the Spirit searcheth all things, yea, the deep things of God.
−1 Corinthians 2:10

We see two extremes in Christianity today; on the one end, we see where man has been elevated to a place where Divine Sovereignty hinges on the whims of man, and at the other extreme, we see God's Sovereignty that nullifies human responsibility. In both persuasions, one common thread is evident; it is human reasoning given credence over revealed truth. Though sincere and preached from the word of God, they lack the crucial element that historical giants of the past had and saw great exploits done for the furtherance of the gospel. Taking the scriptures as is and calling for men everywhere to repent and believe the gospel is just as important as it is to preach the deep things of God, such as Divine Sovereignty. They are both true and meet as friends in the family of truth. We must look to the source of strength that historical preachers had, which was prayer, the clear experience of the fullness of the Holy Spirit, and the word of God; we look to God for our lack thereof rather than how much we can reason our theological position until we die. Though they seemed vastly contradictory on theology, of those we see such as Duncan Campbell or John Wesley, God used them both to shake nations in spiritual awakenings.

REVIVAL

August 18

Crossroads

So shall they fear the name of the Lord from the west, and his glory from the rising of the sun. When the enemy shall come in like a flood, the Spirit of the Lord shall lift up a standard against him. –Isaiah 59:19

In every generation, the church first comes to the crossroads of whether they will obey God rather than men; following a compromise of the church, the nation follows where it finds itself in the crosshairs of the judgment of God. The church decides the nation's spiritual condition, whether they will fulfill their God-given mandate of being a thermostat. The current state of the church of being a thermometer to tell how hot or cold the surrounding social conditions are is of no use; the news media can do that. When a nation turns away from God, the restraint of evil, from the perspective of the God-ordained institution, is placed on the church's shoulders, which is the pillar and ground of the truth, to call evil evil and good good for all the world to hear. It fails to be salt and light when it loses the power of the Holy Ghost, and no amount of preaching, singing, and fellowshipping can substitute for prayer, obedience, and the work of the Holy Spirit in raising a standard against the enemy who comes in like a flood. And in America, the enemy has already come in like a flood, and there has been no standard lifted against it.

REVIVAL

August 19

The Cry of Sin

The simple believeth every word: but the prudent man looketh well to his going.—Proverbs 14:15

There is a danger when one can be content, in light of the encroachment of an enemy, because it does not affect us directly. The subtlety of Satan is in his deception of showing the beginning and not the end. To broadcast a drunkard dying in the gutter drowning in his own vomit is not pleasant to watch, but social drinking of having a beer at a friend's party is seen as enjoyable. Yet while the church sleeps, the sleep of death, Satan is making some significant advances in the continuing infiltration of a self-satisfied and self-righteous church. What will it take for the church to see the approaching storm? Do we need to see fornication on the streets or Christians crucified on crosses before we call for nights of prayer? The astounding statement on the part of God to wonder at the state of a nation and saw that there was no intercessor; in contrast, we see Abraham who stood before the Lord when the Lord said that the sin of Sodom and Gomorrah had come up before Him. Unless we repent and turn to God and seek His face for the sins of our beloved land and unless we live consecrated lives before God to plead for mercy considering the impending wrath of God that is to come, nothing will stay His hand when the cry of sin is complete, and the judgment of God commences.

REVIVAL

August 20

Stemming the Tide of Sin

Go, gather together all the Jews that are present in Shushan, and fast ye for me, and neither eat nor drink three days, night or day: I also and my maidens will fast likewise; and so will I go in unto the king, which is not according to the law: and if I perish, I perish. –Esther 4:16

There is a cost in following Christ. It is an unknown concept in places where persecution is a foreign topic. But Christ's call to take up his Cross and follow Him speaks of submission, forsaking of sin, dying to self, surrendering to the Lordship of Christ, making no provision for the flesh, bringing our body into subjection, and the mortification of the deeds of the body. The cheapening of God's grace makes salvation for the express purpose of going to Heaven as life insurance, but that will never do. Christ's call is not primarily for a life of happiness, but God's call is for His disciples to get on the Cross and stay there at all costs. Apostolic Christianity preached the grave danger of desiring to follow Christ while having one foot in the world like Demas. We are at a monumental time where we are called not to count our lives dear or that we may live long or be silent in our stand, but we are called to stand with Esther and say, if I perish, I perish. If we don't stand against the tide of sin, we will be swept away by it. Contending for the faith is the first call in the book of Jude to preserve what has been given and its truthful witness before reaching the lost who are in a dilemma of what truth really is.

REVIVAL

August 21

The Gospel of Accommodation

How then can man be justified with God? or how can he be clean that is born of a woman?–Job 25:4

The gospel is dreadful news for the sinner for it shows the sinfulness of sin before a thrice Holy God; it shows man as a worm not worthy of eternal life; it shows man's righteousness as putrefying sores and as a leper unclean; it reveals the utter inability of the man to find God on his own; it shows the impossibility of man adding any good works to the scale of God; it shows the eventuality of the eternal fires of Hell for those who die without Christ no matter how moral, charitable or respectable they had been on earth, before a God from whose face the earth and the heavens fled away. On the contrary, the gospel of accommodation shows sin as not exceedingly sinful, that man has some good in him but needs some help, that he does not need to repent, that God is not angry with the wicked every day, that the wicked will not be turned into Hell, that it is about going to Heaven, that has man as the center of attention and not God, that God is hoping that man will choose Him since it is such a good deal. Such a bankrupt gospel produces a bankrupt Christianity and reflects on our downward trend of morality in America. The gospel becomes good news when a convicted sinner sees the way of escape through Jesus Christ by the illumination of the Spirit.

REVIVAL

August 22

Discerning the Times

And when they had prayed, the place was shaken where they were assembled together; and they were all filled with the Holy Ghost, and they spake the word of God with boldness.—Acts 4:31

Relevance is not about being in step with the world's philosophy but being in contrast with it while proclaiming God's unchanging truth in the power of the Spirit. A church that imitates the world will be irrelevant with God, for they are opposed to each other. Our young people lose interest in our churches because the church has lost its fire. There are no burning hearts because there are no burning pulpits. The responsibility to bring change to a community is not in the pew but the pulpit. In the historical account of revivals, when an evangelist came into town, irrespective of the initial state of the pew, when he left, the moral climate of the community was changed, whether it was Mordecai Ham, Wesley, or Moody. The problem we have with the apparent downward spiral of our Nation is in the church's teachings against the anointing of the Spirit of God that these men of the past possessed and preached. Not the manifestation of tongues which none of these evangelists experienced, but an enduement of power for service that was separate from salvation and just as life-changing, which is evident from the scriptures and was preached by the apostles but is sadly lacking in our pulpits today.

REVIVAL

August 23

Without the Camp

As many as I love, I rebuke and chasten: be zealous therefore, and repent.–Revelation 3:19

When the sin of God's people, the church, has reached God's threshold for judgment, God removes His manifest presence from His people. Removal of the manifest presence of God unleashes the encroachment and torrent of evil. Israel knew well when they went a whoring after the golden calf where Moses had to remove the tabernacle and pitch it outside the camp and in a great distance from them, for God will not dwell amongst a people whose heart is not wholly directed toward Him. When we look around us with the moral and spiritual bankruptcy, sin in the church, political chaos, gender issues, and the social upheaval that we are experiencing in our day, we can see that God has removed His manifest presence from His Laodicean church in America and sin has been allowed to prevail. God has been put as it were outside the camp. Where is the glory of Ancient Egypt, Babylon, Assyria, or Rome today? Winston Churchill said, "Those who fail to learn from history are condemned to repeat it." Will the churches in America see the need, raise a call to repentance and stand in the gap for this Nation before it is too late?

REVIVAL

August 24

Spiritual Discernment

Beloved, believe not every spirit, but try the spirits whether they are of God: because many false prophets are gone out into the world. – 1 John 4:1

In a day where there seems to be a prevailing apathy among God's people for spiritual discernment of what is truth and error, the tendency is there to see someone who claims to speak the truth or their love for God and accept their teachings as "truth" irrespective of things which may be contrary to the word of God. We see this evidenced today where the symbols of Christianity are embraced rather than the truths of Christianity that are lived out. We realize that there is a great need for spiritual discernment where we need to ask God for this purpose of defending truth, contending for the faith, and protecting the inner man from deception. There are five principles that God has given us for trying the spirits as commanded by God. We have the principle of the revealed truth of God's word and prayer, the principle of historical teachings of Church fathers who have gone before us, the principle of the witness of the Spirit in leading one to holiness to bring about spiritual fruits, the principle of whether it represents the character of God, and finally the principle of seeing where that starting point leads to in one's spiritual life and as a Church. Anything found contrary when tested against these principles must be rejected as deception of truth no matter how good it sounds, practiced, or propagated by so-called men of God.

REVIVAL

August 25

Judgement of Sin

Then Moses stood in the gate of the camp, and said, Who is on the Lord's side? let him come unto me. And all the sons of Levi gathered themselves together unto him. –Exodus 32:26

One need not go far as one looks around to see the display of the effects of sin. Whether it be racism, exploitation of the innocent, murder, defrauding of another, or genocide, the depravity of man in his sinful condition is seen. Yet, it is not just what we see but to realize that the same seed lies in all of us and is cherished willingly by the desire of our fallen heart. Sin is anything that is against God and deviates from the law of God in thought, action, or intent. And the essence of the whole matter is that God hates sin and judges it. God used Babylon, who were sinful, to judge Israel when Israel crossed sin's threshold for judgment. Babylon was also judged when they did not repent, and their cry of sin came before a Holy God. God was against both in their partaking of sin though He used one against another. And to whom much is given, much shall be required. Israel was given much by her Abrahamic covenant and was held to a higher standard. When we are tempted to look at a situation and try to analyze whose side God is on, it is quite possible that God is not on either side but as the judge of all the earth, He will do right.

REVIVAL

August 26

The Love of Christ

Nor height, nor depth, nor any other creature, shall be able to separate us from the love of God, which is in Christ Jesus our Lord.
–Romans 8:39

There is a love that is far beyond knowledge, experience, and understanding. Such love is too high for the human mind to comprehend. Mankind is still baffled by the magnitude of Creation, intricacies of life itself, and the infinity of the Universe; to take a step back and look at the God who made them, who declares that the nations are as a drop of a bucket and earth as His footstool. To think of God who is so majestic and eternal but yet confined Himself into this robe of humanity and be born in a lowly stable amidst the animals of that dirty stall, to imagine the depth of God's love in letting the soldiers spit on His face and drive cruel nails in His hands and feet, to see Him standing there outside that empty tomb in resurrection power; unable to assimilate such grandeur we turn and look at that one phrase, "for God so loved the world that He gave." Silence speaks when we are awestruck by such love for unworthy sinners such as you and me. Do we comprehend how much God loves us? Mere words cannot pen such love. As one hymn writer wrote, "Could we with ink the ocean fill, And were the skies of parchment made, Were every stalk on earth a quill, And every man a scribe by trade; To write the love of God above Would drain the ocean dry; Nor could the scroll contain the whole, Though stretched from sky to sky."

REVIVAL

August 27

Tolerated, but not Desired

Draw nigh to God, and he will draw nigh to you. Cleanse your hands, ye sinners; and purify your hearts, ye double minded. – James 4:8

In the desperate need to keep the balance of what is expected in religion and my well-being in this life, we can unknowingly come to the place of tolerating the things of God and not sincerely desiring them. God, who is all-sufficient off Himself and having no need for anyone, has opened this sacred portal of friendship through the blood of His dear Son on the Cross. Such privilege has been granted to mortal man where he will be placed as Adam was in the garden to desire God out of love and not out of compulsion. When God is "tolerated" in my life, even as a follower of Christ, it becomes mundane in my necessity to seek Him; if that is my attitude, then God will never make Himself known to me in a warmly personal way. But when I set my heart by the Spirit's sustenance to seek after God daily and look for His coming even during periods of darkness, then God is pleased to make Himself known in what we call as the manifest nearness of Christ. Such encounters are more precious than gold, but they will cost us just as much in purifying the intents and motives of our hearts.

REVIVAL

August 28

Restoring our First Love

Jesus said unto him, Thou shalt love the Lord thy God with all thy heart, and with all thy soul, and with all thy mind.
–Matthew 22:37

We hesitate to mention certain aspects of the Christian walk lest we give a low view of what it means, and people upon embracing it feel deceived and are left in darkness when they sought the light; such is this area where our inner-most motive of service for Christ revolves around the core element of our love towards God. Serving God should be from the outflow of that love that has been imparted into our hearts through salvation and not for earning His love or gaining acceptance from God. This agape form of love [act of will and not primarily based on emotion] that is unconditional and spoken as "charity" in 1 Corinthians 13; and love that is manifested in the agapao form of representation such as "For God so loved that He gave [action]" speaks of the divinity of this love. First, love hinges on this fact that we love [agapao] God because He first loved [agapao] us, and then it goes on to demonstrate that love is an outflow of good works from being in love with Him. One who does not just love someone but is in love with someone does things that others may see as above normal or foolish. But to the one, who is the giver of it, that expression of love is all they see in their desire for the object of their love. Thus, leaving our first love needs careful consideration to go back and find its cause and then seek God in repentance for its restoration and do the first works until we fully experience it. Once we are restored, to continue in it by the renewal of the mind and the power of the Spirit to the glory of God in living out that love-relationship.

REVIVAL

August 29

Spontaneous Revivals

Now when Solomon had made an end of praying, the fire came down from heaven, and consumed the burnt offering and the sacrifices; and the glory of the Lord filled the house. And the priests could not enter into the house of the Lord, because the glory of the Lord had filled the Lord's house. – 2 Chronicles 7:1,2

There are times when God comes down in power to a people set apart and waiting for Him, a heart prepared and a people aware of the need for God to come. During such times of sudden infusion of God's manifest presence, the people fall on their faces before God and, in awe, realize that God has come. As a result, it bleeds into the community where the community as a whole is changed, and the world stops to take notice of the church, not just that they exist but that they are living a supernatural life by the Spirit that they cannot explain away. And we see similar results as we read in the book of Acts repeated; "great fear came upon all the church; and they spake the word of God with boldness; and great grace was upon them all; turned the world upside down." One of the tragedies of our day is that we have not seen such power in our midst and have gotten used to the lack thereof where the next generation thinks that going to church, reading their Bible, praying, witnessing, loving others is all there is to it in the realm of being a Christian. Suppose all we have of "Christianity" is just what we are used to today, lacking spontaneous works of the Spirit. In that case, lack of the supernatural moving's of God in raw, unbridled power, without seasons of the manifest presence of God in the midst of His people, then "Christianity" as we see today is pretty disappointing.

REVIVAL

August 30

Get Out of the Boat

And he said, Come. And when Peter was come down out of the ship, he walked on the water, to go to Jesus.—Matthew 14:29

There is a temptation to accept the here-and-now in the realm of what we have labeled as "Christianity" and be convinced that there is nothing more to it. But Christianity, as we see in the book of Acts, was very different from what we see today. What we call Christianity today comes down to going to church regularly, follow an orderly and predictable service, talk about trivial pursuits and programs, pass out tracts, have our cookie-cutter "revival" services, display our academic accolades, and scholastic abilities, pray and not see any real change. Have we seen unpredictable services like Ananias and Sapphira; experienced prayer meetings like the place shaken and the people filled with the Holy Ghost; saw the supernatural with Eutychus brought to life from the dead; witness that was so powerful that it was either salvation, prison, or stones; people delivered from the bondage of Satan like the woman who was possessed with the spirit of divination; five thousand saved in one anointed preaching? Christianity at best today is not Biblical Christianity; neither can we call our shallow want of decisions without the supernatural witness of the rebirth experience salvation. Can God revive us? Yes, if we are willing, to be honest. If not, we are just fooling ourselves and giving our young people a religion of derision.

REVIVAL

August 31

The Prodigal

If we confess our sins, he is faithful and just to forgive us our sins, and to cleanse us from all unrighteousness. – 1 John 1:9

Having a fear of God while keeping Him in full view is paramount for the life of a Christian. The wanting of the swine feed of this world may be desirous at the beginning to appease the flesh, but it will never satisfy. Realizing the beggarly value of what the world has to offer when compared to the riches of Heaven can make one wiser, but it will never stop the flesh from wanting its way. Putting to death by the mortification of the flesh, submitting to the Lordship of Christ moment by moment is necessary for experiencing the life of victory. There are times when forgiveness is not in a simple prayer, but it is longed for on the way home that one has to endure before he comes to his Father's house and receives it. Usefulness for service and the flow of the Spirit needs to be guarded watchfully lest any trample on the sweet grapes of the vineyard, and it is the little foxes that spoil the vine. In such times of return when the Father's face is hidden, contemplating on the mercy of grace to allow such feelings of love toward God and the conviction of sin by the Spirit should give us the greater desire to persevere until we reach home and fall on our face before God in confession, forsaking, and tears of repentance, seeking restoration. Though healing and restoration can be found in His presence, the scars remain for life.

REVIVAL.

September

September 1

Wings as Eagles

O taste and see that the Lord is good: blessed is the man that trusteth in him.—Psalm 34:8

In the age of technology, where having a conversation is literally in the palm of our hands with phones and smartwatches, the reality of what it means to draw near to God needs to be evaluated if one is to pursue that lofty goal. The more one draws near to God, the lonelier they become where what is seen around them, even in the realm of Christian fellowship, becomes nothing but the chatter of earthly-minded goals which hinder one's longing to look above. Such were the prophets of the Bible from Enoch to John the Baptist. The school of loneliness strips one of self-ability and self-esteem and purifies them for reflecting their Maker. In the chapter on stillness, Moses learned to stay forty days and forty nights on the mountaintop but met God and spoke with Him face to face. The desire of the flesh to keep us occupied and entertained, the reality of a Church becoming a social-betterment influencer and forgetting her mandate, and such, needs to be evaluated if we are to pay the price of loneliness for knowing God. In silence, we hear His voice, and in His stillness, we get to experience Him. Though the eagles soar alone, they fly far about the mountain tops in the pristine air that is untouched by the pollution of the lowlands.

REVIVAL

September 2

Preaching and Revival

Preach the word; be instant in season, out of season; reprove, rebuke, exhort with all long suffering and doctrine.
−2 Timothy 4:2

God in our midst in manifest power is as a glimpse of Heaven with its inexhaustible presence of God. The preparation of praying, preaching, contending, worship, separation, and so forth prepares us for God to come into our midst. In such cases, when He comes, generally, all else ceases, and only worship and adoration persist. And on the part of the sinner, the awfulness of sin becomes overwhelming where we hear the groans and cries of sinners for mercy. The purpose of preaching is to cause the listeners to move from where they are to where God is. Anything else is just giving instruction and becomes teaching. Teaching can be done without the Spirit, but genuine preaching can only happen by the Spirit. The preparation for the tabernacle and the items such as the lamps, table of shewbread, brasen altar, and all others were to prepare them to meet God in the holy of holies. In historic revivals, there is often little or no preaching once God comes since there is no need for it. Thus, there is no preaching in Heaven, for we don't need it to prepare us to meet God, for God is always there.

REVIVAL

September 3

Restraint on Sin

Quench not the Spirit.—1 Thessalonians 5:19

A vacuum cannot stay empty for an extended period since something needs to fill it, or it will implode. Though an implosion of sin can happen, and destruction for the penalty of sin may be delayed, destruction will eventually happen. In the area of God's truth, that God has revealed in His word and expressed by His Spirit, when that truth is spurned or quenched, the restraint on sin is removed, and evil begins to have a free course in a nation. In America, due to compromised churches, shallow evangelism, false converts, and bringing down the purity of the gospel, the restraint on sins such as LGBTQ+, divorce, crimes, and so forth have been withdrawn, and evil has been left unchecked while breeding powerless pulpits and polluted pews to continue that vicious cycle. And unless we seek the face of God in repentance for our part in this, to hold ourselves accountable for where America is, we will never see a revival or a turnaround of the holiness of God and the fear of God manifested in our land. This was how our forefathers sought, through brokenness and repentance, to have true freedom and justice in our land.

REVIVAL

September 4

A Grim Truth

And from the days of John the Baptist until now the kingdom of heaven suffereth violence, and the violent take it by force.
–Matthew 11:12

A nation in moral decline, spiritual bankruptcy, gender wars, political chaos, social upheaval; Americanized Christianity that displays a form of godliness but denies the power thereof, the reality of revivals that shake a community which has become like a fairy tale, the church that is hastening the falling away with shallow evangelism, head knowledge that is emphasized without the supernatural experiences of the Spirit. We have many evangelists but no revivalists who can shake a community for God; we have many preachers, deacons, and teachers but lack anointed preaching that moves the audience from the word of God to the Person of the word; we have many people who pray but no agonizers and travail'ers in prayer that storm heaven to take it by force; we have many conferences but no moving of the Spirit to affect them or the communities that the audience represents; we have religion, but our young people are tired of theoretical Christianity that has no depth. Then I realize that the blame rests upon me for where America and the church are, for I make up the church, and I need to look no further. God does not raise up movements; He raises up people.

REVIVAL

September 5

Fleshly Works during Revival

Then shall ye return, and discern between the righteous and the wicked, between him that serveth God and him that serveth him not.—Malachi 3:18

Whenever there is a move of God, there is always a move of Satan by counterfeit to discredit God's work. The clamorous declaration by the woman who distracted Paul was just as subverting as Peter, who desired Christ not to be crucified. In times of revival, the spirit of the meeting needs to be discerned to execute on the required steps lest Satan plucks the seed before it bears fruit being mixed with faith. To have the proper understanding of what God is dealing with by the working of His Spirit is crucial, and we ought to guard it lest anything, even in the name of "good," turn our focus from it. Our gracious God works in the hearts of the people and raises up those who can discern if something is done in the energy of the flesh in times of such closeness with God. And He has given us His word and His Spirit to equip us in this good fight of faith. The forces of evil do not engage with God's servants in this battle by the principles of warfare but by cheat and deception, even desiring to attack where the saint of God is most vulnerable; such traits are common in his plan. But we have great comfort that God will not allow anything to come our way which He has not permitted; for Satan never debated with God on what he was allowed to do to Job, but at the grant of his request obeyed.

REVIVAL

September 6
A Ray of Hope

And hope maketh not ashamed; because the love of God is shed abroad in our hearts by the Holy Ghost which is given unto us.
—Romans 5:5

Just as our self-view is affected by how we view God, we need to come to the place of beginning with God in all areas of our lives. Knowing what God has done in the past is not enough to be convinced of what He desires to do today. History has shown us a glimpse of the high points of God's working, but we live day by day with things that affect us in all walks of life. Desiring God to come needs to start by realizing that God desires to meet with His people more than our desire for Him. And when we recognize the seriousness of God's desire and align our lives to meet that need as the chief end of man, to glorify God and to enjoy Him forever, then we can make ourselves ready like the virgins who were wise, longing for their Lord. Our prayers should always reflect God's desire before they reflect ours. It should always begin with the cause of Christ's desire for His church to receive her as a pure bride before we see the lack thereof on our part. In its finality, praying for the manifestation of God among His people in transcendent power starts with God's desire for us and our willingness to make ourselves ready to meet Him. The jealousy of the Lord will provoke His working in our midst when we seek His face for the express purpose of joining in a solemn oath of wanting God to be glorified and His exhalation above all things.

REVIVAL

September 7
The Hidden Forces of Evil

For such are false apostles, deceitful workers, transforming themselves into the apostles of Christ. And no marvel; for Satan himself is transformed into an angel of light. Therefore it is no great thing if his ministers also be transformed as the ministers of righteousness; whose end shall be according to their works.
—2 Corinthians 11:13-15

In the demise of a nation or an individual, there is always more to it than what is seen and heard. Lucifer, since his fall, works behind the scenes to subvert the purposes of God and bring destruction. While God is light, Satan is darkness; while God is good, Satan is evil; while God is the source of truth, Satan is the father of lies; while God is the giver of life, Satan is the bringer of death; while God is the creator of beauty, Satan is the embodiment of corruption; while God desires absolute good for His Creation, Satan wants absolute evil for anything God creates. With such a heavenly battle in high places that are constantly taking place, there is a great need for the church to lift her eyes off political parties and things that are happening at the here-and-now and realize the source of the outcome seen on earth. To pray effectively against the onslaught of evil is to begin where God is and desire His victory to be manifested in the lives of His people over sin, to live holy lives that reflect the name we bear, and to pray intercessory prayers of faith against the forces of darkness that fight for the soul of a nation. If America is destroyed, it will be because of the prevailing darkness among God's people who failed to seek God to lift up a standard against the enemy, and not because of politics, laws, or the media.

REVIVAL

September 8

The Burden of Revival

Now while Paul waited for them at Athens, his spirit was stirred in him, when he saw the city wholly given to idolatry. Therefore disputed he in the synagogue with the Jews, and with the devout persons, and in the market daily with them that met with him.
–Acts 17:16,17

A fire left unattended will eventually die out. As in natural causes of physical fire, we have the world, the flesh, and the devil that are constantly pulling us down for drying the wells of the desire for revival, and there is a great need to continually weed out the elements that stifle God's intent for His people. To uphold as it were the great need that lies before us is to have a burden for the manifest presence of God in our midst. And the reason for maintaining this burden stems from the cry of those who need more than what the church or we can offer in monotone Christianity; the responsibility we bear to the younger generation that is desperate for the reality of Christ, the Person; the burden of removing the reproach that is on the name of Jesus; the singular focus of God being glorified in a pagan society; the burden of seeing the gospel to come not in word only, but also in power, and in the Holy Ghost, and in much assurance; the burden of evangelism and seeing people genuinely born of the Spirit of God; the burden of the true expression of the Christ-life in believers; and the burden of seeing the Book of Acts Christianity that was a thermostat to bring about change, and not a thermometer to talk about change, where we find ourselves today.

REVIVAL

September 9

Rediscovering the God of the Bible

Ye are the salt of the earth: but if the salt have lost his savour, wherewith shall it be salted? it is thenceforth good for nothing, but to be cast out, and to be trodden under foot of men.
–Matthew 5:13

If there ever was a message as a two-edged sword in its implication, it is the absolute truth of who God declares Himself to be with "I change not." And an unchanging God in a changing generation, culture, and standards will become more and more contrasted in being viewed of who He is. Over the years, this contrast has been blended with error to make God more acceptable and brought to a place where He can coexist with sin. By focusing primarily on the goodness of God, the love of God, and the mercy of God, and ignoring the justice of God, the holiness of God, and the wrath of God, we have built a cage where we can "manage" how we view God. Thus, God has become nothing more than the object of our imagination and not who He truly is; One worshipped in unimaginable purity by the elders who fall on their faces before Him day and night, along with the seraphims who cannot look upon Him but rather cry "Holy, holy, holy." God has not changed; only our perception has been dulled. Facing the living God will be a terrible thing when we don't know Him anymore other than as a hero in a storybook that soothes our feelings and cheapens Him in the gutter of our imagination.

REVIVAL

September 10

Aftermath of a Revival

All scripture is given by inspiration of God, and is profitable for doctrine, for reproof, for correction, for instruction in righteousness: That the man of God may be perfect, thoroughly furnished unto all good works.—2 Timothy 3:16,17

As with any move of God, such as the 1904 Welsh revival, there is always a time of flowing and a time of eventual subsiding of revival blessing. During those times, there is a great need for two things. One is the need for putting down any manifestations of the flesh and counterfeits that Satan brings during and after the revival, two the need for the called of God who are to disciple those affected by the move of God to be grounded in the word of God. There is a great need for the people's focus to stay in the word of God and desire to continue to find the God of the word by the Holy Spirit. Though manifestations may be seen during a revival, there is always a difference to discern if it attracts attention to the one going through it or brings awe and glory to God. Anything that gives temporal display without the depth of a holy life and a desire to seek the God of the Bible needs to be put down and carefully weeded out from what God has for His people. The application of the word of God that flows through revival power by the Spirit needs to be established as the lifelong journey of one's walk with God, which is critical for preventing any disillusionment of those touched by a visitation from God.

REVIVAL

September 11
Pure Religion Undefiled

This is a faithful saying, and these things I will that thou affirm constantly, that they which have believed in God might be careful to maintain good works. These things are good and profitable unto men. –Titus 3:8

Despite a fallen world constantly deteriorating and breeding chaos, God has ordained His remnant to take the torch of mercy and truth to bring hope amidst a world of despair. Throughout history, we see the effects of true Christianity that moved in places like England and America to abolish slavery; it moved millions of missionaries who left home and went to uncivilized parts of the world and brought true freedom through Christ to those who were bound in superstition and the darkness of the occult; it saw fellowmen as brothers irrespective of color, creed or social standing; it touched the untouchables and lepers; it turned the moral climate of nations through the first and the second great spiritual awakenings; it brought scientists and great minds, who believed in creation and brought the laws of God into their discoveries, radically change human medicine and science; it saw the freedom from child labor, drugs, alcohol, temple prostitutes, built hospitals, schools, Christian colleges and gave worth to man in places such as Africa, Asia, India, Europe, America and all over the world. Though fallen man has used religion as a bludgeon to fulfill his sinful lusts, the true work that God intended always sets man free from the bondage of sin and brings true freedom to those who walk in the Spirit.

REVIVAL

September 12

The Call to Give Up

Save thyself, and come down from the cross. – Mark 15:30

The constant struggle of the world and the flesh, against the desire of the Spirit and the voice of God, is something that a faithful Christian needs to contend with daily. Though the cleansing for past sins, which have been confessed and forsaken, has been given, the remembrance of the scars which remain cries out in enticing echoes in a desire to bring us back to what once was. In the face of persecution, the flesh has a great desire to turn aside and give up the narrow way, to stop bearing the cross and following the Lord. But faithful is He that calleth you, who also will do it. Our responsibility to realize the reality of the shallowness of sin; the way of the transgressors, which is hard; the pleasure in sin for a season that soon fades away; the things that are eternal which are more valuable than the temporal; the realization that our life is but the vapor and what is done for Christ by His Spirit will be as jewels in His crown for all of eternity; these truths ought to be pondered where the flesh can be mortified to resist the call of Demas, when he gave ear to the tempter and loved this present world, turning aside to the fleeting and unfulfilling pleasures of sin that captivated his attention.

REVIVAL

September 13

Spiritual Awakening

So the people of Nineveh believed God, and proclaimed a fast, and put on sackcloth, from the greatest of them even to the least of them. –Jonah 3:5

Why is there no move of God though there seems to be much asking? Is it because we are asking the wrong god? We seem to be asking the god of our imagination, the one with whom we have come to love and preach about from the scriptures. Where we have sought God based on His promises, the true God is Holy and waits for purity; while we have asked God for revival, the true God is just and waits for humility in judging ourselves of our sin; while we have asked God for His presence and God's desire to be fulfilled on earth, the true God waits for man to rediscover the holiness of God who cannot look upon sin; while we have worshipped Him in our songs, the true God waits for a solemn assembly to be still and know that He is God without the clamorous display of music and words that drown the Spirit and feeds the flesh; while we have looked for God to save lost souls as His priority, God waits for a pure Bride where He would be the object of her love and affection; while we have sought God for the fulfillment of His promise of refreshing, God sought for a man whose shuns sports and entertainment with a heart that is perfect toward Him; while we have prayed with fervor and tears, God waits for a man with a broken spirit: a broken and a contrite heart.

REVIVAL

September 14

God's Garden

Come, my beloved, let us go forth into the field; let us lodge in the villages. –Song of Solomon 7:11

It is the Spirit who brings life. While being led by the Spirit, some plant, some water, some do the weeding, but God gives the increase. The focus is not on those who plant, water, or do the weeding; the focus is on God who gave the increase, that no flesh should glory in His presence, for it is God who calleth who also will do it, and He has raised up many for the task. We rejoice together on what God has done, looking unto Jesus and walking by faith, not lingering in the past. Though weeping is part of bearing precious seed and going, the burden of harvest is upon God to bring forth the increase. While we go with expectation, God is the Husbandman, and we are co-laborers with God in His garden, looking to Him for that increase. The old Welsh divines used to state revival as "God visiting His garden." It is for the desire to draw near to the Master that we prepare His Bride so she can meet her God. To bring forth fruit unto holiness, to be in the world but not of the world. The crowning jewel of life is to pay tribute to the giver of life by the response of one who is fruitful in bringing the fragrance of Christ to a world in need. And see the result of carrying it from the garden of God to the world around them.

REVIVAL

September 15

Seeking God Perpetually

I will greatly rejoice in the Lord, my soul shall be joyful in my God; for he hath clothed me with the garments of salvation, he hath covered me with the robe of righteousness, as a bridegroom decketh himself with ornaments, and as a bride adorneth herself with her jewels.—Isaiah 61:10

To seek God is not for reaching an expected end on earth but a lifelong enjoyment of seeking God and finding Him. New heights to climb and new joys to have when seeking after the One who loved us so. When we find Him, we desire more0 of Him to continue to seek Him. Seeking God for the Christian is not primarily based on meeting our physical needs; instead, it is based on love and the Bride's desire for her betrothed Husband, the One she longs to see. "That I may know Him" is a lifelong desire and goal that one should aspire as a journey that they have undertaken by the express hand and impetus of God at the point of regeneration. Though there may be times where the face of God is hidden from us, the faithfulness of God in loving us should reciprocate with fresh love toward Him that finds rest in His presence. And anything that this world offers as an alternative, as attractive as it may seem, would be as dung when offered on the platter of sin. The temporal culmination of seeking after God could be in seasons of revival, with its finality realized when we see Him face to face. Such love needs the supernatural infusion from above and sustenance by the Person of the Holy Spirit.

REVIVAL

September 16
A Cause for Anguish

Yea, truth faileth; and he that departeth from evil maketh himself a prey: and the Lord saw it, and it displeased him that there was no judgment. And he saw that there was no man, and wondered that there was no intercessor:–Isaiah 59:15,16a

There is a tendency at times where a concern is raised with no valid justification for it. If such were the case, one would be right to ignore what is being conveyed. When dealing with the things of God, the reality is evident that God rules in the affairs of men, and nations are held accountable for the light that they have been given and to the obedience of it. The overwhelming evidence of the amount of light from the founding of our beloved land, portrayed in our Declaration of Independence to the moral construct of our system of law and values, is seen throughout our history. The danger of receiving blessings from the kind hand of God and rejecting His rightful place, which we see prevalent today, should be a cause of great concern and fear for those who see this trend that is happening in our land. The trickery of Balaam to cause Israel to commit whoredom for bringing God's judgment upon Israel when he could not curse them is being repeated, where the tipping point will soon be reached to the place of no return, to incur the wrath of Almighty God upon this Nation. Would God say of the American church today, "And I sought for a man among them, that should make up the hedge, and stand in the gap before me for the land, that I should not destroy it: but I found none."

REVIVAL

September 17

Filling the Void

Then goeth he, and taketh to him seven other spirits more wicked than himself; and they enter in, and dwell there: and the last state of that man is worse than the first.—Luke 11:26

In many instances, when reading about historic revivals, there is intense persecution after a genuine move of God. The early church experienced great multitudes of people being swept into the Kingdom of God and the great persecution that followed. In reading accounts like these, specific patterns emerge. While persecutions may lead to strength, blessings in the long term generally led to apathy among God's people. When a void is created, something must fill it, or it will be filled with whatever the world can give. After the Pyongyang revival of 1907, we see great persecution that came, to where today North Korea is one of the most repressive countries in the world. We can say the same for the evangelical revival in England, where after the blessings that followed, England today is a barren land. The void will be filled, and it depends on who gets to it first. The same happened in China, which allowed Christian missionaries before the Boxer Rebellion; when a void was created, communism filled that void. The natural principle of a void that must be filled is being seen today in America, where Americanized Christianity is unable to meet the Nation's spiritual needs, and every diabolical element that contends for the soul of this Nation is starting to fill that void.

REVIVAL

September 18

Marks of Genuine Revival

Then said I, Woe is me! for I am undone; because I am a man of unclean lips, and I dwell in the midst of a people of unclean lips: for mine eyes have seen the King, the Lord of hosts.–Isaiah 6:5

The restoration of one's view of revival must begin with one's restoration of their view of God, for revival is God in our midst. And as such, there are certain traits that one can observe from historical revivals. It is the manifest presence of Christ, deep conviction of sin and exuberant worship in the beauty of holiness, the free course of the word of God as a flood which invades into the community with lasting effects, the arrest of sin by the Spirit and His transformative power among God's people, the revelation of the nature of Christ among His children to be Christ-bearers. On the contrary, the works of the flesh are manifested by the exaltation of self that hinders the working of God, the elevation of personalities and their abilities, the eclipse of the deep work of God replaced with the shallow result of one's effort that brings reproach to the name of Christ, the delusional views of pride elevated over the Biblical view of humility. The grave danger that persists where one can be deceived must be combated by desiring the God of the word at all costs, the willingness to examine the events in light of scriptures, and the effect of any movement on the presence and manifestation of wickedness that would be contrary to the nature of God. Seeking God for who He is and not for how He can affect our emotions should be our primary goal in this matter of desiring genuine revival.

REVIVAL

September 19
Broken and a Contrite Heart

Against thee, thee only, have I sinned, and done this evil in thy sight: that thou mightest be justified when thou speakest, and be clear when thou judgest.–Psalm 51:4

The great need of our day is for an honest re-evaluation of ourselves before God in this matter of our heart attitude towards our Creator. "Lovest thou me?" is a question that needs serious pondering for many hours, if not days, to see our love toward God in our service towards Him. Our giving, our going, our obeying, and even our life of separation unto holiness needs to be born out of love for the express purpose of loving God with all our heart, soul, and mind. Many times, in our walk with God, we find ourselves in times of barrenness and a sense of being "distant" from the presence and favor of God. In those seasons as in all times, nothing can truly bring us to that place of restoration than an honest recognition of this deadness, breaking up of one's fallow ground by desiring the Spirit to bring us to the vision of His love on Calvary; God in the flesh dying for unworthy sinners. Having a broken spirit that cannot be mended but by God and contrition from seeing the wickedness of our pride that is subtle and inherent in everything we do should cause us to flee to Him for mercy and cleansing. Such sacrifices bring the pleasure of God to His children and can set us on the path of restoration and usefulness. And moments like these should be guarded and remembered as a memorial since we constantly wage war with the flesh that desires to rule over the Spirit.

REVIVAL

September 20
The Manifest Presence of God

In the year that king Uzziah died I saw also the Lord sitting upon a throne, high and lifted up, and his train filled the temple. Above it stood the seraphims: each one had six wings; with twain he covered his face, and with twain he covered his feet, and with twain he did fly. And one cried unto another, and said, Holy, holy, holy, is the Lord of hosts: the whole earth is full of his glory. And the posts of the door moved at the voice of him that cried, and the house was filled with smoke. –Isaiah 6:1-4

It is a fearful thing to be in the manifest presence of God. It exposes sin, it brings conviction of truth, it demands a response, it breaks down all our facades, it condemns the nominal "Christian," it is unpredictable, it causes those who are affected by it to examine themselves and at times cause one to hesitate to enter into His presence, it challenges and changes our view of God, it terrifies the lost and brings to bear the full brunt of His holiness. On the other end of the spectrum, it brings the nearness of Christ; it edifies the true believer, it produces the speechless adoration of love in response to God's love and the joys of enjoying Him, and so forth. Such effects of the overwhelming presence of God have been seen in times of revival where God comes down. Mortal men are privileged to gaze on the glory of God and to fall prostrate on the ground and worship Him with one voice with the host of heaven that He is worthy of honor, glory, and praise for time without end. Such heavy presence of God cannot be built up by any works of man with choirs, music, lights, preaching, or any human instruments. They are brought by the work of the Spirit in the soul of man to prepare, purge and lift those who are of a broken and contrite heart and lay hold of His promise with the eye of faith.

REVIVAL

September 21
What is Our Supreme Goal?

But it is good for me to draw near to God: I have put my trust in the Lord God, that I may declare all thy works. –Psalm 73:28

Paul uttered while approaching his final years, having followed Christ through starvations, persecution, privations, great deliverances of those bound by Satan, seeing the gospel witness spread with immense force, and many other exploits that God did, his maturing in Christ brought him to place where he uttered those famous words "that I may know Him." The necessity of knowing God becomes supreme when we realize that everything else hinges on that. Whether service to man, contending for the faith, preaching, witnessing, dealing with social issues, and so forth become secondary. When you come to the place of knowing Him, you see everything else as an outlet from knowing God, which flows into those other avenues. The primary intent of the Father is that Christ is lifted up, and Christ is lifted up when we know God; and in that sacred cloister, we commune with Him knowing His heart, plow through the word and learn His ways in intimate fellowship. Such knowledge of God brings forth the joy of sharing Him with others that they may know the One who is the joy of our hearts, in times of fruitfulness or during our times of trials in the backside of the desert. To rejoice in the God of our salvation irrespective of anything else that vies for our attention.

REVIVAL

September 22

Serious Indictments to Consider

But they rebelled, and vexed his holy Spirit: therefore he was turned to be their enemy, and he fought against them.
–Isaiah 63:10

Repeating the same mistakes and expecting a different result is a sure sign of insanity. In the realm of far-reaching implications and unfathomable consequences, specific questions need to be asked, at least to ensure they are considered, even if they are found to be inaccurate. Are we aware that God has withdrawn His manifest presence from our midst? Have we realized that He has become America's greatest enemy because of our iniquities against Him? That God will hold us accountable for the blessings that He has bestowed upon us? Do we know that we serve a God who is angry with the wicked every day? and that the wicked shall be turned into hell and all the nations that forget God? Have we realized that God is long-suffering, but we don't know how long He will suffer? And that God's Spirit will not always strive with man? Do we realize that God is good, but the justice of God will demand His wrath upon ungodly sinners? Are we aware that we can come to a point in time in the life of a nation where when the fullness of sin has come before God, He will not be able to find ten righteous to stay His hand of judgment?

REVIVAL

September 23
Conveying Truths

Then opened he their understanding, that they might understand the scriptures,–Luke 24:45,
For the kingdom of God is not in word, but in power.
–1 Corinthians 4:20

There is always the unbroken relationship of the Sovereignty of the Holy Spirit, the sufficiency of the Holy Scriptures, and the necessity for holy supplication. It is a crucial truth for seeing the effectiveness of the gospel to be preached in power. Where man tends to think he needs the word of God alone and preaches with passion and zeal, without the Spirit, the word falls flat on the ground. Just as claiming a Bible verse won't save anyone but rather, being born-again is an experience of the Holy Spirit who regenerates the lost soul into the Kingdom of Light, just as that act the unity of the Spirit who wrote the word and His effectiveness to use it as an aul to penetrate the shell of a hardened man and bring life is irreplaceable. In preaching, the empowered word becomes the word that will not return void. In contrast, the quoted word that may be uttered in the flesh becomes a sequence of alphabets arranged in a particular fashion and is powerless. The word of God "says," but it is the God of the word who "shows" in effectual calling. We need to wait for the Spirit of the word to "show" and not lead someone into a decision because they are intellectually convinced of what the Bible says. Fundamental orthodoxy has made the grave error of equating the assurance of the word, of itself as good enough for the impartation of eternal life, but that will never do for God looks at the witness of the Spirit on the soul of man for the presence of that eternal seed. Anything else will hear the dreaded words "I never knew you: depart from me, ye that work iniquity."

REVIVAL

September 24

Three-fold in Purpose

Faithful is he that calleth you, who also will do it.
–1 Thessalonians 5:24

Meditating on the eternity of God brings us to the edge of our understanding, where we may plunge into the depths of His love toward us and gladly follow His will for our lives. Yet, there are three significant areas of self-examination that one needs to consider. First, Paul's grand declaration of "that I may know Him," second, Christ's heartbeat of "that they might know thee the only true God, and Jesus Christ, whom thou hast sent," and finally, the response of an overwhelmed heart that cries out to a lost and dying world "O taste and see that the Lord is good." To be enabled for treading on such holy ground, one must realize the absolute necessity of being filled with the Spirit of God. God's desire for those disciples at Pentecost to shew forth His glory has not waned in our day and age where He desires to enlarge our weak vessels by breaking them, remolding them, cleansing them, and filling them to fulfill His Sovereign plan in the lives of men and paint the grand panorama of God's intent. The hindrances of our flesh, pride, self, covetousness, and so forth always cause one to stagger at the promises of God. And He has promised to back up His word upheld by His Spirit and is well able to bring it to pass.

REVIVAL

September 25
Self-satisfied Christianity

Because thou sayest, I am rich, and increased with goods, and have need of nothing; and knowest not that thou art wretched, and miserable, and poor, and blind, and naked:–Revelation 3:17

We are in grave danger when we come to a place where we don't expect anything more than what we are used to. Anytime God has worked in the past was when the people of God began to realize that something was amiss. Being self-satisfied in critical areas in the life of a congregation will become the death knell of a Church. Revival? We have a "revival" service once a year that gets forgotten within a week. Regeneration? We have people making decisions to go to Heaven, though they don't show any desire for God or have lasting change. Prayer? We have a Wednesday night prayer service to petition for the needs of the body. Presence of God? We meet in church and worship and go home talking about what's for lunch. With such shallow representations of what it means to meet God, those who suffer are the hungry sheep who desire to be fed from the Father's table but are left starving. Examining ourselves to see if we are experiencing the power of the Spirit as displayed in the Book of Acts and see the greater works that Christ promised should be a good starting point, to be honest with ourselves as we begin to question the "norm" and to desire what God intended for His Bride.

REVIVAL

September 26

The Need for Extreme Caution

But in vain they do worship me, teaching for doctrines the commandments of men. –Matthew 15:9

In alignment with the word of God, one must consider the need for reevaluating what is done as "normal" in Christendom today. While God has blessed "the call" in certain instances and the sincerity, in general, cannot be questioned, the validity of such practices is not found in the word of God. Popularized in the 19th century by Charles Finney as the "new measures," it continues to be the trojan horse of evangelical Christianity. Today's understanding that a physical movement to the altar or praying a "sinners" prayer repeated after someone or in a tract can be equated to the conviction of sin and repentance; and calling the act of intellectual process as being converted and passed from death unto life, given a new heart, in-dwelt by a new Spirit; having such skewed understanding is not only faulty but detrimental to the sincere soul who is made into a proselyte. Such a system needs constant feeding where seeing no change is accepted, and a person who has no interest in the things of God is called a Christian, always pointing to that time when they prayed a prayer. The response to preaching seen in the scriptures was the sinner crying out in realization of their need and not the preacher making an invitation. A person can be raised in external adherence to what one may consider as traits of a good Christian and never be truly born of the Spirit of God.

REVIVAL

September 27

Waiting on God

Wait on the Lord: be of good courage, and he shall strengthen thine heart: wait, I say, on the Lord.—Psalm 27:14

There are times where the natural tendency of man to react when having the ability to solve what he perceives as delay can become hugely detrimental to what God desires to do. In seeking God's direction or answer to something one is waiting for, one can have the idea of waiting until our perceived time runs out and we go-ahead to do as we already intended to do. In truth, waiting is God bringing us to the place where we are ready to receive. A child who is held back from receiving something because of his immaturity until he comes to a certain age is appropriate— and waiting until that time helps him by growing and learning to accept that which was intended for him from the beginning. Thus, waiting on God must rely on the foundation that God as our perfect heavenly Father, desires to give good things to His children, but in waiting, we strive to know of Him, to mature and be able to come to the place where we can receive what God intends for us to have in His time. The time factor involved for Moses, who was unknown in the backside of the desert for forty years, was not a wasted period, for the metal was being forged to withstand the brunt of the Israelites, to become the meekest man on earth from what he was forty years prior.

REVIVAL

September 28
God will Require of Us

But if I tarry long, that thou mayest know how thou oughtest to behave thyself in the house of God, which is the church of the living God, the pillar and ground of the truth. –1 Timothy 3:15

When blessings are showered because of our obedience to the truth in desiring the living God, there is much at stake to prevent deviation from that path. America, in founding its principles from the word of God, has reaped the blessings of God for such desire bountifully. But the same God who gave also requires us to bring forth fruit unto holiness for the light we have been given and the blessings we have enjoyed. When a Nation forgets the God who blessed them, they open themselves for what follows in the lack of God. Every oppression, occult, idol worship, and darkness that has gripped nations, be it in India, North Korea, Africa, or any other culture, has been because of the absence of God, who is all Truth. And where we have rejected God, His truth will be replaced with lies, freedom with bondage, and prosperity with oppression. "For unto whomsoever much is given, of him shall be much required" is something that the church needs to give serious consideration to. For the church of the living God has been called the pillar and ground of the truth, and God will require of our hands at the destruction of the Nation.

REVIVAL

September 29
The World Stage

Woe unto you, scribes and Pharisees, hypocrites! for ye are like unto whited sepulchres, which indeed appear beautiful outward, but are within full of dead men's bones, and of all uncleanness.
–Matthew 23:27

Irrespective of how one may attempt to redefine a nation according to their whim and pleasure with political correctness, diversity, inclusion, gender choices, and so forth, the world will not look kindly upon our way of thinking. Instead, it is harsh in its scrutiny of a nation based on her resilience and strength on the world stage. Regardless of who agrees, God is the one who made America great, and as a consequence of His exclusion, America will fall. Not to the tyranny of a foreign nation but to the moral leprosy within herself. The truth that made America a beacon of freedom came from the Author of liberty, God, and in the demise of true Biblical Christianity that made America great, the tottering stilts of moral pollution, political correctness, convenient but silenced Christianity, calling evil as good, redefining gender and marriage, and such will destroy her from within. Rome was not conquered; it was destroyed from within, and America is ripe to follow Rome's path. Would to God that true Bible-believing churches across our beloved land would call a fast for repentance from our evil ways, to put away sham Christianity, to confess in humility our barrenness, our inability to stem the tide of sin, and seek the Lord for His face to once against shine upon us. In Ezekiel, we read this fearful statement of God who said to His people, "I am against you."

REVIVAL

September 30
Divine Judgement

Righteousness exalteth a nation: but sin is a reproach to any people.—Proverbs 14:34, Behold, the days come, saith the Lord God, that I will send a famine in the land, not a famine of bread, nor a thirst for water, but of hearing the words of the Lord:—Amos 8:11

The picture of God's dealing with men and nations as revealed in the scriptures and history speaks of the conditions that must be met to stay the hand of God before final judgment. The need for a church or calling a Nation to repentance must rest on the fact that those who cry out against sin do so realizing the judgment that is inevitable unless the wicked forsake his way, and the unrighteous man his thoughts. The call to return is a call of mercy, for the prodigal will destroy himself by eating the husks meant for the swine. Where destruction is unavoidable, the voice that cries in the wilderness calls for a turning away from sin and turning to righteousness, in the slim hope that it will be heeded, and God's hand of judgment will be stayed. Repentance brought by the conviction of sin and seeing one's offense before a Holy God and turning from it in thought and action is needed for desiring that healing and restoration that only God can bring. Those convinced of the grave danger that America is in, in following the path that she is headed, will need to awaken to the great need that we have for preachers to call their people to repentance in tears and brokenness, instead of preaching why they are correct, and others are wrong in their theology and practice.

REVIVAL

October

October 1

Who moved the Truth?

His watchmen are blind: they are all ignorant, they are all dumb dogs, they cannot bark; sleeping, lying down, loving to slumber.
–Isaiah 56:10

To see forward, one must have the courage to look back to make sure they are not already on the wrong pathway. What has changed in what we call "Christianity" today? Prayer has been changed from being essential to being just important; Saved from sin to saved for Heaven; Victorious Christian life to sin as something to be expected; Salvation in a Person to salvation in a decision; Repentance from sin and believing to just believe; Born of the Spirit to saved by agreement of facts; Sin as revelation from God to agreement with the text of Scripture; Inner witness of the Spirit to believing the text of the word; Practical everyday Christianity to convenient Christianity; Repentance in daily living to a one-time event; God be merciful to me a sinner to reciting the sinner's prayer; Convicted crying out to God to Altar calls; Soldier of Jesus Christ to personal rights; High view of God to elevated view of self; God of the word as the end to the word of God as the end; Expecting a changed life to teaching a changed "God" and educating in self-reformation; Change from within to change from without; Spontaneous revival affecting a community to scheduling a week of meetings; Being filled with the Spirit and knowing it to just yielding to the Spirit and staying barren; Christianity as a way of life to a title you identify yourself with; War, blood and trials Christianity to sentimental Religion.

REVIVAL

October 2

Americanized Christianity

Blessed is the nation whose God is the Lord; and the people whom he hath chosen for his own inheritance. —Psalm 33:12

With great prosperity comes the temptation of ease and convenience. The things that can only be accomplished by prayer and fasting are being substituted instead to preaching, fellowshipping, youth camps, and activities. We have built an add-on Christianity. There are no Altar calls in the New Testament, sinner's prayer, raise your hand and tell me what you should tell God. We are losing the next generation by the masses from High School to College. It is not because of the strength of secular education; it is because God was not made real when they grew up in fundamental and Bible-believing churches. Instead of having corporate prayer meetings, we were having program planning meetings; instead of desiring the witness of the Spirit, we were giving them some intellectual reasoning to hold on to; instead of expecting the work of the Spirit from conviction to regeneration, we were busy with how we can get them to believe and get baptized; instead of giving the God of the word they were told to "make a decision" on what the word of God declares about Christ; instead of living the gospel in helping those of the street in washing their wounds and receiving them with open arms, whether they smelled bad or were of another culture, we gave a few coins, wished them warmth and sent them away. We, of all men, are guilty before God for our Americanized cookie-cutter Christianity that has no semblance of Biblical Christianity.

REVIVAL

October 3

The Eastern Influence

There shall not be found among you any one that maketh his son or his daughter to pass through the fire, or that useth divination, or an observer of times, or an enchanter, or a witch. Or a charmer, or a consulter with familiar spirits, or a wizard, or a necromancer. For all that do these things are an abomination unto the Lord: and because of these abominations the Lord thy God doth drive them out from before thee.–Deuteronomy 18:10-12

The cultural revolution that we see around us is a testament to the minimal impact the Church has had on the world in this generation. It is not the culture of generalities based on a people group but the influence of practices accepted into the Church. Instead of earnestly contending for the faith, we were humming to the likes of rhumba and mime "gospel" skits. The Church is to be the pillar and ground of the truth and truth which is blended or blurred ceases to be the truth, and for it to be effective, it needs to stand alone. Truth must be in stark contrast to everything around it to provide a beacon of hope to the lost and one who is confused about what truth really is. Whether it is yoga, transcendental meditation, social gospel, doing good for fellowmen at the compromise of unity with religions, etc., all these speak to the desperate need we have to realign our perspective of why Christ came. He was that perfect standard that stood in stark contrast to the world around Him, so much so that they put Him to death. We reach out in love as Christ did, a love that rejoiceth not in iniquity, but rejoiceth in the truth. The truth can set the individual free if they will only repent and believe the gospel.

REVIVAL

October 4
Silencing the Pulpits

What I tell you in darkness, that speak ye in light: and what ye hear in the ear, that preach ye upon the housetops.
–Matthew 10:27

The war of the heavenlies began when Lucifer rebelled against God and started a fight he was destined to lose. That war still rages today in our time, and the fruits of it are seen all around us in generations past and will continue until God puts an end to it. It is not a war of man's perception of good vs. evil; it is a war of Truth who is Jesus Christ against the doctrine of lies in Satan. The manifestation is endless in evolution, transgender ideologies, rebellion, racism, sexual exploitation, social media censorship, politics, counterfeit "Christianity," mother earth, religions, atheism, etc. While the fruits have been manifested in various forms, the responsibility has always been to the true church in every generation to expose sin by calling for repentance and stand even at the cost of their own lives and livelihood. Then why is the church silent today in public? Why are the pews hearing a strange sound that leaves them confused about what truth is? Have we become as the German church, who when the Nazis were taking the Jews by the trainloads to the gas chambers all around them, sang Amazing Grace to drown their pitiful cries in fear of reprisal? Darkness only prevails in the absence of light, and the darkness of America has been allowed to prevail by the sin of the church and her pulpits that have been silenced.

REVIVAL

October 5

Biblical Christianity

And by the hands of the apostles were many signs and wonders wrought among the people; (and they were all with one accord in Solomon's porch. And of the rest durst no man join himself to them: but the people magnified them.—Acts 5:12,13

"The early church was married to poverty, prisons, and persecutions. Today, the church is married to prosperity, personality, and popularity."–Leonard Ravenhill. Biblical Christianity is not how well we follow the Bible or stay close to the Bible; it is the truth of the scriptures that brings about the manifestation of the power of the word by the acts of the Holy Ghost. The other day I was sitting in a large gathering where the one who was to preach was introduced as this famous preacher with so many accolades and so forth. Suddenly I was struck by the Holy Ghost with this verse "That no flesh should glory in his presence."–1 Corinthians 1:29. We can have man's glory or God's presence, but we cannot have both. Christianity is not primarily based on facts but based on truth, and the facts speak for themselves. We can get intellectual fireworks and be impressed with someone's ability to put words together and preach, but it is the Holy Ghost who gives life to the word, and He never comes where men are lifted up.

THE CHURCH

October 6
Same God, different Results?

And Gideon said unto him, Oh my Lord, if the Lord be with us, why then is all this befallen us? and where be all his miracles which our fathers told us of, saying, Did not the Lord bring us up from Egypt? but now the Lord hath forsaken us, and delivered us into the hands of the Midianites.–Judges 6:13

If the backslidden Peter got right with God and preached in the power of the Spirit at Pentecost and saw three thousand get saved in one sermon, how can we have millions of sermons, book resources, blogs, internet, websites, commentaries, podcasts, music, worship teams, the completed canon of scripture and maybe thousands claiming to be filled with the Holy Spirit, how can we not see the same or greater results? The first-century disciples didn't have the New Testament, finances, church buildings, college degrees, political support, or ministerial approval. Yet, they turned the world upside down. Jesus said, "greater works than these shall he do" in John 14:12. In the book of Acts, it was either revival, imprisonment, persecution, or martyrdom. No matter where the Apostle Paul went, either the community got transformed, or they were chased out; there was no middle ground. If we claim to serve the same God, then why do we see different results?

THE CHURCH

October 7
Rebirthing the Natural Man

Even when we were dead in sins, hath quickened us together with Christ, (by grace ye are saved;). For by grace are ye saved through faith; and that not of yourselves: it is the gift of God: Not of works, lest any man should boast.–Ephesians 2:5,8,9

The need for those dead in trespasses and sins is more than getting a new perspective on the truth of who Jesus is and why He came. Instruction of knowledge and application of it can by no means produce that good fruit of salvation. Mental assent to what one may agree to, physical response to come forward and such does not prove that such response is the reason of the Spirit's working in their heart. Eloquence and the ability for one man to convince another can invoke a physical response, such as those who follow a leader into battle at the loss of their own lives. The natural man is dead and is an enemy of God, and the work of regeneration is much more than his understanding and agreement to the gospel. It is the giving of life as in Ezekiel's valley of dry bones; it is the hearing of God's voice as in "Lazarus come forth," it is the blowing of the wind as in being born again of the Spirit of God. The sap of the tree produces the kind of fruit it carries, so is a man who is genuinely converted and ingrafted into Christ will produce the good fruit of prayer, devotion, and love because of the sap inside of him and not for proving that he is a Christian. Having the wrong view of God will cause us to have the wrong view of sin, which will produce the wrong idea of salvation and cause one to get the assurance of his regeneration from means that God has not approved.

THE CHURCH

October 8

The Wrath of Almighty God

And in hell he lift up his eyes, being in torments, and seeth Abraham afar off, and Lazarus in his bosom. And he cried and said, Father Abraham, have mercy on me, and send Lazarus, that he may dip the tip of his finger in water, and cool my tongue; for I am tormented in this flame.–Luke 16:23,24

There is a time we know not when that the cup of God's wrath comes to the utmost when looking upon the sins of men or a nation. "Arise, go to Nineveh, that great city, and cry against it; for their wickedness is come up before me"–Jonah 1:2, "For we will destroy this place [Sodom and Gomorrah] because the cry of them is waxen great before the face of the Lord; and the Lord hath sent us to destroy it."–Genesis 19:13. When God's wrath is poured out, it is a consuming fire where none can stand in its way, for our God is a consuming fire. It would have been foolish to pray for rain when God said through Elijah that there would be no rain for three years; it was a time for repentance. We need to come trembling before a God who is "angry with the wicked every day" and plead for mercy. It is not a time for speaking about the love of God or seeking a God of comfort. Instead, it is a time to call the Church to repentance. God is long-suffering, but we don't know how long He will suffer. If we don't intercede for our nation, confessing our sin and obeying His voice, at an appointed time, God's mercy will end, and judgment will begin. While Nineveh repented, Sodom did not.

THE CHURCH

October 9

Spiritual Experiences

For there shall arise false Christs, and false prophets, and shall shew great signs and wonders; insomuch that, if it were possible, they shall deceive the very elect.–Matthew 24:24

The scriptures are truth, and any spiritual experience contrary to the scriptures is not from God, no matter how convincing they may be. God warns us to try the spirits, whether they be of God. When God deals with the inner man, there may be an outflow of spiritual experience from that work, but it will never be contrary to the word of God. God does not contradict Himself from what He has revealed to us in His word. While experiences are real, they must never be sought as the primary source or substitute for truth. "If an archangel from heaven were to come, and were to start giving me, telling me, teaching me, and giving me instruction, I'd ask him for the text. I'd say, 'Where's it say that in the Bible? I want to know.' And I would insist that it was according to the scriptures because I do not believe in any extra-scriptural teachings, nor any anti-scriptural teachings or any sub-scriptural teachings."–A. W. Tozer. The saneness of the teaching is not in the excitement of the senses or the "peace" that one may suggest that they have. Still, it is in the validity of the soundness of the foundation it finds itself in, on the word of the living God.

THE CHURCH

October 10
Lowering our Expectation

And also all that generation were gathered unto their fathers: and there arose another generation after them, which knew not the Lord, nor yet the works which he had done for Israel.–Judges 2:10

There are four significant areas that the church of Jesus Christ has lowered what's to be held in high view and being accountable before God's people. One is the high view of God; two is the discernible traits of God working in our midst; three the genuine results of conviction of sin and regeneration; and fourth, the reality of the manifest presence of God and what it produces when He comes. Suppose we are content to call our sham Christianity the true book of Acts Christianity. In that case, the next generation will have a lower expectation of what it means to meet God, and we aid in the falling away of our young people who see it as nothing dramatically different in going to church than going to a social club. They walk away for better things that the world has to offer. By lowering our sails, we may sound right and give the people a false sense of comfort that we are healthy, while God sees us as wretched, miserable, poor, blind, and naked. The sooner we acknowledge our need before God and man, the sooner we can expect God to work when we cry out to Him to send repentance in mercy for the glory of His name and the healing of His people. Can we be honest?

THE CHURCH

Watchman of the Soul October 11

So thou, O son of man, I have set thee a watchman unto the house of Israel; therefore thou shalt hear the word at my mouth, and warn them from me. –Ezekiel 33:7

God holds those who preach the gospel accountable for the message, for discerning the truth of its impact and the outcome in the heart of the hearers. If an uncertain sound is uttered and the people follow the wrong path, their blood is required at the hand of the watchman. And watching for the souls of the people, the preacher of the gospel is to be diligent and question when someone professes to know Christ but does not show the fruit thereof. It is better to provoke one another to good works and awaken them to the actual condition of their lost soul than not to question and give them a false assurance of hope and send them to Hell. Though one cannot discern the intents of someone's heart, given that the truth of the gospel and what it produces has been revealed to us in the scriptures, we are held accountable to be faithful to our calling. The fundamental nature of the gospel to deal with the universal problem of mankind, which is sin, should cause one to discern if the gospel elevates God's holiness, His character, and displeasure upon sin; if it brings the hearer to conviction and repentance from sin and after their profession to examine their lives if they bring forth fruit unto holiness.

THE CHURCH

October 12

Church Unity

Behold, how good and how pleasant it is for brethren to dwell together in unity!–Psalm 133:1

The fundamental construct of unity demands the question of the purpose for unity. If the goal is man-centered or earthly, then it becomes the unity of devils that leads to compromise within a short time, though it may have started well or with sincere intentions. Agreement in a church or a movement must always begin as God-centered, for upholding His holiness, His character, having the conviction of the essential foundational elements of Christian doctrines, and for the glory of God alone. Desiring the praise of men, unity for the sake of spreading the gospel while compromising on fundamental doctrines of the faith, trying to get a larger platform for being able to get a larger audience or impact, calling evil as good for the sake of inclusion, etc., are all following the paths of unrighteousness which has the Anathema of God upon it. The purity of Christ, while it drew His disciples and flowed into a deeper walk with Him, nevertheless, drove most of the crowds to reject Him and cry out, "crucify Him, crucify Him." Darkness always rejects light, and narrow is the way that leads to life everlasting. With these in mind, it becomes crucial that unity be found within the walls of truth and not for the acceptance of error or numbers.

THE CHURCH

October 13

The Object of Worship

God is a Spirit: and they that worship him must worship him in spirit and in truth.—John 4:24

In "Let the word of Christ dwell in you richly in all wisdom; teaching and admonishing one another in psalms and hymns and spiritual songs, singing with grace in your hearts to the Lord."–Colossians 3:16, our singing should be prayers or praises directed to God in the form of lyrics. The primary focus of special music (of itself) is not to entertain or edify the people or prepare their hearts for the preaching of the word but rather to focus the hearer's eye of faith to look upon God. The primary goal of worship in a congregation or a special is to focus our attention on the object of our worship, God. When God is desired in such a manner in all aspects of the service, then God purifies the hearts of His people by the Holy Spirit to be able to hear from heaven through the Spirit-filled preaching of His word. Thus, in the finality of this interaction, the focus is on God alone. When this is our motive, the Spirit can have a free course to work in our midst. The result of such worship would be an awareness of the manifest presence of God. The more we are made aware of someone's talent or ability in any aspect of the service, the less we are aware of God.

THE CHURCH

October 14
The Cycle of Corruption

But when he saw many of the Pharisees and Sadducees come to his baptism, he said unto them, O generation of vipers, who hath warned you to flee from the wrath to come?–Matthew 3:7

No truth established with human sources, though it is based on the scriptures and by the conviction of the Spirit, stays pure for more than the generation that brought it to pass. The corruption that came when Constantine made Christianity the religion of the State saw the rise of paganism that was combined with the teachings of Christ to form lifeless orthodoxy and elaborate ceremonial rituals in the place of a personal encounter with Deity. Such is the state where we find ourselves in where fundamental Christianity that was founded upon truth and conviction has given place to intellectual assent, church membership based on another Church's recommendation, and lifeless worship, with dead men bearing the name of Christ. The forsaken truths of repentance and regeneration, which have already been exchanged for mental assent of "believe" on the name of Jesus, are preached while missing out on the Person of Jesus and the Spirit's inner witness. While the outer veneer of what it means to be a fundamental Christian may seem to be appealing, the inner rottenness of dead men's bones symbolizes the predicament of the Pharisees. They were confronted by Christ where they had lost the purpose of the law and followed the letter of the law superficially, denying the personification of the law, Jesus Christ.

THE CHURCH

October 15

A Jealous God

Thou shalt not bow down thyself to them, nor serve them: for I the Lord thy God am a jealous God, visiting the iniquity of the fathers upon the children unto the third and fourth generation of them that hate me;–Exodus 20:5

When Balaam realized that he could not curse the people of God, all he had to do was to cause Israel to sin against Jehovah, and God became their judge and smote twenty-four thousand Israelites (Numbers 25). You can see similar judgments for sin recorded in Jeremiah, Zephaniah, and in other portions of scripture. Scorning God, who is jealous of the purity of His people that are called to be set apart and reflect His nature to the world around them, is a sure way to bring the judgment of God upon us. The problem with America is not politics, democrats, or moral relativism that has invaded her; the problem with America is uncleanness in the Church, forsaken nights of corporate prayer, denominational arrogance, and shallow evangelism. Has God become our enemy? "But they rebelled, and vexed his holy Spirit: therefore he was turned to be their enemy, and he fought against them."–Isaiah 63:10. The jealousy of God cannot be brought under the sinful scrutiny of man; instead, it is the nature of God to desire the purity of His Bride and aggressively undertake the formation of Christ in us, the hope of glory.

THE CHURCH

October 16
The Fear of God

That thou mightest fear the Lord thy God, to keep all his statutes and his commandments, which I command thee, thou, and thy son, and thy son's son, all the days of thy life; and that thy days may be prolonged.–Deuteronomy 6:2

"Fear not" is the general outcome first uttered when a man encounters God or an angel. In the sense of a natural response, fear has the thoughts of intimidation, torment, and self-preservation. But the fear of God has the healthy response of meeting with someone who is infinitely powerful with awe and wonder. Like Mary, it almost has the thought of uneasiness when facing a God who knows all things. It is not just a sense of reverence that signifies deep respect, but also the solemnness of dealing with holy things and sacred things, which has intense consequences. It speaks of God's moral perfection against our imperfections, God's excellent majesty and power, His unapproachableness, His wrath, His infinite attributes of Omniscient, Omnipotence and such, God's role as our Maker, as our Creator, the high view of God and the vilest view of ourselves. First, this creates the response of reverence (proper view of God), secondly a sense of awe, third to be afraid of what it means to face this Holy God (accurate view of self), fourth our inescapable accountability toward Him, fifth in creating a sense of worship, sixth to depart from evil, and seventh our gratitude in salvation and being able to draw near to Him in love through the provision of Jesus Christ. The fear of God is the natural response when confronted with the reality and truth of who God is.

THE CHURCH

October 17

The Judgement Seat of Christ

For we must all appear before the judgment seat of Christ; that every one may receive the things done in his body, according to that he hath done, whether it be good or bad.
–2 Corinthians 5:10

As Christians, when we think of the judgment seat of Christ, we think of rewards. But judgment has an intent of something that we are judged against, our works. It will be a trial by fire in the presence of a Holy God. All of God's gifts are expensive, and those who have plowed through by the Spirit to live the Christ-life will be rewarded with gold, silver, and precious stones; and those who were content to be saved as by fire will receive wood, hay, and stubble. It is not what is seen or how well-known someone was or how much was displayed that God rewards, but the unseen stream of what one's life was in the secret place which will be treasured before a God who probes the intents of men in the deep recesses of their hearts. It will be a terrible day to face God with men and women like Paul, Samuel Chadwick, Wesley, C. T. Studd, and Perpetua, who will give an account of their lives before God. I will be called upon in that same arena to provide an account of my deeds done in my body that falls way short of the Spirit-filled giants that God has used in the past. Nothing can be hidden before the penetrating eyes of a Holy God.

THE CHURCH

October 18

Compromise

And what agreement hath the temple of God with idols? for ye are the temple of the living God; as God hath said, I will dwell in them, and walk in them; and I will be their God, and they shall be my people. Wherefore come out from among them, and be ye separate, saith the Lord, and touch not the unclean thing; and I will receive you.—2 Corinthians 6:16,17

Hating truth has far-reaching and eternal consequences, for it brings with it certain death. But in the interest of the gospel, one is confronted with the reality of preserving its purity, not only for the next generation that will be tempted to dilute it further but also for the present generation that must embrace it in its fullness. The tremendous and historic doctrines of conviction, repentance, regeneration, propitiation, and so forth must constantly be protected and purified, as in Apollos, to a more perfect way. The world hates truth and will not have any part of it. In an attempt to win the world's ear, one who takes the truth and hands it over to the world to analyze and modify it will find that the world will rape the truth to fit it to its own lusts. Truth ceases to be true when mixed with error, even in the sincerest of intentions that one may have to reach the lost. The truth, from God, remains, and the effectiveness of truth is not in its content but in the Author of it, God. It is not word alone but in Spirit and in power. Anything less than that forces one to reevaluate what they preach and adjust the message to placate the lost, not to expose sin but to make them agree by intellectual assent to doctrines that can only be understood by the illumination of the Holy Spirit.

THE CHURCH

October 19

The Purity of the Bride

And I John saw the holy city, new Jerusalem, coming down from God out of heaven, prepared as a bride adorned for her husband.
–Revelation 21:2

Jesus is not coming back for a harlot; He is coming for a pure Bride. We wear white at weddings to symbolize the beauty and purity of the bride, and God has given us such imagery as a picture of what He intends for us to be as a church when we see Him. The bride's beauty is not in her ornaments, apparel, talents, or ability; instead, the bride's beauty is in her character, in keeping herself pure for the bridegroom, of holiness unto the Lord, set apart unto her God. In a fallen world, we expect a woman getting married to be faithful and pure, given solely to her husband; how much more does God require of that from us and for us to be a holy people, for He is Holy. God has made provision for us through the blood of the Lamb to be pure before our God by the renewing of the Holy Ghost for being unspotted from the world. By calling sin "normal" in the life of a Christian, we are defiling the bride. Leonard Ravenhill states, "To be part of the bride, you have to be divorced from everything in the world."

THE CHURCH

October 20
Authority vs Authoritarian

And the servant of the Lord must not strive; but be gentle unto all men, apt to teach, patient, In meekness instructing those that oppose themselves; if God peradventure will give them repentance to the acknowledging of the truth;—2 Timothy 2:24,25

There is a vast difference between imparted authority that comes from the Spirit and authoritarian leadership. When Jesus spoke, it was an authority that astonished the people, and contrarily the Pharisees were authoritarian who demanded strict obedience to their self-imposed teachings, or one would be kicked out of the synagogue. With Christ, there was the unmistakable touch of God that caused the people to take notice, pay attention and obey or disobey to their peril. The authority that Jesus showed caused His followers to have the proper fear of God and willing obedience grounded in love. This authority penetrates the conscience and brings life. The authoritarian, on the other hand, irrespective of where you see it, causes you to rebel or act in fear which can lead to following a man in unquestioned loyalty at the expense of one's convictions. True authority comes from God and not from one's intellectual prowess or the academic qualifications that one has attained.

THE CHURCH

October 21

Goal of Missions

And without controversy great is the mystery of godliness: God was manifest in the flesh, justified in the Spirit, seen of angels, preached unto the Gentiles, believed on in the world, received up into glory.–1 Timothy 3:16

The great commission of God given to His disciples and us is to go into all the world and preach the gospel and make disciples; in light of that command that we are to obey, we must realize the motive of our obedience to go. If we only desired the comfort of man, such as the needs of the body, social betterment, and avoiding the pains of Hell, then we have done a disservice to our fellowmen and God Almighty. Our motive should be upward before it can be outward. Paul's drive of the love of Christ which constrained him, Christ's desire of the Father "that they might know thee the only true God, and Jesus Christ," should be addressed before we look at the hands of men. While compassion for the lost can flow in helping physically while ministering spiritually, the order must be carefully maintained to let our love for God be the foundation before love for people. The Moravians from that outburst of the outpouring of the Spirit in 1727 went into all the world and, as someone commented, did more for spreading the gospel in twenty years than all the evangelical church had done in two hundred years. The two young Moravians who had sold themselves into slavery for the gospel who uttered, "May the Lamb that was slain receive the reward of His suffering!" calls us to consider Him above all else.

THE CHURCH

October 22

That which is Unseen

And Elisha prayed, and said, Lord, I pray thee, open his eyes, that he may see. And the Lord opened the eyes of the young man; and he saw: and, behold, the mountain was full of horses and chariots of fire round about Elisha.–2 Kings 6:17

The natural man is completely unaware of the spiritual forces that are operating around him. God is always at work in intersecting the natural (flesh and blood) and the supernatural. This is evident at the point of regeneration when the heart of stone is taken and replaced with a heart of flesh, one that is sensitive and now has the ability to hear the voice of its Maker. Thus, the act of salvation is not about flesh and blood in intellectual assent to historical truths or facts. Instead, the intersection of God with a man in the blending of forces in moving man to see his Creator and the chasm of his fall, to cry out for mercy in seeing the way of escape through the Lord Jesus Christ. A historical gospel will stay such and have no impact on the listener on how it applies to him. The gospel needs to not come in word only, but also in power, and the Holy Ghost, and in much assurance. Such a gospel cannot stay alone but will penetrate the soul of man and bring him under conviction. In its finality, the blending of the natural and the supernatural worlds allows mankind to realize that life is more significant than what he sees around him and the one race that God created as His treasured jewel, where we cry by paternal bond, Abba, Father.

THE CHURCH

October 23

Taking Responsibility

For what the law could not do, in that it was weak through the flesh, God sending his own Son in the likeness of sinful flesh, and for sin, condemned sin in the flesh:–Romans 8:3

The curse of having a low view of God manifests itself in a myriad of ways in the life of a church and the individual. And as goes the church, so goes the nation. One of the areas of how it affects society as a whole is in the way credence is given to individuals who don't want to take responsibility for their actions but try to divert it as a cause and effect of something that "happened in their past" to move them to commit acts of violence. The temptation of Adam, who shifted the blame to Eve and ultimately to the serpent in the garden when God confronted them, is the same tactic that is repeated today. Christ came to set humanity free from the onslaught of sin, not only by defeating it at the Cross but by offering a way of escape from the infinite cycle of cause and effect. Thus, the regenerated man rises above the blame game, realizes his position in Christ, and takes responsibility for his actions, whether in restitution or in accepting fault. When society tells God to stay out of their business, blaming God for the evil of our day is ludicrous and the height of foolishness. In God is our protection, and when that protection is taken away, anything goes, from mass shootings to the abounding of wickedness in society.

THE CHURCH

October 24
External vs Internal

But they that wait upon the Lord shall renew their strength; they shall mount up with wings as eagles; they shall run, and not be weary; and they shall walk, and not faint.–Isaiah 40:31

In our desire to see God work, one can be tempted to ask for seeing great manifestations of external displays and miss out on the deeper things of God and His moving's. While man desires external displays such as a crowd at the Altar or some extraordinary impression of a message, God desires the inner depth of creating a hunger for God Himself; while man desires the fullness of the Spirit for power, God desires fruit unto holiness; while man wants to reach far and wide with some representation of the gospel however shallow it may be, God desires him to see the ways of the nearness of Christ and plunge deep to drink of the water of life; while man desires Heaven and captivating people with the reward of eternal life, God desires a broken spirit and a contrite heart that is repentant; while man desires to know and display his knowledge of the scriptures, God desires man to know the God of the word and do exploits; while man desires acts and feats done for God because of his denomination, God desires those who long after the high view of God and zealous for the glory of God alone. God's call remains the same. While there may be outbursts of what man desires in the externals, God's starting point is always internal, in exploring the deep chasm of knowing God and having the tranquility of still waters that run deep.

THE CHURCH

October 25

The Reckoning of Eternity

But when the Comforter is come, whom I will send unto you from the Father, even the Spirit of truth, which proceedeth from the Father, he shall testify of me:–John 15:26

Truth is self-evident and always remains. It is our acceptance of the truth that reflects on the need for man to agree and embrace it, leaving all else behind. The scriptures, the existence of God, the uniqueness of man, the reality of death and life after death, the deity and purpose of Christ, the bodily resurrection of Christ from the grave, Creation, the infinite sources of evidence that point to the truth, are all present and self-evident. There is no necessity to prove that truth is truth, for nothing can be added to the truth to make it more acceptable or plausible. The response of man requires humility which is the antithesis to the nature of man. For the light of truth to shine into darkened hearts, there must be an infusion of input from outside to awaken the deadness of man and bring life to it so that he can hear the voice of God and come under conviction of truth. The work of the Holy Spirit is paramount in this crucial step, for without Him, the scriptures become just another book, and the self-evident truths become just the ploy of man to those rejecting it. The finality of man when he faces his Creator after death will settle this matter of truth no matter where they stood in this life, for eternity brings the reckoning of truth with its full weight and is a great revealer of the reality of it.

THE CHURCH

October 26

Satan's End Goal

The thief cometh not, but for to steal, and to kill, and to destroy:
–John 10:10a

When surveying the events of our day and age, one can be overwhelmed with the variety of challenges that humanity faces. From wars, social chaos, perversion of truth, enslaving and exploiting the vulnerable, addictions, suicides, philosophical destruction of the minds to the killing fields of the body, death is the finality of sin, and Satan desires to bring it about with great haste. But underlying in all this is the silent war by the enemy of the man's soul who comes to steal, kill, and destroy that good and perfect will of God. The fruits of the mayhem we see in the world are only the product of his myriad ways to bring destruction, feeding upon man's response to commit sin. Those who follow the cancel culture have themselves been canceled, fulfilling God's truth that those who live by the sword will die by it. When evil prevails, there is no discrimination for the method of destruction, only that destruction happens. Such is the tactic of the enemy to use the world, flesh, and himself to send men to their eternal destruction and face the wrath of Almighty God. But God is faithful who is willing and fully able to save the penitent sinner to the uttermost; for whosoever will, let him take the water of life freely.

THE CHURCH

October 27

Thick Skin, Tender Heart

And the serpent said unto the woman, Ye shall not surely die:
– Genesis 3:4

In dealing with truth and the chief end of man, the consequences of error are incalculable and eternal. A variation in the fundamental nature of man, forces of the unseen, and their impact on the soul of man is of tremendous proportions. The three areas that are seen are first, the attack of Satan on the foundation of the truth of the word of God by deception, false science, relativism, and such; second, his attack on the deity of Jesus Christ in skewing our view of God and who He is by false religions, compromise, boisterous voices of error and such; finally, the blending of the lines of the truth of the nature of the man who is created in the image of God by lies of gender fluidity, evolution, expressions of "self," media, philosophies and such. The Christian desires to look beyond these to have, as it were, an outer layer that is unmoved by falsehood and human response of anger or frustration but has the inner man who is in tune with God with the spirit of humility, compassion, and love while reflecting on the holiness of God. Such a response needs to have a threefold counter-response to Satan's attack. First, to be settled on the truth of the word of God; second, to rest upon Christ who is our foundation by the Spirit; finally, in desiring to reach the person in selfless love, for their deliverance who stands behind the facade.

THE CHUCH

October 28

ICHABOD

And he wist not that the Lord was departed from him.
–Judges 16:20b

It is a state where there can be much activity but no progress, much preaching but no praying, much exhorting but no weeping and pleading, much talk about the reality of Christ but no moving of the Person of Christ, many avenues of outreach but prevalent barrenness. In all this, a core element is missing, the power of the Holy Ghost. The glory has departed from the Church when the world can sneer at the powerlessness of the Church and get away with it; can compare Christianity to any other religion and not be able to tell the difference; can excel in the superficial but lack in the supernatural; can have numbers but have no reflection of the holiness of God in its people; can be rich in goods but just exists as another religion; can blend well with the world where it can coexist with no friction; is looking to politics for regaining its voice; can function without nights of prayer, fasting and tears; is only a news item for the exposing of sin in its ranks; is unable to discern her plight. Ichabod means death, and with all the advancements of the gospel witness that we have tried, do we see any lasting impact on the Nation to move her to God, or has our message been compromised where the precious Spirit has taken His flight from us, and our words are falling on deaf ears?

THE CHURCH

October 29

Smearing Christ's Name

But the fearful, and unbelieving, and the abominable, and murderers, and whoremongers, and sorcerers, and idolaters, and all liars, shall have their part in the lake which burneth with fire and brimstone: which is the second death. –Revelation 21:8

In a day where naming the name of Christ is as easy as having a penny, one needs to realize that Christ's name signifies the magnitude of being a Christ image-bearer; to be conforming to His image in holiness, in the purity of character, in the piety of Christian living, in being harmless and blameless, in bearing His reproach, and so forth. Such magnitude demands that we take seriously who we call a Christian. The time is now for the church to stop calling everyone "Christians" because they say some mental assent or show a shadow of believing while their lives have not changed but are as worldly as anyone else. It could be a sports player, movie actor, businessman, and others who claim it but don't show it in the least bit. The high cost of giving credibility to that holy name by association needs to be considered soberly lest they bring shame to that name that is above every name. If one claims it, then let them show it. The response does not change whether they are a Pastor who falls into gross sin, or a layman who lives like the devil, or someone baptized who continues to enjoy their depraved lifestyle; it should always be of the utmost importance to stop labeling someone with the name of Christ when they are comfortable to partake of the filth of this world. Let the world see our Christlikeness and label us rather than we label ourselves.

THE CHURCH

October 30
Our Plague of Shallowness

But watch thou in all things, endure afflictions, do the work of an evangelist, make full proof of thy ministry. – 2 Timothy 4:5

In an age where the church of Jesus Christ has been afforded with unlimited access to resources of sermons, books, blogs, commentaries, and sorts of every stripe and kind, one thing seems to stand glaring in nearly every sermon, special effort, or program; the presence of shallow truths presented on a platter of convenience. A topic such as God, who is vast, immeasurable at an unfathomable depth, deserves His children to plunge into the ocean of His ways that are past finding out and bring forth treasures of purest gold for the ears of the hearers. Instead, all we are given are good-natured truths, humor, and surface-level gospel presentations with no power or ability to bring the listener to lift up their eyes and behold God as this Being who is high and lifted up. "God is just a friend" is the cry of a generation that has been content to build their lives around the trivial things of this world and keep God as optional, and American Christianity is, as someone said, "five miles wide and one inch deep."

THE CHURCH

October 31

Moratorium on the Gospel

And when the day of Pentecost was fully come, they were all with one accord in one place. –Acts 2:1

The question comes in evangelical circles on the plight of the Nation, the ideologies being pushed by the progressives, and so forth, and the need for Christians to stand up. But have we considered why we are in this state? Is it not because of the bankruptcy of the church and our shallow gospel presentation, which is nothing more than a pretense of the truth? We have such a low view of God that we don't preach the holiness of God, repentance from sin, accountability of those professing to know Christ to prove it by their works before we accept their profession. We preach escape from the penalty of sin while the sinner is not concerned about the person of sin that needs to be repented of. We call an intellectual assent as a Christian and do not expect a supernatural rebirth experience. And every time we accept such sham converts, we dull the light and allow evil to prevail. It would be better off if we stopped preaching this tainted gospel for a period of time and fall on our faces before God in repentance and seek for restoration of the worthy view of God before we look around at the state of our land. It would be better to stop our "revival" meetings, programs, and special efforts that get forgotten within a week and seek God for the true moving of God that changes the moral climate of the community.

THE CHURCH

November

November 1

True Love is Action

For as the body without the spirit is dead, so faith without works is dead also.—James 2:26

There are certain mysteries in life that cannot be explained, but the outcome can be seen. Such is the nature of love, where it demands action for it to be evident, an act that could be known by the person giving it or experienced by the person receiving it. But we are confronted with the need for a foundation and an absolute standard that love needs to be defined by, lest it is corrupted and be given to or associated with corrupt behaviors. One could be in love with money where it affects them to acquire it at all costs; one could be in love with their appearance that brings them to the place of vanity and pride; one could be in love with inordinate affections that bring about lust exposing the depravity of man; one could be in love with self where it brings them to the place of pleasing themselves at all costs even to the point of gender transitions. But true love must reflect the giver of it, God, and He has defined true love as the love that rejoiceth not in iniquity but rejoices in the truth, and that love is the fulfilling of the law. Our benevolent God has given us His word for us to have that proper view and response of love. And God had shown us that selfless, humble, fulfilling love when Christ came and lived among us and gave His life a ransom for many.

THE CHURCH

November 2
The Normal Christian Life

Nay, in all these things we are more than conquerors through him that loved us. –Romans 8:37

Consistent from the early church to today, God commands that we present our bodies as a living sacrifice, one who has counted the cost, obeyed His voice and submitted to Christ in absolute surrender. It is not our ability to be a witness for Christ but God's ability to fill us and use us. We are to be empty vessels. Boldness, a burden for the lost, seeing as God sees, feeling as God feels, are all traits that are unnatural to the flesh of the regenerated man. God's call to those people at the upper room of disciples, women, laymen, others, was not for them to work themselves up but to be filled with the Spirit for service, which we call as the work of grace apart from His work in salvation, also called as the anointing of God or the baptism of the Holy Ghost and fire. And we see multiple fillings that were just as sudden in the lives of that early church. Thus, the normal Christian life is a constant inflow of the Spirit for the consistent outflow of the Christ-life through us, with prayer and obedience. This is the repetition of the exploits of those early Christians in the book of Acts by the power of the Spirit in exponential power that was not of themselves.

THE CHURCH

November 3

Worship

Let all the earth fear the Lord: let all the inhabitants of the world stand in awe of him. –Psalm 33:8

"Worship must be by the Holy Spirit and truth. We cannot worship in the spirit alone, for the spirit without truth is helpless. We cannot worship in truth alone, for that would be theology without fire. Worship must be in spirit and in truth!"–A. W. Tozer. Worship is not just an event that happens when we attend Church; it is a way of life. The woman in Luke 7 did not care about the audience, her presence among men, the stigma of her act. Her only focus was on the Lord Jesus Christ. It was an offering of worship that moved her to perform the action of silent adoration while anointing the Lord. Her audience was Christ, and no one else mattered. In its finality, worship is speechless adoration. It could be experienced as an individual or in a solemn assembly, but it is the spontaneous response when the Spirit of God leads the humble disciple to behold their God.

THE CHURCH

November 4

Children's Ministry

But when Jesus saw it, he was much displeased, and said unto them, Suffer the little children to come unto me, and forbid them not: for of such is the kingdom of God. –Mark 10:14

The desire to bring the truths of Christ and the gospel to little hearts and minds can be seen as an opportunity to reduce some of the critical nature of the gospel to manageable terms. In narrating the act of redemption to children, we see the absence of the sense of the majesty of God or the seriousness of sin, or the depth of God's love to bring us unto Himself. On the contrary, the trust of a little child where impressions can be made is such that the truth of the greatness of God, when adequately emphasized, can be something that can last with them for a lifetime. Their early years to mold their impressions of Christ and His love and work should be made such that we desire the Spirit to impart the magnitude of the majesty of God and for His teachings to be remembered. Similar impressions were made in varying degrees of those in the past who spoke of their parents instilling in them habits such as memorization of scriptures, explaining in depth the beauty and glory of Christ, learning of hymns, etc. which bore fruit much later in their lives when they were headed to destruction in their path of sin. When deviating from Biblical methods, our desire to give the gospel ought to be scrutinized in greater detail so we can ensure that the high view of God is not diminished when looked through the eyes of a child.

THE CHURCH

November 5

Preaching

Then Jesus answering said unto them, Go your way, and tell John what things ye have seen and heard; how that the blind see, the lame walk, the lepers are cleansed, the deaf hear, the dead are raised, to the poor the gospel is preached. –Luke 7:22

With the advent of this century, the emphasis on instruction and the desire for keeping the audience occupied with homiletics, stories, and such, can leave the audience, in its finality, unmoved and minding earthly things. Genuine preaching has the ability to move, to perform as it were an operation of the heart to bring the hearer to God and leave them with a sense of eternity in meeting the eternal God. The awe that a sermon should impart must accompany the audience when they leave, those who have been captivated with the glory of God. This encounter with the living God with whom they have just met is crucial in preaching the truths of Christ and the gospel. Such transactions require four things: the impotence of man; two, the omnipotence of God by His Spirit; third, the means of grace given of holy supplication and the Holy Scriptures; finally, the glory of God alone. Such flow of the Spirit comes from knowing God and carrying His fire in one's belly, dying to self, and preaching unto Christ. In all this, there is a time factor in bringing oneself to be taught by the burning bush where they meet God and have sacrificed who they are and have exchanged it with what God has wrought in their hearts and lives.

THE CHURCH

November 6
The Great White Throne Judgement

Knowing therefore the terror of the Lord, we persuade men; but we are made manifest unto God; and I trust also are made manifest in your consciences. – 2 Corinthians 5:11

There are fewer topics that make one tremble than to see the lost standing before a thrice Holy God and face the full wrath of Almighty God in the nakedness of their sin. With no covering to hide their wretchedness, they present the veneer of good works or morality or ignorance to a God who sees the hearts of men and finds none righteous, no not one. One of the most fearful words uttered in scriptures is, "I never knew you: depart from me, ye that work iniquity." This is unbearable to hear when one realizes what that means of one who is without hope to be cast into the lake of fire that burns forever time without end. While it is a fearful thing to fall into the hands of the living God, it is an even more fearful terror to fall into the hands of an angry God. Especially when one has spurned the grace of God and trampled over the blood of His Son to face the One whose wrath will be poured out in full and without restraint, and there will be no appeal or false verdicts for the judge of all the earth will do right. It is not just those who have spurned the grace of God who will be there, but also those who may have been religious or made a profession of faith but were never regenerated by the Spirit of God.

THE CHURCH

November 7

The Persecution of the Church

And others had trial of cruel mockings and scourgings, yea, moreover of bonds and imprisonment: They were stoned, they were sawn asunder, were tempted, were slain with the sword: they wandered about in sheepskins and goatskins; being destitute, afflicted, tormented; (Of whom the world was not worthy:) they wandered in deserts, and in mountains, and in dens and caves of the earth.–Hebrews 11:36-38

Christian history is a history of persecution. Someone once said that the blood of the martyrs is the seed of the Church. Even today, Christians in India, China, N. Korea, Middle East, Africa, and other countries go through dismemberment, death, torture, or lose everything they have for Jesus' sake. Maturity in Christ doesn't come on flowery beds of ease but in the intense crucible of God's cleansing. While we utter "come blessed Lord, we are ready for the rapture," a man in Sudan who lost all he had said, "I am most aware of God's presence when I am suffering," while we groan, "we cannot go to church because of Super Bowl," persecuted Christians in Vietnam said, "they would rather have open heavens than open borders." While we thank God for the freedoms that we have for the time being in America, let us not for one moment think that persecution is abnormal. It is the hill of difficulty that strengthens the muscle and builds endurance for the race that is set before us, and the strongest metals are forged in the hottest furnace. If we are to hear anything close to "Well done, thou good and faithful servant," our shallow up and down living of the Christ-life is not going to cut it.

THE CHURCH

November 8
The Counsel of Balaam

For the vineyard of the Lord of hosts is the house of Israel, and the men of Judah his pleasant plant: and he looked for judgment, but behold oppression; for righteousness, but behold a cry.–Isaiah 5:7

From the underlying cause for the destruction of perfection in the garden of Eden to the compounding of sin unto homosexuality that bought judgment of God upon Sodom, there is a silent river that runs which pollutes everything that it touches. Though it hides in secret regarding its true nature and promises happiness, acceptance, and worship of the self-image, this river of death, which is Satan himself, gave counsel to Balaam in allowing sin in the camp at Peor, bringing the judgment of God upon Israel. Thus, we sin because we love our sin and are born into it. The sinner, though he does not realize his worth of being born in the image of God and desired by God to repent, if he continues in his sin will bring the judgment of God upon himself in the eternal fires of Hell for his rebellion against the most High. And a nation that forgets that light that she has been given and gives into the widespread talk of inclusion of sin as a norm is edging that threshold of the fullness of sin, which Sodom and Gomorrah crossed. Where are the prophets of our day who cry out in the power of the Spirit, "Woe unto them that call evil good, and good evil; that put darkness for light, and light for darkness; that put bitter for sweet, and sweet for bitter!"?

THE CHURCH

November 9

Separation

But ye are a chosen generation, a royal priesthood, an holy nation, a peculiar people; that ye should shew forth the praises of him who hath called you out of darkness into his marvellous light;–1 Peter 2:9

The words ring clear of what God expects of us as one carrying the mark of Jesus Christ. Statements such as come out, touch not, love not the world, make no provision for the flesh, have no fellowship with the unfruitful works of darkness, be ye holy, and so forth. The message of separation is not based on our preference but built on the One who redeemed us by His blood. The root of separation starts with ownership. Because of salvation, God rightfully owns us, and we are not our own, and God does not own us for our pleasure but for Himself. However, there is great joy in being owned by God. If we realize that we are not our own, but another's, then everything I have, do, or say has the tremendous implication that it needs to represent the One who owns me, for I carry His mark for the world to see. Separation does not affect just our lives but also the lives around us, for if we are to shew forth the glory of Christ to a world in darkness, living the Christ-life will be in stark contrast to the nature of this world. A regenerated life is a changed life, and there are no alternatives. When Satan was my master, it was unto death, with God as my Master it is unto life, and His commandments are not grievous.

THE CHURCH

November 10

The Reproach of Jesus Christ

Let your light so shine before men, that they may see your good works, and glorify your Father which is in heaven.
—Matthew 5:16

The chief tragedy of the Laodicean Church was its unwillingness to bear the reproach of Jesus Christ, and instead, they laid it upon the Son of God. When we desire the trinkets of what the world offers and expect to be spiritual, we are willing to exchange pearls for swine feed. Some time ago, I was standing near Times Square in New York, and I noticed a young lad who had stopped in the sidewalk being enthralled with the glitter of a storefront with an empty outstretched arm that was supposed to have been holding his father's hand. It was a forceful picture that the Holy Ghost painted in my heart of the Church, which has an arm outstretched to the Father, but it is oblivious to the fact that He is not holding it; meanwhile, the Church is very much indulged and fascinated by the glitter of this world. Today the Church is experiencing Ichabod being polluted with worldliness, plucking unripe fruits, having no desire for the purity of the Bride, and the world has grown sarcastic to her claims. And so, the precious Son of God bears the reproach of the world while the Church is neither hot nor cold.

THE CHURCH

November 11

Purpose of Contending

He healeth the broken in heart, and bindeth up their wounds.
–Psalm 147:3

Revelation and restoration are the core objects of contending. Our goal in exposing error must be bathed in love for lifting up those who oppose, for the express desire of the purity of the Bride of Christ. It would not mean new truths but breaking up of wrong ways and weeding out error so that foundational and historical Biblical truths can replace them and take root. The different stages in this process are the same, breaking up, deep plowing, weeding, seeding, watering, and seeing the harvest. There is a time factor involved in all this with the final goal of meeting and knowing God, preserving the truth for the next generation, zeal for the glory of God alone, desiring personal holiness. In being wise as serpents and harmless as doves, we must be swift to hear, slow to speak, slow to wrath, which must be our attitude for contending. It is not about man or man's word agreeing with our beliefs; instead, it is God and God's word, however agreeable or disagreeable it may be to us. Contending is to align us to God and what He has said rather than seeing how God's word can be made to fit us; it is about my need for realignment of how I view God. The foundation of desiring God's best for those we speak against is that they might know the living God and be restored to love and worship their Creator, rather than trying to contend for the purpose of making the other angry because you know better than them.

THE CHURCH

November 12

Obedience to Christ

And Samuel said, Hath the Lord as great delight in burnt offerings and sacrifices, as in obeying the voice of the Lord? Behold, to obey is better than sacrifice, and to hearken than the fat of rams. – 1 Samuel 15:22

Service for Christ is primarily about being obedient to Him before anything else. We are unprofitable servants: we have done that which was our duty to do. It is God's pleasure as to how He chooses to use us. It is not "I just want to be a blessing"; instead, it should be, "I just want to be obedient." Being a blessing is a subjective term of perception. John the Baptist was obedient to stand against Herod in the power of the Spirit and was martyred for it; Jeremiah wept as he pronounced judgment against Judah. Nonetheless, it was about obedience and truth, though it was not necessarily seen as a blessing to the ears of the hearer. Love rejoiceth not in iniquity, but rejoiceth in the truth, and love starts with a love for God, love for truth, and then love for others. In tandem with such obedience to Christ is humility. Humility begins with the proper view of God and the accurate view of self, a flesh that is weak and desperately desiring the daily sustenance of God lest we fall. Obeying the voice of God and proclaiming the truth in love supersedes the desire to be known, accepted, loved, or heard. The spirit of the prophet is bred in the crucible of God's cleansing. And prophets are lonely men who desire to be alone with God than spend their day in the clatter of trivial pursuits.

THE CHURCH

November 13

The Dawn of Creation

And God said—Genesis 1:3a

In the beginning God created, and everything we know and see came from the first five words of the Bible. All the laws of science, life, logic, math, laughter, etc., burst forth when the first dawn of creation made its way into the darkness when time leaped from eternity and beauty sprung forth from the void. An Omnipotent God who is self-contained and self-existent and needed nothing apart from Himself chose of His own will to impart from the goodness of His heart the beauty of creation. Though because of man's sin, death surrounds everything we touch and enjoy in this fleeting moment called time, creation still testifies the beauty of the One who made them when we, with awe-inspired expression, gasp at something that captivates us. Death came by sin, and the fallacies of evolution which declare death as essential to the progress of life forms from one kind to another can never satisfy the beauty and nature of God in its teachings, for it is diametrically opposed to a Creator who in His own power created the world in splendor in six literal days around six thousand years ago by the word of His mouth.

THE CHURCH

November 14
Baptism, Our Position in Christ

Therefore we are buried with him by baptism into death: that like as Christ was raised up from the dead by the glory of the Father, even so we also should walk in newness of life.–Romans 6:4

Someone once said that a picture is worth a thousand words. Baptism by immersion is a picture of our position in Christ. It is not just an acknowledgment of salvation and obedience to Christ's example; it is an active agreement of our standing before God. In immersion, we recognize and embrace that we are dead unto sin because we died with Him; in rising from the waters, we identify our standing with Him in desiring the resurrection life that we may know Him. In showing that picture of grace to the world, we bear witness to what Christ has done in saving us from sin. Baptism is the fruit because of salvation and not for salvation. It is done with all consideration of what one is about to partake of, that in so doing, one identifies with Christ to the world around them, which may be a death sentence in many places. In baptism, we acknowledge that we are called to be dead unto sin that we should no longer serve therein, and we are not our own, for we belong to another.

THE CHURCH

November 15
The Age of Illusion

For we have not followed cunningly devised fables, when we made known unto you the power and coming of our Lord Jesus Christ, but were eyewitnesses of his majesty.—2 Peter 1:16

When reality is made to blend with what is unreal to the point where the illusion becomes more real than the physical world, we see a grave danger that conditions men of this generation to sacrifice faith on the altar of sight and emotions. In the age of humanoids, video games, super-heroes, virtual partners, and Artificial Intelligence, one's perceptions are blurred by what is portrayed as fantasy or popular with people. Truth is fallen on the streets where what feels good is elevated, and the desire for temporal pleasures is encouraged. The reality that man still faces death and the eventuality of meeting his Creator never enters his mind. He hides behind this illusion hoping that the reality of life and death goes away. In this age of technological revolution, preaching Christ by intellectual reasoning and instructions is not enough; the younger generations are the future, and they have the illusion to play with. At the same time, Bible truths are seen as fairy tales. The only way we have to penetrate this impregnable wall is the aul of the Holy Spirit, who brings the reality of God and our accountability to Him for life on earth and awaken us to the world that is to come. Without Him, Christianity becomes part of that illusion that man has created in the blending of the worlds.

THE CHURCH

November 16
Erosion of Truth

Even so then at this present time also there is a remnant according to the election of grace.–Romans 11:5

It is incredible how a small crack in a building's foundation can cause significant damage over time. This is the law of cause and effect, which is so often seen today in Christian denominations. Once began in Spirit and truth, cracks have been allowed and not repaired over time, and now they have become gaping holes in the proclamation of truth and practice. Whether it is regarding the teachings on the Holy Spirit, regeneration, repentance, revival, or any other crucial topic, without exception, there has been an erosion of truth. The evidence of it can be easily seen when comparing the historical teachings of their forefathers to where one is today. Whether it is Methodism, Lutheran, Anabaptists, fundamental Baptists, or others, it becomes a system of beliefs that has dramatically changed, seen by its practice and denominational attachments. What was once based on conviction of truth by the Spirit is now based on an intellectual agreement to historical beliefs. God raises people for His cause in their generation, and the foundation, no matter how well they were established, will erode, for it will be challenged at the altar of convenience and ease when passed from one generation to the next.

THE CHURCH

November 17

Following God

And he said to them all, If any man will come after me, let him deny himself, and take up his cross daily, and follow me.–Luke 9:23

Don't try to validate everybody's ministry by their claims or change your message or convictions based on someone else's claim of truth or how God had worked through their lives. Thank God for what He does in someone's life and leave it at that, but you follow God and go on with Him. There comes a time when following God becomes the greater reason to leave a denomination or a church where you see a watered-down version of the truth that you find yourself in. Still, the preservation of truth in its purity is more critical than the persistence of religious affiliations. You cannot change fundamental flaws by staying in a denomination when they are not willing to evaluate where they are headed. Preservation of truth needs to be done in humility and with discernment, realizing that we let God be true and every man a liar, lest we fall. The goodness of God will preserve the truth for every generation, and He has a remnant whom He calls, and following Christ is never easy or without a cost. The only other option is to quench the Spirit and sear the conscience and continue the decay of truth into the next generation.

THE CHURCH

November 18

Solemn Assembly

And the king commanded all the people, saying, Keep the passover unto the Lord your God, as it is written in the book of this covenant. Surely there was not holden such a passover from the days of the judges that judged Israel, nor in all the days of the kings of Israel, nor of the kings of Judah; But in the eighteenth year of king Josiah, wherein this passover was holden to the Lord in Jerusalem. –2 Kings 23:21-23

Today, there is too much clatter in the name of fellowshipping that the awe of meeting with God has been lost. We bring to the sanctuary the fleshly pleasure of what we have indulged in over the week and entertain ourselves in finding agreement with another of the same mind. This shallow desire of gathering makes the church nothing more than a social club, with just the exception that we turn a switch and expect to jump into being solemn and worship the God of eternity. And after the last amen, we turn the "god-switch" off and continue our sports and conversations from where we left off before the service. There is a lack of understanding of the magnitude of what it means for God to come among us, the God who dwellest between the cherubims. Claiming a verse does not in itself make anything happen. God comes among His people when they desire Him and prepare their hearts to meet Him. This heart preparation is a way of life that one must be willing to live for, for God to come, and when we have these solemn moments of expectation as a Church body, we can have a solemn assembly where God can come. Anything less is a cheap imitation of spirituality.

THE CHURCH

November 19

Changing Times

For when for the time ye ought to be teachers, ye have need that one teach you again which be the first principles of the oracles of God; and are become such as have need of milk, and not of strong meat.–
Hebrews 5:12

In every generation, there is an enormous need for the challenge faced in the declaration of truth to be proportionate to the answers given to meet that need. When we are faced with biblical illiteracy at an alarming rate, our messages that are presented as half-truths add to our nation's deplorable condition. The high view of God, being born of the Spirit, the conviction of sin, repentance, regeneration, the witness of the Spirit, and so on must be preached in its entirety for the very reason that those listening are used to a fast-food Christianity which desires convenience over truth. To someone who has no knowledge of God other than Santa Claus, baby Jesus, benevolent genie, and Easter bunnies, the starting point is not the problem of sin; instead, the starting point is the existence of God as revealed in the scriptures; for sin is a problem only because of the existence of a Holy God. The less we take time to preach the whole counsel of God's word and plow through the hard topics, the more illiterate they become of the deep things of God. One who has no interest in the things of God does not need to be sweet-talked about the eternal security of the believer; instead, they need to be awakened to the false security of their state to examine themselves whether they be in the faith, whether their salvation was of the Spirit of God or a desire of the flesh for going to Heaven. The more we water down the gospel message, assurance, and so on, the less sound the next generation will be when facing the world, the flesh, and the devil.

THE CHURCH

November 20

Statistical Christianity

Sow to yourselves in righteousness, reap in mercy; break up your fallow ground: for it is time to seek the Lord, till he come and rain righteousness upon you. –Hosea 10:12

In a drive towards numbers and show tangible results, one is tempted to ascribe works of the flesh to works of God by looking at surface-level results and claiming as good, even by using the name of Christ and the "grace" of God. The great danger of using religious talk and terms to direct a conversation into some mental assent and call them "Christians" or add numbers to boost one's justification of God working in our midst needs to be seriously scrutinized in light of the Holy Spirit and the word of God. Suppose there is no abiding fruit unto holiness. In that case, no victory over sin, no pulling down of strongholds, no immediate change of passing from death unto life and knowing it by the inward sacred witness of the Spirit, no thirst for righteousness on the part of those professing Christ, then the honest evaluation of what is being done needs to be seriously considered. The great danger of where one is called a Christian without any evidence of it in their lives is detrimental to them and to the cause of Christ, where it brings shame to the name of Christ. Our repentance as a church needs to start with our methods and reevaluating the results based on what God has promised and not what was taught in a seminary. We can get numbers and be smug about it, but it will never stand in the trial by fire before God.

THE CHURCH

November 21

Worshipping an Unknown God

Having a form of godliness, but denying the power thereof: from such turn away. – 2 Timothy 3:5

Though we hear sincere Bible teaching, laboring, special efforts, and so forth, there seems to be a gaping hole that is continuing to be conveniently ignored. For the most part, we don't know what a true revival is, we don't know what the awful presence of God is, we don't know what genuine regeneration by the Spirit and the immediate change He brings is, we don't know what conviction of sin and what it produces is, we don't know what the baptism of the Holy Spirit and its impact on a soul is, we don't know what the book of Acts Christianity is, we don't know what it means to see God come down and to tiptoe into an auditorium for the reason that God is there lest we quench the Spirit by dealing with sacred things using unholy hands, we don't know what prevailing prayer is, we don't know what the inward witness of the Spirit is; with all these unknowns, week after week and year after year we are content to go and do the same thing of what we've always done, and no one seems to care. It looks like we don't want God in our services since He will disrupt us too much, and we are too comfortable where we are to desire anything else, so we end up worshipping an unknown God.

THE CHURCH

November 22

Pride and Prejudice

Judge not according to the appearance, but judge righteous judgment.—John 7:24

Judgment always has to do with one's dealing with sin. Judging righteously has the idea of comparing a practice or deed to what God has said and in humility exposing the unrighteousness in it. Any other judgment is just based on prejudice. If it is not sinful in nature or deed, critiquing a personal preference or another person's disposition or practice would not be the right motive for judging. When we look at a mote in our brother's eye and ignore the beam in our own eyes, it leads to hypocritical judgment that overlooks one's own need and condemns another. To reflect the holiness of God, judgment must begin by examining our own lives before God before we look at others that we are burdened about in the same realm. In its final summary, pride is the exaltation of self, and prejudice is the devaluation of another, and God hates them both.

THE CHURCH

November 23

Preaching without the Spirit

And she named the child Ichabod, saying, The glory is departed from Israel: because the ark of God was taken, and because of her father in law and her husband. – 1 Samuel 4:21

If you preach on Hell without the Spirit, you will frustrate the people and cause them to either get scared or get cold; if you preach Christ without the Spirit, you will only reveal Christ as a historical figure; if you preach salvation without the Spirit, you will be plucking unripe fruits; if you preach repentance without the Spirit, you will only cause someone to desire self-reformation for salvation; if you preach Christian standards and purity without the Spirit, you will only be sowing discord among the brethren; if you preach on sin without the Spirit, you will only cause them to intellectually agree on facts where it may even cause them to come to the altar, but it will never penetrate their hearts; if you preach good works without the Spirit, you will only breed apathy among the believers; if you contend for the faith without the Spirit, all you have done is to try to prove your point of view; if you preach the word of God without the Spirit, all you have done is to convince the listeners that it is a good book; if you give assurance without the Spirit bearing witness in their hearts, all you have done is that you have made them technically converted but spiritually lost.

THE CHURCH

November 24
Preservation of Truth

Ephraim is joined to idols: let him alone. –Hosea 4:17

Is preservation of unity more important than the preservation of truth? Truth is like a dying flame; unless stoked, cleansed, and fed with a pure source of fuel, it will die out in a short time. For truth to be preserved, one must evaluate where they are spiritually against what God has promised. It is not that God has failed but man, for God is always faithful to His servants whose desire is the Lord. To be taught of God is the great need of our day instead of being taught of men. The property of a fire is crucial to understand our role in embracing it. Fire purifies the dross from the gold and reveals that which holds up, attracting one to something genuine. The fire from God cleanses but never destroys, reveals but restores, attracts but never boasts on the pride of man. To hold the fire of God in one's bosom is to burn from within and contrast the corruption that is without. God does not need vessels that are soaked with the teachings of men; He needs dry ones that He can set on fire and shew forth to a lost world that there is still hope for the sinner to turn from their sin to the Savior or burn in the fires of Hell forever.

THE CHURCH

November 25
Blending of the Lines

Behold therefore the goodness and severity of God: on them which fell, severity; but toward thee, goodness, if thou continue in his goodness: otherwise thou also shalt be cut off. –Romans 11:22

In the natural world, we see many examples of absolutes. There is light and darkness, and any other state is either an increase of one or the lack thereof, but foundationally there are only two states. Similarly, when we look at the moral world around us, there are only two absolutes, right and wrong. God always deals with absolutes, whether in the matter of gender with male or female by birth for life, the marriage which is the union of one man and one woman for life, Jesus who is the only way, the only truth, and the only giver of eternal life, and so forth. Any variations to those absolutes have intense consequences, and the more significant the deviation, the more severe the impact will be, which can affect generations to come. Anything that we hear must be put through the filter of God's viewpoint and His word on what He has said lest we fall into the subtle call of this world to put down our guard and give in to relativism. Compromise is the blending of the lines, a semblance of truth mixed with error in small doses, an attractive way to accept the lie in light of an influential culture or a person sharing it. The valley of compromise has no end, for it desires the purity of a virgin to be exchanged for the defilement of a harlot at the altar of convenience.

THE CHURCH

November 26

The God who Gives

Or despisest thou the riches of his goodness and forbearance and longsuffering; not knowing that the goodness of God leadeth thee to repentance?–Romans 2:4

When we think about God on the topic of giving, we are overwhelmed by the goodness of God. He didn't just give one stalk of corn for every seed; he provides a bushel; He didn't just give one grain of rice, but provides bountifully, enough to feed the farmer's family and a multitude of others; He did not just give black and white, but He gave a myriad of colors; He did not just give sunrise and sunset, but He gave the beauty of the various shades of a twilight; He did not just create one animal or one bird, but an infinite variation in beauty and complexity. When worshipping a God who does not give miserly but abundantly should cause us to be overwhelmed at the tenderness and love of God for His creatures, He feeds the righteous and the unrighteous, He loves the lovely and the unlovable, He gave off His bosom His only begotten Son for a world that did not deserve Him, desire Him or delight in Him, but finally crucified Him. Yet God calls us out of the abundance of His grace that was manifested at Calvary, to a world devoid of hope and enduring love, unto the One who is the embodiment of love and peace, and all that humanity is longing for in the realm of sanity. Oh, that men might see the goodness of God and repent.

THE CHURCH

November 27

The Deceit of Riches

No man can serve two masters: for either he will hate the one, and love the other; or else he will hold to the one, and despise the other. Ye cannot serve God and mammon. –Matthew 6:24

There is a constant call of this world that demands that man takes notice of the treasures it offers and gives into its philosophy, which seems to provide popularity, position, and acceptance. The gospel of Jesus Christ is never about any of them, for a man's life consisteth not in the abundance of the things which he possesseth. Its message is that the world is on the path to destruction and has given into the vanity of temporal things and the deceitfulness of riches that has blinded them. Any importance given to this vapor of life in areas such as money, health, creature comforts can soon eclipse the source from whom it came and cause us to take our eyes off Him, the One true God from whom we receive all good things. To compromise is to be concerned with the things that pass away and succumb to whatever it takes to get it and keep it even at the cost of freedom. The man who lives in freedom is the one who can look at riches, earthly possessions, health, trouble, and so forth as secondary and desires God alone as the only goal worth living for. A man who lives in deep poverty but is in step with God can be the freest man than someone who lives with everything this world can offer and allows himself to be pierced with its sorrows, which are many.

THE CHURCH

November 28
Exposing a Lie

For they being ignorant of God's righteousness, and going about to establish their own righteousness, have not submitted themselves unto the righteousness of God. For Christ is the end of the law for righteousness to every one that believeth.—Romans 10:3,4

There is only one truth, but many lies. In the revelation of truth, there is no need to catalog all the errors because errors propagate in abundance and transform with the culture, governments, media, and societies. The scriptures show us what's true in its instruction of absolutes, such as Jesus calling marriage as between one man and one woman for life; in the matter of true love, it is that which rejoiceth not in iniquity, but rejoiceth in the truth; that love is not about a feeling, man's definition or relativism but love is the fulfilling of the law; love in its essence is obeying God's law with a pure heart, one whom the blood of Jesus has redeemed; the law of labor and reward; the traditional home, to teach and raise their children in the nurture and admonition of the Lord; of salvation which is only through Jesus Christ and not of works or religion and so forth. By its revelation of that which is true, it helps contrast the lie irrespective of the changes around it, for the bedrock of truth stands for all generations to expose error and dispel darkness and evil, which tends to prevail in the absence of what God has defined as true and right; For God shall bring every work into judgment, with every secret thing, whether it be good, or whether it be evil.

THE CHURCH

November 29

Indoctrination of Evil

The foolish shall not stand in thy sight: thou hatest all workers of iniquity.—Psalm 5:5

The loudest voice is the most heard, and the squeakiest wheel gets noticed. When told long enough and loud enough, a lie will become "truth" to those hearing it. The church which once was is now a has-been, with teachings that are the ministrations of men, rather than being a beacon of truth and its workings supernatural. The church is good business if you shut up and go with the flow of society, but it will be as a harlot in the eyes of God, the One who sees all things. Where are the churches that preach against the social evils of our day and raise up their voices to warn their people and preach Christ in the power of the Spirit to lift up a standard against it? Where are the churches that preach against evolution and its dogma of man became a god? Where are the churches that call their people to repentance to get on their faces before God in corporate prayer and weep for the sins of their nation? The New Testament church had poverty, persecution, and prisons, but they had the power of God resting upon them and could change the moral climate of nations; the 21st-century church has prosperity, popularity, and pomp but has lost the fire of God and exists as just another institution of education in religion.

THE CHURCH

November 30
The Deafening Silence

Thus saith the Lord, Stand ye in the ways, and see, and ask for the old paths, where is the good way, and walk therein, and ye shall find rest for your souls. But they said, We will not walk therein.
–Jeremiah 6:16

The silence within the Church of not addressing realities is deafening. There is talk of fellowshipping and feasting but no urging to fasting; talk of the cross but no reflection of the crucified life; talk of joy but no exhortation to suffer for the cause of Christ; talk of fruits of the Spirt but no desire for enduring hardness as a good soldier of Jesus Christ; talk of Biblical truths but no call to repent to a lukewarm church that is comfortable in the midst of a nation that is burning itself to death with racism, unrest and gender issues; talk of prayer but not in practice of having a weekly church-wide prayer meeting; talk of going to Heaven but not calling sinners to repent and turn from their wicked ways; talk of wanting "their" man in the White House but no talk of the judgement of God that is already upon us no matter who rules the White House; talk of going into all the world and preaching the gospel but no discernment of the message that we are taking abroad, a message that has produced false converts in our own churches; talk of purity and holiness but no desire to shy away from sports and entertainment, the gods of America. Since we are silent, God has become silent, and in so doing, many perish with no hope because of the sin of the Church.

THE CHURCH

December

December 1

The Mode of Education

And Moses took the tabernacle, and pitched it without the camp, afar off from the camp, and called it the Tabernacle of the congregation. And it came to pass, that every one which sought the Lord went out unto the tabernacle of the congregation, which was without the camp. –Exodus 33:7

The role of a seminary is not to give head knowledge to those enrolled in their university about God and clever tips to get the message across to those they are preaching to. The role of the seminary is to make sure the students have an encounter with God the Holy One. Man shall not live by bread alone; to provide means for a man to do well so he can impress his congregation and apply what he learned in histrionics, homiletics, Greek, and human interpretations is to fall short of the God-called man. One of the primary roles of preaching is to hear the voice of God for the people rather than satisfying the want of a man to help in his social betterment. If they walked into the seminary and had a head knowledge, do they now possess a heart knowledge of God by the Spirit; have they learned to seek after the deep things of the Spirit such as brokenness, tears, anointing, and prevailing in prayer; have they learned to plow through the word to find the God of the word in incandescent beauty; have they come to times where they can discern the voice of heaven and learned the lessons of stillness, patience, and faith lest they touch and disturb the waters. Anything less is just the intellectual ability to get a summa cum laude and walk out with a big head and a shrunken heart.

THE CHURCH

December 2

Deep Ploughing

He that is slow to wrath is of great understanding: but he that is hasty of spirit exalteth folly. –Proverbs 14:29

Today, there is a danger of being content with things that appeal to look upon but have no depth upon a more thorough examination. It is a fast-food mindset with an impatient desire for results, wanting more from less. Anything in the spiritual realm is nothing but hard. Evan Roberts prayer for thirteen years before the fire of the Spirit shook Wales. The old Puritan preachers used to call their sermons "Deep Ploughing" that laid the hard and laborious groundwork for planting on good ground. This shallowness has permeated into many aspects of our lives as Christians, be it in the matter of our prayers, "revival meetings," devotions, worship, or evangelism. And so, we serve a utility God who is subject to our whims, timelines, and wants. The laborer today is busy with his time schedules and things to do that he has no time for delay, but this is the very reason why with all our activities and programs, our churches remain the same. The spiritual condition of our nation in recent decades continues to decline.

EVANGELISM

December 3

Unction / Fullness of the Spirit

And be not drunk with wine, wherein is excess; but be filled with the Spirit;–Ephesians 5:18

We see a pattern in the scriptures on how great exploits were done when people were filled with the Holy Spirit, be it Samson, Elisha, or the disciples in the book of Acts. We see multiple fillings similar to Pentecost (Acts 2:1-4), which was given to the gentiles (Acts 11:15-17), and for service in Luke 1:15,41,67, Acts 4:8,31, 7:55, 13:9, 19:2,6, where it was not a gradual process. The disciples in Acts 1 already had the indwelling Spirit when the risen Christ breathed on them in John 20:22 to "Receive ye the Holy Ghost." John R. Rice, in his book "The Charismatic Movement," explains, "... there is deadness in the Plymouth Brethren position about the Holy Spirit. If you simply tell people, "You already have all there is; if you just obey the Lord, that is all you can do now to be useful," then people do not wait on God nor seek nor pray for the mighty power of God for soul winning. That means there will be no great evangelists among people who hold very clearly to the teachings of Plymouth Brethren on the Holy Spirit." For reaching the heart of fallen man, it takes more than one's ability to reason; it is the truth that must be mixed with fire that breaks through, and the fire of the Holy Ghost cannot be purchased with mammon but must be sought with tears.

EVANGELISM

December 4
Plucking Unripe Fruits

Be patient therefore, brethren, unto the coming of the Lord. Behold, the husbandman waiteth for the precious fruit of the earth, and hath long patience for it, until he receive the early and latter rain.–James 5:7

There is a law in nature that teaches us the reality of the stages from seedtime to harvest. God is never shallow in dealing with the hearts of men. Where man may see someone getting saved as unexpected, like Saul, who became the Apostle Paul, God works all things together for His good in His time. Some sow in tears, some water with prayer and preaching in the Spirit, but it is God who gives the increase. There are no shortcuts to the work of regeneration. There is a danger of having zeal with impatience. In desiring to see people saved, we can convince someone to make an intellectual assent of what they need to believe, have them pray a prayer, and call them converted. Still, the final step of regeneration is an exclusive work of the Holy Spirit and not something that we can produce or rush. Though it may be with sincerity that we try to steady the ark of God, if we rush into forbidden matters, we are plucking unripe fruits. We can make a proselyte out of him, but we will be found guilty of making him twofold more the child of Hell. The underlying stream of salvation always has these five foundational pillars in them. Conviction of sin deals with the nature of sin, which reveals the nature of the transgression; second, Repentance deals with the attitude about sin that brings about your action against sin; third, Faith deals with the revelation and work of the Person of Christ; fourth, Believe deals with the way of escape; fifth, the Lordship of Christ which deals with the identification and obedience to His authority.

EVANGELISM

December 5
Focus of Missions

Whether therefore ye eat, or drink, or whatsoever ye do, do all to the glory of God. – 1 Corinthians 10:31

There are four sorrows that those redeemed by the blood of the Lamb need to weep for on the plight of humankind that is lost and without God. One is that they are running away from God who created them and loves them; two that they are treading on the blood of Jesus and calling it unholy while being devoted to religion, atheism, philosophies, and so forth; three that they serve the god of this world being bound and blinded by sin trying to find fulfillment, hope, and pleasure that satisfies, in the web of deceit; four that they are running blinded to their plight into a devil's Hell to be damned forever. Yet, amid our tears, we realize that these are not the focus of missions though they represent the need for missions. The primary focus of missions should be because we love God and desire to see Him receive the reward of His suffering. From such love that is imparted by the Spirit, in absolute surrender of self on the altar of holiness, we rise up to see a world that desperately needs to hear the voice of the Savior calling out to them. Though desiring to meet the physical needs of those around us is necessary for its proper context, seeing as God sees is paramount for having the right start.

EVANGELISM

December 6
Cheerful Giver

And they spake unto Moses, saying, The people bring much more than enough for the service of the work, which the Lord commanded to make. And Moses gave commandment, and they caused it to be proclaimed throughout the camp, saying, Let neither man nor woman make any more work for the offering of the sanctuary. So the people were restrained from bringing. For the stuff they had was sufficient for all the work to make it, and too much. –Exodus 36:5-7

Giving, whether in finances, talent, or time is not primarily to further the gospel, which is a byproduct of giving; or because it belongs to God, which it already is His; or because God has blessed us, for giving back is part of the response; instead, giving is for recognizing God's Lordship over us, for He owns all things; to acknowledge God's enablement, for everything I have is from God, from my life to my ability; and a form of worship, by giving up that which is tangible to me for He is worthy of it, such as Abraham who was willing to sacrifice Isaac. Regarding what one can give to a benevolent Creator, the question does not come with a fear of a threat that one must give, or God will afflict them. The focus of the giver is, in essence, the overflowing love that they have for the One who has given Himself for them and redeemed them. It is the ability of the Spirit to lift up our eyes and see a world beyond our needs and a God who desires to meet that need above and beyond what we can ask or think when we do it in love. That we might experience in some small way the gift of love that God gave of His only begotten Son to a world that received Him not. Giving cheerfully shares a small reflection to the beauty of what God gave that we might remember His sacrifice and wholeheartedly give of our time, talent, and treasures.

EVANGELISM

December 7
Repentance toward God

When Simon Peter saw it, he fell down at Jesus' knees, saying, Depart from me; for I am a sinful man, O Lord. –Luke 5:8

The crucial element of salvation is the need for a man to come to the place where he realizes that he cannot, but God can. Conviction of sin by the Holy Ghost that prepares the heart crashes the righteousness of man against the woodshed of the law to remove everything that man hopes to give as his defense for eternal life. When a man has thus been stripped of his good works and sees that he is utterly hopeless before God, only then is he ready to see the utter depravity of his sin, which has now become exceedingly sinful. Repentance is always toward God; Judas repented himself and committed suicide; Esau sought repentance with tears but was rejected. The common theme that we see is when sin becomes an element of disgust, it is then that he is willing to repent and turn from his sin. The foundational truth about man's condition is his transgression towards God; only after this comes his offense towards man and never the other way around. When someone shows their need for repentance toward God, we know that he is ready to believe on the Lord Jesus Christ, the only way of escape, and be regenerated by the Holy Ghost. Preaching a gospel that despises the need for repentance is to fall into the snare of the devil by diluting the gospel and not dealing with this indispensable step of salvation.

EVANGELISM

December 8
The Fullness of Sin unto Death

And the Lord said, Because the cry of Sodom and Gomorrah is great, and because their sin is very grievous;–Genesis 18:20

God's Spirit will not always strive with man is the truth that one must tread with fear when dealing with the fullness of sin. Sin progressively hardens the heart, and you can see the many facets of sin and its manifestations as it has been revealed to us in the scriptures. We see a facet of sin where the man who is often reproved but hardeneth his neck, shall suddenly be destroyed, and that without remedy (Proverbs 29:1). In another facet you see the plight of the believer who has repeatedly quenched the Spirit of God, where God gives him over to his sin for the destruction of the flesh, that the soul may be saved so as by fire (1 Corinthians 5:5). Finally, we tremble at the unpardonable sin, where when a lost person blasphemes the Holy Spirit and crosses that unseen line, at which moment God will never shed grace in his life, and he can never be saved but is sure of Hell as if he has already gone there (Matthew 12:31,32). Sin is not something to be trifled with, for it tolls a heavy price that cannot be paid for by mortal men. The central theme of Scripture contends with this antithesis that God is perfectly Holy, and man is exceedingly sinful, and the inevitable consequence that sin must be paid for.

EVANGELISM

December 9

Hell

Therefore hell hath enlarged herself, and opened her mouth without measure: and their glory, and their multitude, and their pomp, and he that rejoiceth, shall descend into it.—Isaiah 5:14

The controversy of Hell is not because it is so little preached in our churches. It is the nature of Hell that should terrify the reader. Every good gift and the essence of life itself is from God and has been given to mankind out of God's abundant mercy and goodness. Hell is the absence of God where the unrestrained wrath of God is poured out in that literal place of an everlasting burning, torment of the mind, soul, and body; it is the place that was prepared for the devil and his angels. The name-calling and making of light of Hell don't change the fact that one day man will stand before the Judge of all the earth and answer for the full weight of his sins that he has committed with no ability to pay for them. If one sin of disobedience caused Adam and Eve to be banished from the garden forever, the collective acts of the sinner in word, thought, and deed demands justice from a Holy God. To pay its penalty in that place called Hell for all of eternity is the just reward for the man who has spurned the grace and love of God bleeding on that cross for the sins of mankind and trampling on the blood of Jesus to write his own condemnation into Hell. The man who has lost the vision of Hell is playing at the threshold of Hell that is one heartbeat away.

EVANGELISM

December 10
Packaging God's Methods

He removed the high places, and brake the images, and cut down the groves, and brake in pieces the brasen serpent that Moses had made: for unto those days the children of Israel did burn incense to it: and he called it Nehushtan. – 2 Kings 18:4

In every move of God, we always see the Sovereign nature of God dealing with the heart of man. And it is the Spirit who holds the absolute authority on how He interacts with an individual to bring him to the point of repentance. Even during historic revivals where God used methods such as the mourner's bench or dealing with someone using the book of Romans, it was evident because the Spirit led in that way. Though that was the case during certain seasons, it does not allow subsequent generations to package that as a winsome method and place it in the scheme of desiring the conversion of lost souls. It would be as the people of Israel who idolized the bronze serpent Moses had raised many generations prior. In repeating these incidental methods God used and packaging it into an altar call, sinner's prayer, taking it by faith, making a decision, or the Romans road, it brings us into the same wreckage that the Israelites fell for. The Holy Spirit is Sovereign in how He deals with the heart of man, and our responsibility is to remove the hindrances to the gospel so men may hear the voice of God and repent and believe the gospel. The general declaration of the gospel is the foundation of what was preached to the Jews and the Greeks in Acts 20:21. Then there is the specific application of the gospel based on the direction of the Holy Spirit's effectual working. You cannot take the specific application and apply it to the general declaration to an audience, for the Spirit is Sovereign in the method that He uses.

EVANGELISM

December 11

Bearing Fruit

Verily, verily, I say unto you, Except a corn of wheat fall into the ground and die, it abideth alone: but if it die, it bringeth forth much fruit.–John 12:24

A child of God is to yearn for two areas of fruit, fruit unto holiness and fruit unto childbearing. One is for life from within to affect the person without, the other is to reproduce and bring to birth someone from death unto life. Yet the impetus for the desire of a newborn is seeded into the heart of the sower by the Spirit, watered by the burden of prayer, manured by the testimony of their life and witness, and God brings the increase. For those desiring to bear fruit in those two areas, one has to be in a place where the goodness of God and the worthy portions that the Lord blesses them with, though they are incredibly thankful for, drives them to realize that, in their barrenness, they have nothing to give in return to their Lord; where the role of the Wife in childbearing drives them to long for that day when she can truly say "for this child I prayed." The process of conception, gestation, and birth can be fulfilled when one comes to the place where they cannot remain barren in birthing a lost into the kingdom of God or unable to stand the reality of the reproach that is on the name of Jesus. They thus seek the enablement of the Holy Spirit in the enduement of power for service, to go and tell and be as vessels through whom flow the testimony of God and sets the listeners free.

EVANGELISM

December 12

Opening Blinded Eyes

He answered and said, Whether he be a sinner or no, I know not: one thing I know, that, whereas I was blind, now I see.—John 9:25

In preaching eternal truths and desiring spiritual fruits, it is imperative that we stand on the right platform. If our foundation of truth is incorrect, the building that is built upon it will remain flawed. And in matters of eternal importance pertaining to salvation, sincerity of belief, purity of motive, or lack of proper instruction, is no excuse for a false outcome. Having the proper view of God and the impossibility of spiritual truth to be able to penetrate the natural man, these must be taken with great significance. The great salvation doctrines and the call to repent and believe begins with the revelation of God in the soul of man and the reality of man standing before a Holy God in the conviction of sin by the Holy Spirit. Without this foundation, those saying a prayer or believing in a scripture verse or being religious will be as tares on the day of judgment. The great responsibility rests upon those conveying these truths to make sure that the revelation of sin by the Spirit has been made to the darkened heart before they are given the hope of the way of escape. To the great question of "who then can be saved?" one needs to seriously consider the response of Christ, "with men this is impossible; but with God all things are possible."

EVANGELISM

December 13
Who Art Thou?

And then will I profess unto them, I never knew you: depart from me, ye that work iniquity.—Matthew 7:23

It will be a day of terror when many who have called Jesus as "Lord, Lord" stand before a God they didn't expect. An atheist or a heathen who worshiped an idol upon crossing the veil of death will be confronted with the One true living God; where he may have expected to have been reincarnated or to be in some state of bliss or maybe meet one of his deities that he worshipped while on earth, instead, he finds himself standing before a God, he doesn't know. The greater tragedy will be for someone who made an intellectual decision for Christ, grew up in a Church, believed, memorized scriptures, and read the Bible through, supported missions, passed out tracts, maybe even went as a missionary or served as a Pastor; when they stand before a God who they don't recognize to ask the question "Who art thou?" One of the most fearful words in the scripture that I see beyond this life is God declaring, "I never knew you: depart from me." Without the experience of regeneration by the Holy Spirit and Him bearing witness in our hearts of our sonship towards Christ, no scripture or human reasoning will hold weight before God who ruleth eternity and whose all-seeing eyes pierce through the veneer of religion.

EVANGELISM

December 14

Regeneration

Jesus answered and said unto him, Verily, verily, I say unto thee, Except a man be born again, he cannot see the kingdom of God. –John 3:3

There is an opposing truth that seems to have been forgotten in our day and age. A veil of darkness rests on every man, which cannot be penetrated by any means that men may use. Flesh and blood are dead in trespasses and sins, and no man can receive the things of God except it be given him from above. Only the Spirit can reveal the things of the Spirit, which are foolishness to them that perish. By desiring to remove the veil, one can be sincere in making scriptural assertions, logical conclusions, historical significance, scientific reasoning, archeological excavations, and so forth. But the final illumination needs to come from the Spirit, or else there is only darkness. The beauty of the gospel is not in its story but in its spirit of what it accomplishes. One who is dead and has no life is given life, one who is an enemy of God is made a friend of God, one who is bound in sin is set free to serve Christ, one who flees to Christ for mercy who has been revealed of their corruption is made pure, one who is eternally damned is declared righteous. Regeneration is an act as big as the conception, gestation, and birth of Jesus. We are birthed into the family of God by the Holy Spirit, where we pass from death unto life.

EVANGELISM

December 15

Authority on Truth

God forbid: yea, let God be true, but every man a liar;
–Romans 3:4a

In one's desire to be accurate with the word, one tends to believe that a particular denomination has exclusivity on truth. Denominational arrogance can blind us to the fact that no one individual or denomination has a corner on truth. Truth reigns as evident from the truth-giver God who is infinite, and for someone to have the notion that they know everything there is to it in its entirety is coming close to claiming themselves as gods. We see towering intellectuals like John Wesley and George Whitefield who had a deep knowledge of the word of God and walked in union with the Spirit of God but had vast theological differences on certain key doctrinal areas regarding the Sovereignty of God and the responsibility of man, with all this they were mightily used of God in spiritual awakening on both sides of the Atlantic during the 1700s. God used them not because they agreed on specific points of doctrine but because He is God despite the fragility of man.

EVANGELISM

Nearer, Still Nearer
C. H. Morris

Nearer, still nearer, close to thy heart,
Draw me, my Savior, so precious thou art.
Fold me, O fold me close to thy breast;
Shelter me safe in that haven of rest,
Shelter me safe in that haven of rest.

Nearer, still nearer, nothing I bring,
Naught as an off'ring to Jesus, my King–
Only my sinful, now contrite heart;
Grant me the cleansing thy blood doth impart,
Grant me the cleansing thy blood doth impart.

Nearer, still nearer, Lord, to be thine,
Sin with its follies I gladly resign,
All of its pleasures, pomp, and its pride;
Give me but Jesus, my Lord crucified,
Give me but Jesus, my Lord crucified.

Nearer, still nearer, while life shall last,
Till safe in glory my anchor is cast;
Through endless ages, ever to be
Nearer, my Savior, still nearer to thee,
Nearer, my Savior, still nearer to thee.

Public Domain

December 16

A Call to Repentance

The night is far spent, the day is at hand: let us therefore cast off the works of darkness, and let us put on the armour of light.– Romans 13:12, Let the priests, the ministers of the Lord, weep between the porch and the altar, and let them say, Spare thy people, O Lord, and give not thine heritage to reproach, that the heathen should rule over them: wherefore should they say among the people, Where is their God?–Joel 2:17

Christ's last call to the church was "repent." In the book of Revelation, we see Jesus knocking outside the church's door to get in. Today in our day and age, I see the church fighting for rights in the government, blaming the "left" for the onslaught of sin, self-righteous in their own eyes with denominational supremacy, boasts of numbers, and grieves over the plight of its closed-door in governmental overreach. God's call to the church is not more rapport with the world; God's call to the church is a call to repentance. We need to take personal responsibility for where America is and plead with God for the sins of her people. If we spent as much time in corporate prayer weeping over our nation's sins, be it abortion, pride, homosexuality, worldliness, apathy, sensuality, and so forth. If we wept over these instead of entertaining ourselves to death, God could do something about it. It is not the White House that is the answer for our generation but God's people who are broken and contrite; such sacrifices are those that God does not despise. It's time to call the church to repentance, lest God spews us out of His mouth and America along with it.

RESTORATION

December 17
Forgiveness and Restoration

For ye have not received the spirit of bondage again to fear; but ye have received the Spirit of adoption, whereby we cry, Abba, Father.—Romans 8:15

In the life of a Christian, there are times when he is confronted with the reality of the flesh taking over in subtle or open ways for the exploitation of inordinate desires that causes one to sin against the goodness of God. At such times the grief that we may experience and the desire for forgiveness and cleansing weighs heavily on the transgressor. Psalm 51 is a perfect example of such a time, and the fruits meet for repentance are directed solely at God and not for personal vindication by blaming Bathsheba. At such times when the Spirit convicts and brings him to the place of repentance, one is confronted with the truth of what they rightly deserve, judgment, but instead with what they have been given, mercy, because of their position of sonship in Christ. This ought to produce a heart of gratitude and love towards the God who is plenteous in mercy. During such times though forgiveness is granted, the outcome of that restoration is up to God. For Abraham, it was the loss of Ishmael; for David, it was the death of his baby and the rebellion of Absalom; for the Corinthian, it was the giving him off over to the devil for the destruction of the flesh. The response of rewards for the life that has been lived on earth when we appear before the judgment seat of Christ ought to motivate us to put our soul, might, and strength in loving God with all our hearts, lest we forfeit our rewards for eternal loss, for much will be required of us.

RESTORATION

December 18
Knowing God

Forasmuch as ye are manifestly declared to be the epistle of Christ ministered by us, written not with ink, but with the Spirit of the living God; not in tables of stone, but in fleshy tables of the heart. –2 Corinthians 3:3

There is a price to pay for knowing God. It is not the God of one's knowledge of the scriptures; instead, it is intimacy with Christ by the fullness of the Spirit where one has plowed through the word to find the God of the word. It is a price that is costly not because God is not willing but because we are naturally engrained into this world that the other world does not seem worth it until God takes our worldly pleasures away from us so we can realize the true meaning of the riches we have in Jesus Christ. The man who thinks he knows God is most probably thinking of his standing in the knowledge of scriptures. The man who truly knows God is too engrossed with God to give heed to the clamor and the vain boastings of man. It is victory over the world, the flesh, and the devil, that brings one to the place where he can ascend into the hill of the Lord with clean hands and a pure heart. The casual man is too occupied with this world and is looking for shortcuts on how he can know God, but that will never do, for the Creator of heaven and earth will not share His glory with another or be the object of divided attention from His subjects.

RESTORATION

December 19
Looking unto Jesus

Looking unto Jesus the author and finisher of our faith; who for the joy that was set before him endured the cross, despising the shame, and is set down at the right hand of the throne of God.
–Hebrews 12:2

A battle rages within the regenerated man, a struggle with the influence of the old nature that is engrained in this body of flesh against the new inner man. The daily awareness of one's dying to self makes no provision for the flesh and keeps it crucified as in subjection, by which the flesh can have no power over the renewed man. We do so as His child because we love Him, hating even the garment spotted by the flesh. Sin lieth at the door, and when one yields to temptation without obeying the leading of the Spirit, one finds out that the wretchedness of sin is always willing to keep one blinded to the calling on their lives as a soldier of Jesus Christ. One could be in presumptuous sin and "serve" God, not knowing they are serving their flesh in its subtlety. Only the God who set us free from sin, the precious Spirit of God, the word of God, and a conscious and constant looking unto Jesus can keep us in close awareness of this Adamic nature that desires to have the preeminence. It is the desire to be a doulos or a slave who beholds the face of his Master and standing in the foundation not of himself but rather upon Jesus Christ. In true preaching, the focus is not on the message bearer but the message, for it comes from God and carries with it the voice of God by the Holy Spirit and affirmed by the Holy Scriptures.

RESTORATION

December 20

Self-examination

But seek ye first the kingdom of God, and his righteousness; and all these things shall be added unto you. –Matthew 6:33

The church is married to the world when the world can instruct the church on how to get a bigger crowd and what the world would like to hear in a sermon, when the people can enjoy entertainment and sports rather than spend a night of prayer weeping before God for the sins of their nation, plan meetings and programs and have a rhetoric of desiring God to work but not putting into action with what God moves one to do, can offer prayers that are sincere and heartfelt but no desire to sustain those prayers with obedience and faithfulness, can follow a political party of the greater good but fail to see the greater danger in not being a watchman in where God has placed them to call evil evil and good good. When a church can exist and not be noticed because the message that it preaches does not cause friction with the world around them, you can be sure that the church has been compromised. The clarion call of God for the church is not to have affiliation with the government, political party, or political sympathy. But its supreme command is to pledge absolute allegiance to Christ over political parties, governments, denominations, family, or friends.

RESTORATION

December 21

Embracing our Cross

Whosoever is born of God doth not commit sin; for his seed remaineth in him: and he cannot sin, because he is born of God. – 1 John 3:9

The cross is a symbol of death, and it is at the cross where the exchange for failure to the experience of victory happens. At the cross was where sin was paid for, and the gates of Heaven were opened wide with access to the holy of holies. The cross for the believer is not a burden to bear but a gift to embrace. Taking up the cross and following Christ is the supreme call of God for the Christian. Being freed from sin is preceded by recognizing our present position of being dead to self by Christ's death; it is at the cross where we see the reality of death and the liberating flow of life from above where we die to who we are and live to who Christ is. We are most vulnerable at the point of death. Being crucified with Christ and abiding in Him allows us to experience that exchanged flow of the Christ-life in us which is the hope of glory. Following the Lord with all our hearts is more than saying a few prayers, reading the Bible, and doing our best in serving Him; it is a daily life of looking unto Jesus, counting the cost and taking His yoke upon us, and following Him in absolute surrender with the purposeful intent of not my will but Christ's be done.

RESTORATION

December 22

Obey God rather than Men

Ye shall walk after the Lord your God, and fear him, and keep his commandments, and obey his voice, and ye shall serve him, and cleave unto him.—Deuteronomy 13:4

When the restraint of evil has been withdrawn, whether, through a compromised church or the false gospel of convenience, the world sees its opportunity and rushes into the dangerous ground of the legalization of sin. There are three principles that a serious follower of Christ needs to pay careful attention to. The foundational principle states that the law of God supersedes the law of man. The situational principle states that our response is based on where the alignment of man's law is to the law of God. The consequential principle states that the law of God permanently binds a Christian before he is bound by the law of man, where humility and the love of truth should precede the rejection of the law of man. When we stand before God, we will not be judged by the law of man but by the law of God. We are saved from sin to the savior, and whether it is the legalization of sins such as homosexuality, abortion, pornography, or marijuana, the law of God still stands, to which we are to obey and reject the law of man that has gone against the law of God. Though God's reward may be deliverance by life or by death, compromising for the here-and-now will be worthless when we enter eternity.

RESTORATION

The Eternal Purposes of God

December 23

John answered and said, A man can receive nothing, except it be given him from heaven. –John 3:27

Whenever we find ourselves in a valley that we did not see coming or in a mountaintop where we wish we could stay longer, we are tempted to look at the here and now and desire an end to our problems or be hesitant to move from our place of ease. We must start with God in either situation before looking into our pocketbooks or human provisions to meet the need. If our foundation is that all things work together for good to them that love God, to them who are the called according to His purpose, if that is our foundation, then we realize that if I am right with God, then nothing has come without the express hand of God to shape me and mold me into the image of Jesus Christ. Though it is hard to comprehend this in a valley that may be looming in front of us, it is not for seeking an immediate solution that one needs to start with; instead, we seek the all-knowing God on how to respond, needing to know what to ask of His loving hand. Absolute trust in God and walking in the Spirit is the key to a fulfilled Christian life.

RESTORATION

December 24
Being Thankful

In every thing give thanks: for this is the will of God in Christ Jesus concerning you. – 1 Thessalonians 5:18

The foundational reason for being thankful is not for the cause of favorable circumstances, provision, health, possessions, or even family; the foundational basis for being thankful is God. Everything else changes with time, social conditions, etc. but to know a God who is beyond time and space, One who never changes, is a truth that gives us great comfort irrespective of everything happening around us. Being thankful does not depend on man's perspective of good that can be used to evaluate his thankfulness and its sum. If all our thankfulness is based on what we deem as good, it would seem proper for someone in prison or a hard-labor camp in North Korea for their faith to be ungrateful. But God's call is in everything give thanks. We must divorce our thankfulness from being about what we possess and marry our thankfulness to God for God Himself, and after that being grateful for everything which has or has not flowed from His loving hand. If God is all we had, would we still be thankful?

RESTORATION

December 25
Steadfastness of Heart

Therefore, my beloved brethren, be ye stedfast, unmoveable, always abounding in the work of the Lord, forasmuch as ye know that your labour is not in vain in the Lord.—1 Corinthians 15:58

A heart grounded upon God in hearing His voice and walking with Him can look at the world's philosophies and excuses and see their fallacy. To have a revelation of God by the Spirit in salvation and to be set free from sin and see what God made you for; to see the whole sphere of life, world, and death align in a perfect synchronized union is a treasure that a steadfast heart cherishes. To have intimacy with Christ in the closeness of hearing His voice, seeing His hand, is more desirable than all the treasures of Egypt where one can say with godly resolve, "the world behind me the cross before me, no turning back." And what is there to turn back to? Pleasure in sin for a season? Way of the transgressor that's hard? An uncertain future? To wholly follow the Lord through mountaintops and valleys yet beholding His face that seems hidden at times is a journey worth living for. Such closeness with God causes one to weep for those who deny God, see the error of their ways, and intercede for them. To know the God who orchestrates the present to bring the future to an expected end that He has ordained can cause us to look toward Him to lead us through paths of righteousness for His name's sake.

RESTORATION

December 26
Counting the Cost

For which of you, intending to build a tower, sitteth not down first, and counteth the cost, whether he have sufficient to finish it?
–Luke 14:28

Being a follower of Jesus Christ has great joys, purpose, and a genuine love relationship with our Creator. But it is also a sobering matter to consider when realizing the seriousness of such a path. One needs to come to the place early on in their Christian journey, recognize that this world is not our home, and be willing to lay down all worldly possessions, wealth, family, and even our comforts in exchange for the cross even unto death. Such was the tenor of the early Christians who stood at the precipice of death as they were ushered into Nero's garden to be put up on crosses, covered with tar, and set on fire. The crossroads of life constantly have their pull to direct us to the vanity fairs of this world, but God desires to bring us through green pastures and still waters that cannot be compared with anything this world has to offer. The ecstasy of following Christ at all costs has of itself the challenges of dry grounds, gushing streams, and the burden of the cross that at times seems too much to bear, but the Master has promised to be with His children until the very end; to those who have counted the cost and left all and followed Him.

RESTORATION

December 27
An Expected End

Either make the tree good, and his fruit good; or else make the tree corrupt, and his fruit corrupt: for the tree is known by his fruit.
—Matthew 12:33

In the realm of God's response to man's need, we see two crucial areas that are displayed in full view. The source of the problem and the result of the outcome. The means to the outcome varies from person to person, be it using drugs, lying, alcohol, pornography, and so on; the source is man's sin, and the outcome is death and judgment in its finality. Though we can misdiagnose the problem, if we stay consistent with the right source and the right outcome, we can come to the proper diagnosis and what needs to change. In salvation or revival, if we commit to seeing the same implication of having the right source, and seeing the right outcome, then the means can belong to the Sovereignty of God on how He chooses to conduct the means. God is always the source of salvation, and a changed life that has been given new desires, hope, and a personal relationship with God is the outcome. The means can vary in each situation. If the outcome is not present where we have desired the correct source, we need to reexamine our means of what we are using in wanting spiritual offspring. The grave danger will be when one does not see the outcome that God has promised in His word but still go our way and ignore the warnings and continue to use the wrong means while being self-satisfied that we are focusing on the correct source.

RESTORATION

December 28

Endureth to the End

Let us draw near with a true heart in full assurance of faith, having our hearts sprinkled from an evil conscience, and our bodies washed with pure water. Let us hold fast the profession of our faith without wavering; (for he is faithful that promised;) And let us consider one another to provoke unto love and to good works:–Hebrews 10:22-24

The analogy that Christ gave concerning the ground and the fruit thereof, shown in the tree that has been allowed to grow into its full strength, is seen all around us in this generation. Judas was among the closest circle of Christ, yet he betrayed Him, showing forth his true seed by the fruit thereof; Demas was dedicated with his travels with the Apostle Paul, and yet he loved this present world and left Paul for following his true nature. In all this, we see that the beginning of a person's so-called conversion or even their "Christian" witness is not to be heralded but instead their fruit that is unto the reflection of their Master, which is holiness, ought to be desired, enduring until the very end as a legacy for the work that God has done. The end matters more than the beginning, where Judas and Demas might have been seen as a good beginning. With the so-called "Christians" who claim the name of Christ but in lifestyles and works, reprobate, should cause a great realignment of our discernment of people, to align them with the nature of God and His word rather than being led by the display of sincerity and emotion. In the end, the wheat will be separated from the chaff, where the wheat will be taken into the Kingdom of God, and the chaff sent for the burning. Jesus said, "Not every one that saith unto me, Lord, Lord, shall enter into the kingdom of heaven."

RESTORATION

December 29

I Change Not

God is not a man, that he should lie; neither the son of man, that he should repent: hath he said, and shall he not do it? or hath he spoken, and shall he not make it good?–Numbers 23:19

To grasp a concept of no change is hard for the human mind to comprehend; we are subject to change and are bound to it as the natural outflow of life and things around us. Yet we come to an area of immense importance when dealing with the God of the Bible. The possibility of isolating ourselves for a moment from this period and traveling back to when Isaiah saw the throne of God and the incredible sight of the heavenlies is something we should desire to dwell in as we meditate on the pages of God's word. In a rapidly spiraling out of control generation, having the proper view of God who declares His immutability is paramount to be aware of the immensity of God and the consequences of earthly philosophies. God Omnipotent, Omniscience, and the only Wise God. No matter how the lines are drawn, the plumbline of God's grace will extend beyond man's definition of "good" in the absolute standard of God Himself, who never changes. To have an honest view of God is crucial in this day and age that we live in, where public opinion determines "truth" and fluctuates with every whim and complaint of man.

RESTORATION

December 30

The Three Pillars

And with great power gave the apostles witness of the resurrection of the Lord Jesus: and great grace was upon them all.—Acts 4:33

"Never man spake like this man" was uttered because of the authority that Christ displayed. This speaks to the benediction of God upon the words that He said where the people could not deny it; they were as it were, confronted by Truth, and they had to obey or disobey it to their detriment, but could not ignore it. The innermost desire of knowing God who comes in the power of a whirlwind but in the gentleness of a soft breeze, to have that intimate supernatural communion with God, a closeness that is sacred and hidden from others all around in ecstatic love, the penetration of the heart of blinded men by words spoken by the vessel that has the spear of the Spirit given to the word with the thrust of effectual force applied to be able to break through to the listener; brings us to the place that all three are lofty goals that one may dream of but never see it become a reality in their lifetime as a Christian. But the faithfulness of Christ to His children to ask for His disciples to tarry in Jerusalem until they were endued, were spoken to those fearful men who already had the Holy Spirit, and further evidenced in the multiple fillings in that early church speaks of the empowering ministry of the Holy Spirit. Not only to do exploits against the enemy to the pulling down of strongholds but to see God move as it were as an unstoppable flood, for the glory of His name.

RESTORATION

Path to Recovery **December 31**

Now unto him that is able to keep you from falling, and to present you faultless before the presence of his glory with exceeding joy, To the only wise God our Saviour, be glory and majesty, dominion and power, both now and ever. Amen.–Jude 1:24,25

One needs to consider two key milestones when dealing with the context of recovery of forgotten truths for our generation and to move from shallow shores to still waters that run deep. First, the motivation to change, and second, the persistence of putting into action with an end goal in mind, where they are sought after daily. This motivation hinges upon God's truth that has been shed abroad by the Spirit to illuminate us to the prize of the high calling of God in Christ Jesus. Persistence to study, pray and discern as a good Berean while practicing the eternal elements of truth should cause us to be diligent in our seeking. We so often sacrifice the eternal truth of God, which has immense consequences with the temporal trinkets of pleasure for the here and now. Seeking God is like a dying fire that must be constantly stoked and fed to continue the burning. Yet, it is God who raises up individuals to set their hearts to seek after Him. May He find a sea of people with whom He might share His heart, and they in reciprocal love share His love which when shed abroad might live to the glory and praise of the Father, Son, and the Holy Ghost. Amen.

RESTORATION

Be Thou My Vision
Dallan Forgaill

Be thou my vision, O Lord of my heart;
naught be all else to me, save that thou art.
Thou my best thought, by day or by night,
waking or sleeping, thy presence my light.

Be thou my wisdom, be thou my true word;
I ever with thee, and thou with me, Lord.
Born of thy love, thy child may I be,
thou in me dwelling and I one with thee.

Be thou my buckler, my sword for the fight.
Be thou my dignity, thou my delight,
thou my soul's shelter, thou my high tow'r.
Raise thou me heav'nward, O Pow'r of my pow'r.
Riches I heed not, nor vain empty praise;

thou mine inheritance, now and always.
Thou and thou only, first in my heart,
Ruler of heaven, my treasure thou art.
High King of heaven, when vict'ry is won

may I reach heaven's joys, O bright heav'n's Sun!
Heart of my heart, whatever befall,
still be my vision, O Ruler of all.

Public Domain

You have come through this one-year study of a lifelong journey of getting to behold your God. Being bound by truth is the most incredible pinnacle of fulfillment rather than being bound by falsehood to the death of the soul, and Christ is that truth who dispels error and floods in life for now and for all eternity. Your journey has just begun, and if God has so pleased to use this study to further your exploration of Himself, praise be to God, for everything that has been said thus far and will be uttered in the future have been received from the kind hand of God.

Additional Resource for Consideration

In continuing this journey, this section is a simple resource for having a proper high view of God and see how it affects our view of life and what we live for in our earthly pilgrimage.

Type	View of God	View of Life	Scripture Reference	
Low	God needs man's companionship.	Man is indispensable, so God has to work around our schedule, Man centered.	To whom then will ye liken me, or shall I be equal? saith the Holy One.–Isaiah 40:25	SELF-EXISTENCE of GOD
Proper	God is self-sufficient in need of nothing or anyone.	Privilege to go to God for He desires it, and I am the one in need, God-centered.		
Low	Sin is normal in the life of a Christian, and God understands that we fail.	I can indulge in sin since everyone does it anyway, and it is to be expected.	For, brethren, ye have been called unto liberty; only use not liberty for an occasion to the flesh, but by love serve one another.–Galatians 5:13	HOLINESS of GOD
Proper	God hates sin, and God is angry with the wicked every day. God became Israel's greatest enemy because of their sin (Isaiah 63:10).	I need to put away things that will hinder my walk with God. I need to evaluate areas such as sports, entertainment, the internet, and friends.		
Low	God wants me to go to Heaven; I can "believe" so I can have fire insurance when I have to die.	I can live as I please since I am going to Heaven anyway. No desire to turn from the sin that separates me from God.	But now being made free from sin, and become servants to God, ye have your fruit unto holiness, and the end everlasting life.–Romans 6:22	JUSTICE of GOD
Proper	God wants us to know the Father and restore the relationship of holiness that was lost in the garden; Heaven is a fringe benefit. (Acts 20:21)	God desires fruit unto holiness. Repentance from sin is crucial for the sinner. For the believer, it is essential to keep his fellowship with God.		
Low	God is waiting at the whim of man for salvation, hoping man will make the right choice.	I can choose when I please, and salvation is secondary since I have to live, make money, and sow my wild oats.	The Lord looked down from heaven upon the children of men, to see if there were any that did understand, and seek God. They are all gone aside, they are all together become filthy: there is none that doeth good, no, not one.–Psalm 14:2,3	OMNIPOTENCE of GOD
Proper	The holiness of God, the sinfulness of sin, and the utter unworthiness and inability of a man to reconcile himself to God. God comes as a conquering King in the soul of man, godly fear of rejecting God.	Conviction of sin to cry out, "God be merciful to me a sinner." Grateful for anything we receive from God daily and see it as a gift bestowed upon us for our good.		

Type	View of God	View of Life	Scripture Reference	
Low	God cannot reject my works of charity, religion, and good works since He is all about love and helping others.	I can do as I please as long as I give for some works of charity and do good to others and follow the golden rule.	Not by works of righteousness which we have done, but according to his mercy he saved us, by the washing of regeneration, and renewing of the Holy Ghost;–Titus 3:5	HOLINESS of GOD
Proper	The holiness of God invokes the wrath of God on man's polluted offering of good works, originated from a heart of sin. Sinner by nature and by choice.	Fall upon the mercy of God for salvation, being revealed of His mercy by the Spirit to show the way of escape through Jesus Christ, having the witness of the Spirit. Salvation from sin and not the penalty of sin.		
Low	Seeing God as a friend and nothing more than that.	I can treat Him just like a friend and not talk to Him when I don't like Him.	So likewise ye, when ye shall have done all those things which are commanded you, say, We are unprofitable servants: we have done that which was our duty to do.– Luke 17:10	SOVEREIGNTY of GOD
Proper	God is holy, and the friendship of Christ is one aspect of my relationship with Him. Slave (translated as "servant" from the Greek word Doulos in the Bible) is another, along with many others, serving a loving Master who is perfect.	He is God and my Lord, and I view my life (as His child) as belonging to Him and desire His heart in whatever I do.		

Type	View of God	View of Life	Scripture Reference	
Low	God primarily cares about my physical needs.	I want God to make me fulfill my goals of fame, popularity, and riches.	After these things the word of the Lord came unto Abram in a vision, saying, Fear not, Abram: I am thy shield, and thy exceeding great reward.– Genesis 15:1	OMNIPOTENCE of GOD
Proper	God is my provision and reward. He is the source of my job, health, family, material possessions, etc.	Willing to let go of things God asks of me and to be able to give myself as a living sacrifice. Living for something above and not for the things below.		

Low	God created me for my good, and everything He does is for my good.	It's all about me, and I can obey God as long as He is good to me according to my definition of good. If I don't like something, that must not be of God.	Thou art worthy, O Lord, to receive glory and honour and power: for thou hast created all things, and for thy pleasure they are and were created.—Rev 4:11	LOVE of GOD
Proper	I was created for His pleasure.	Having a proper fear of God lest I incur His displeasure or disappoint Him, for the benevolent God that He is.		
Low	God wants to heal all my sickness	Life is about happiness and living carefree.	That the trial of your faith, being much more precious than of gold that perisheth, though it be tried with fire, might be found unto praise and honour and glory at the appearing of Jesus Christ:—1 Peter 1:7	RIGHTEOUSNESS of GOD
Proper	God molds a man using persecution, sickness, and death.	The greatest desire is to love the Lord with heart, soul, and mind. Seeing everything in life as God's desire to conform me into the image of the Lord Jesus Christ. Desiring God's will to be done on earth as it is done in Heaven.		
Low	God lets me continue in sin since I struggle with it, and He understands that we are weak.	I can categorize sins into small sins, white lies; the end justifies the means.	But if ye be without chastisement, whereof all are partakers, then are ye bastards, and not sons.—Hebrews 12:8	LOVE of GOD
Proper	God whips and corrects His rebellious child to bring him back to Himself using many means and trials.	Having the proper perspective of God as our Father to have the fear and respect that He deserves should affect how I view sin.		
Low	When I see God in Heaven, I will jump on His lap, and He will show me around.	I can be a Sunday morning Christian and live like the world the rest of the week. Sentimental Christianity.	And when I saw him, I fell at his feet as dead. And he laid his right hand upon me, saying unto me, Fear not; I am the first and the last:—Revelation 1:17	HOLINESS of GOD
Proper	God in His holiness is fearful to look upon where the seraphims cover their faces crying Holy, holy, holy; and the elders fall on their faces and worship Him night and day.	Daily consecration and dying to self, realizing that I get the privilege to pray to and commune with the God of the Universe with clean hands and a pure heart to desire the beauty of holiness.		

Type	View of God	View of Life	Scripture Reference	
Low	God is love, which means that my definition of love is all that matters.	Love can be as I imagine it, even at the expense of contradicting God's commands.	(Charity or love) Rejoiceth not in iniquity, but rejoiceth in the truth;–1 Corinthians 13:6	LOVE of GOD
Proper	God is love that complements the other characteristics of God, such as His holiness, judgments, etc., along with His eternal attributes.	I realize that love is the fulfillment of the law and that it doth not rejoice in iniquity, causing me not to justify my position if it is against God's word.		
Low	God forgives all the time.	Have a low view of the consequences of sin and its effect on my fellowship with God. Keeping God as a backup helper.	Then shall they call upon me, but I will not answer; they shall seek me early, but they shall not find me: For that they hated knowledge, and did not choose the fear of the Lord:–Proverbs 1:28,29	JUSTICE of GOD
Proper	God's spirit will not always strive with man. The God of the Bible kills people in judgment (Acts 5:1-11). Fear of having a seared conscience.	I need to ensure that Conviction to Repentance follows Restitution and that it is led by the Spirit. Seeking God for the victorious Christian life		

Type	View of God	View of Life	Scripture Reference	
Low	God can be worshipped according to the feelings that make me feel good.	If I am elevated by music, message, or a feel-good environment, I must have pleased God or God met with me.	Now when Solomon had made an end of praying, the fire came down from heaven, and consumed the burnt offering and the sacrifices; and the glory of the Lord filled the house.–2 Chronicles 7:1	HOLINESS of GOD
Proper	Worshipping God must be with reverence and soberness of a Solemn Assembly. Having a godly fear that we are dealing with sacred vessels that have intense consequences.	I need to make sure I understand the serious nature of coming to Him in worship and have the active involvement in knowing and meaning what I am singing, praying, etc.		

Low	It is easy to get to know God, which can be easily learned in a classroom.	I can do a checklist when I need to get more of God. Convenient Christianity reduces God to intellectual ability.	For all those things hath mine hand made, and all those things have been, saith the Lord: but to this man will I look, even to him that is poor and of a contrite spirit, and trembleth at my word.–Isaiah 66:2	INFINITUDE of GOD
Proper	God is holy and how I approach Him determines how much He will reveal Himself to me. It takes purity, discipline, prayer, and studying the word of God to plow through and find the God of the word, the Person of Jesus Christ.	I need to realize the potential for the world, the flesh, and the devil to hinder my walk with God. And how much I sow is in what proportion that I will reap in the things of knowing God. And knowing God is the greatest fulfillment of life.		
Low	Being holy is optional, depending on our circumstances and social conditions.	As long as I am well-intentioned, I can give into some temptations since it is harder now to live for God.	That ye may be blameless and harmless, the sons of God, without rebuke, in the midst of a crooked and perverse nation, among whom ye shine as lights in the world;–Philippians 2:15	HOLINESS of GOD
Proper	God expects His children to be blameless and walk perfectly before Him. Separation, modesty, piety, etc., are all part of Christian living.	I can claim the provisions through Christ, who is my victory and has fulfilled God's requirement for living a joyful life in victory.		
Low	God of the Old Testament was harsh; God of the New Testament is loving	I can take what I like in Jesus's life for my benefit.	For I am the Lord, I change not; therefore ye sons of Jacob are not consumed.–Malachi 3:6	IMMUTABILITY of GOD
Proper	There is but One God, high and lifted up, perfect in holiness.	Seeing the Bible as one book, speaking of One God and His dealing with humanity that I need to obey in love.		
Low	God is about making sure I have everything I need to serve him and making it easy for me.	Service to God is easy, do it when I please, how I like to do it. It's about what I can do when I have time for God.	And seeing a fig tree afar off having leaves, he came, if haply he might find any thing thereon: and when he came to it, he found nothing but leaves; for the time of figs was not yet. And Jesus answered and said unto it, No man eat fruit of thee hereafter for ever.–Mark 11.13,14a	OMNIPOTENCE of GOD
Proper	God requires more of us than is humanly possible. It reminds us to realize the reality of our inability and His ability, for we can do nothing without Him.	I need to realize that I cannot, but God can through me, as I die to self by doing all things through Christ which strengtheneth me.		

Type	View of God	View of Life	Scripture Reference	
Low	God is easy to approach however I please; sentimental pictures of Christ caring for us give me pleasant feelings.	I can have a god of my imagination who fits my perspective or expectation of Him and how I think.	And if ye call on the Father, who without respect of persons judgeth according to every man's work, pass the time of your sojourning here in fear:–1 Peter 1:17	OMNIPRESENCE of GOD
Proper	The fear of the Lord is the beginning of wisdom. Purity is a requirement to approach God (Psalm 24:3-5).	I get to enjoy the nearness of Christ and His presence while desiring a life that brings joy to His face.		
Low	God meets with His people whenever we can schedule a meeting.	Put God in a box and easily justify any lack of God's working in our midst.	For the eyes of the Lord run to and fro throughout the whole earth, to shew himself strong in the behalf of them whose heart is perfect toward him.–2 Chronicles 16:9	SOVEREIGNTY of GOD
Proper	God is Sovereign and takes great pleasure in meeting with His children.	Preparation for meeting our Lord, longing for His presence as a Bride who desireth her Bridegroom.		
Low	The church is about getting to know others, chit-chat, food, fellowship, having clean "fun," and throwing God in the mix.	Go to church when I feel like it and when it is not too much inconvenience to my schedule.	Sanctify ye a fast, call a solemn assembly, gather the elders and all the inhabitants of the land into the house of the Lord your God, and cry unto the Lord,–Joel 1:14	HOLINESS of GOD
Proper	God desires a Solemn Assembly that understands the magnitude of God meeting with His people.	I need to make sure I understand the serious nature of coming into His presence in worship.		
Low	God's primary concern is the lost.	I need to see people saved using any human means possible, irrespective of my standing before God.	And, behold, I send the promise of my Father upon you: but tarry ye in the city of Jerusalem, until ye be endued with power from on high.–Luke 24:49	GLORY of GOD
Proper	God desires His children to walk in holiness; a vessel made ready for the Master's use for reaching the lost.	We need to be right with God, being fit for service, and reaching the lost in the power of God using His methods.		

Type	View of God	View of Life	Scripture Reference	
Low	I have my rights, and God will use the government to keep me from persecution or lose my rights.	Give excessive time and energy to politics, media, and government at the expense of eternal things.	The king's heart is in the hand of the Lord, as the rivers of water: he turneth it whithersoever he will.–Proverbs 21:1	OMNIPOTENCE of GOD
Proper	God is the Alpha and the Omega; He sets up kings and puts down kingdoms. We submit to His plan for all the ages.	My rights come from God, and I serve Christ by surrendering my rights to the judge of all the earth. Humility is desired above all else.		
Low	God adapts to a culture based on how we want to live today.	I look at life from my perspective and see how to adopt God into it.	Jesus Christ the same yesterday, and to day, and for ever.–Hebrews 13:8	IMMUTABILITY of GOD
Proper	God is unchanging, and I align myself to God and His revealed will and the word, which does not need to change	I desire to enjoy God based on who He is and not how I think about Him in my current cultural persuasions.		
Low	God is a genie who wants me to be happy. I am so blessed because God is always about keeping His promises.	I don't hold myself accountable but shift the blame to others, self-pity. See sin as a disease or justifiable because of my circumstances.	[Habitual sin] Whosoever is born of God doth not commit sin; for his seed remaineth in him: and he cannot sin, because he is born of God.–1 John 3:9	JUSTICE of GOD
Proper	God is holy who cannot look upon sin. Many of God's promises are conditional upon my obedience.	I see sin as an abomination before God which affects how I see it or interact with it. To rise above my circumstances.		

Type	View of God	View of Life	Scripture Reference	
Low	God wants me to be rich and prosperous.	I can keep getting ahead in life and making money the priority, and God will enable me.	How that in a great trial of affliction the abundance of their joy and their deep poverty abounded unto the riches of their liberality.–2 Corinthians 8:2	SOVEREIGNTY of GOD
Proper	God is Sovereign in how He deals with His children; none of God's disciples were rich.	My greatest desire is to follow Him with all my heart, soul, and might, irrespective of the financial rewards.		
Low	The Bible is about man and what I need to know about God. It is primarily about man's best interest.	I learn to see the importance of man in my daily life and how God fits into the puzzle and man's response to God etc.	In the beginning God– Genesis 1:1a That at the name of Jesus every knee should bow, of things in heaven, and things in earth, and things under the earth; And that every tongue should confess that Jesus Christ is Lord, to the glory of God the Father.–Philippians 2:10,11	SELF-EXISTENCE of GOD
Proper	The Bible is about God and His dealing with man from creation until the end of time. It is about God's pleasure in creating man and for His eternal purpose and glory.	I see the importance of God and how He deals with me, what my life is about, which should affect how I view life, historical, political events, and the future.		

Type	View of God	View of Life	Scripture Reference	
Low	God of the Old Testament is just mean who wants to kill people.	I have to find a way to keep God at bay while I do my own thing or push my boundaries on what I can get away with.	I have no pleasure in the death of the wicked; but that the wicked turn from his way and live–Ezekiel 33:11	MERCY of GOD
Proper	God hates sin but desires the sinner to repent and turn to Him for mercy.	My view of sin should be one of offending a good God who loves me.		
Low	I walk in fear and torment of getting in trouble with God.	Nervous about life and what it means to serve God out of terror.	The Lord, The Lord God, merciful and gracious, longsuffering, and abundant in goodness and truth, Keeping mercy for thousands, forgiving iniquity and transgression and sin, and that will by no means clear the guilty;–Exodus 34:6,7a	LOVE of GOD
Proper	God has His goodness displayed before us in His benevolent actions in creation, blessings, provisions, etc., and correction is for those who forsake the truth and follow the path of Cain.	I can live in total freedom and happiness when I live within the gracious path and will for my life that a benevolent God has placed before me. God has original-claim upon mankind through creation and double-claim upon me through salvation in addition to creation.		

Low	Only the New Testament applies to this Church age. Creation, as God said it is irrelevant.	I can interpret scriptures to my liking. I can follow my feelings and adjust the scriptures to my beliefs.	All scripture is given by inspiration of God, and is profitable for doctrine, for reproof, for correction, for instruction in righteousness:–2 Timothy 3:16	IMMUTABILITY of GOD
Proper	God has no beginning and no end, and He is perfect in all His ways and able to preserve the word for every generation, Old and New Testament.	I align myself to the word of God and reject anything contrary, no matter how I feel or am led to believe. I see life as God's gift to me.		
Low	God has done His part, and now it is up to me to decide if I am convinced or what works for me.	I see life and salvation as flesh and blood (natural processes) and not supernatural intersections that affect everything I do.	And Jesus answered and said unto him, Blessed art thou, Simon Barjona: for flesh and blood hath not revealed it unto thee, but my Father which is in heaven.–Matthew 16:17	OMNIPOTENCE of GOD
Proper	God is intricately involved with the human soul; He is the author of life and the One who draws me to Himself.	I see salvation as an encounter with God that begins a lifelong journey of being faithful to God, who has saved me and matures me as His child.		
Low	God is about my best interest and is concerned about my place in society.	I see God as a means to satisfy my perspective of social justice with fellowmen. A utility God for my benefit.	And we know that all things work together for good to them that love God, to them who are the called according to his purpose.–Romans 8:28	JUSTICE of GOD
Proper	According to His standard, God is the giver of justice, His judgment against sin, His righteous anger on the evil, and the sanctity of life itself.	While God has ordained the institution of justice, I realize that I need to submit to God's standard of justice and see the world's injustice through it.		

Type	View of God	View of Life	Scripture Reference	
Low	God conforms to changes in society as society progresses; we need to translate the Bible to our culture and make it relevant.	Trying to accommodate my lifestyle to what fits me and adapt spiritual things to what makes me feel good as I follow my heart or my perspective of love, gender, marriage, etc.	God is not a man, that he should lie; neither the son of man, that he should repent: hath he said, and shall he not do it? or hath he spoken, and shall he not make it good?–Number 23:19 Jesus Christ the same yesterday, and to day, and for ever.–Hebrews 13:8	IMMUTABILITY of GOD
Proper	God created all things as how He planned, and it was good. Sin corrupted our view of God and self. God preserved His word for all generations, and it is relevant to every culture.	I realize I am part of a great purpose that God made me for, and I am an image-bearer of God and have eternal worth, and I am as how God made me (as when I was born) in all matters of gender, identity, marriage, etc. I need to fit myself to the message of God and His word.		

Type	View of God	View of Life	Scripture Reference	
Low	God is one of the standards, among others, to help me in navigating through life.	I see God accommodating my needs since there are many "standards" from the Bible, science, laws, and human ideas of morality.	For by him were all things created, that are in heaven, and that are in earth, visible and invisible, whether they be thrones, or dominions, or principalities, or powers: all things were created by him, and for him:–Colossians 1:16	SOVEREIGNTY of GOD
Proper	God is the absolute standard and authority in all areas of life and practice, though He speaks through various means.	I can have total confidence in the God of the Bible who rules as Sovereign over all His creation and is well able to accomplish His purpose, realizing that true science reveals the greatness of God as seen in the Universe.		

Low	The God of the Bible is just one of the ways to Heaven since God is about love and will not send anyone to Hell.	All religions have some truth in them and are their own ways to God.	Neither is there salvation in any other: for there is none other name under heaven given among men, whereby we must be saved.—Acts 4:12 And whosoever was not found written in the book of life was cast into the lake of fire.—Revelation 20:15	RIGHTEOUSNESS of GOD
Proper	Sin makes us an enemy of God. God is love, but He is also Holy, as a righteous judge will judge sin and not let the guilty go free. The death and suffering we see on earth are because of man's rebellion against God.	There is one God and one way of salvation that is through Jesus Christ. The wickedness of sin is so great that nothing I do in life can atone for it, but rather it is by His mercy that I am saved. I see life as a gift from God and see His love magnified in His redemptive work and the price that was paid.		
Low	The prosperity of the wicked causes me to be constantly thinking about the inadequacy of God's response.	Being troubled at the unknown, wickedness that is around me causes me to get frustrated and anxious	Can any hide himself in secret places that I shall not see him? saith the LORD. Do not I fill heaven and earth? saith the LORD.—Jeremiah 23:24	OMNISCIENCE of GOD
Proper	God knows all things and is in absolute authority over events everywhere, on earth and in the heavens.	Realize that God works all things to an expected end that He has planned. He will glorify His Son, and I can have the confidence to depend on Him.		
Low	God is not involved in the day-to-day activities of men and is not actively involved in everything I do.	What I do does not affect how God views it; I need to plan and act as I see fit and add God in the mix for formality.	Whither shall I go from thy spirit? or whither shall I flee from thy presence? If I ascend up into heaven, thou art there: if I make my bed in hell, behold, thou art there. –Psalm 139:7,8	OMNIPRESENCE of GOD
Proper	God is intricately involved in the affairs of men, from birth until death. He sees all things and knows all things, and there is no place where He cannot be found.	I realize my accountability to God in seeking His face for my life choices, my fear of offending Him, and my communion with Him for all my decisions and ways.		

Type	View of God	View of Life	Scripture Reference	
Low	God can be limited by knowledge about Him. There is everything to know about God by reading books about God, reading the scriptures, and memorizing them.	The point of regeneration becomes the end of seeking after God; knowledge of God is sought in intellectual prowess.	O the depth of the riches both of the wisdom and knowledge of God! how unsearchable are his judgments, and his ways past finding out! For who hath known the mind of the Lord? or who hath been his counsellor?—Romans 11:33,34	UNKNOWNNESS of GOD
Proper	God is infinite and cannot be known entirely through all of eternity. We are finite creatures, and God is infinite, endless in wisdom, knowledge, understanding, holiness, and all His attributes.	The desire to know God is a lifelong journey to seek after Him, study and meditate on the word of God, desire Him by the revelation of the Holy Spirit, persevere, and prevail through prayer. Have a constant understanding that there are depths where God cannot be known fully in our finite minds.		
Low	God's faithfulness is expected. He is held accountable to be faithful.	Limiting God to our expectation of Him in interpreting things around us.	It is of the Lord's mercies that we are not consumed, because his compassions fail not. They are new every morning: great is thy faithfulness.—Lamentations 3:22,23	FAITHFULNESS of GOD
Proper	God's faithfulness is given out of His love to sustain His creation. Of His own will, He sustains us.	Realize that we are subject to His Sovereign rule and see all things as reflecting His faithfulness.		
Low	I can live my life as I please since God understands and will always forgive me.	See sin as inconsequential, see God as love, and plan life independent of God.	For the Lord thy God is a consuming fire, even a jealous God.—Deuteronomy 4:24	JEALOUSY of GOD
Proper	God is a jealous God who constantly refines and draws His children to Himself in holiness to produce the reflection of His Son in them.	Desire separation from the heart to love and please God, who is great and worthy of our love and adoration. See sin as provoking the jealousy of God.		

"That the God of our Lord Jesus Christ, the Father of glory, may give unto you the spirit of wisdom and revelation in the knowledge of him:"–Ephesians 1:17

Let all mortal flesh keep silence
Gerard Moultrie

Let all mortal flesh keep silence,
and with fear and trembling stand.
Ponder nothing earthly minded,
for with blessing in his hand
Christ our God to earth descending
comes, our homage to demand.

King of kings, yet born of Mary,
as of old on earth he stood,
Lord of heaven now incarnate
in the body and the blood,
he will give to all the faithful
his own self for heav'nly food.

Rank on rank the host of heaven
streams before him on the way,
as the Light of light descending
from the realms of endless day
comes, that pow'rs of hell may vanish,
as the shadows pass away.

At his feet the six-winged seraph,
cherubim with sleepless eye,
veil their faces to the Presence,
as with ceaseless voice they cry,
"Alleluia! Alleluia!
Alleluia, Lord Most High!"

Public Domain

Title Index

January	February
1 God, our Supreme Goal	1 The Gospel Witness
2 Desiring God Alone	2 The Implication of the Gospel
3 The Triune God	3 One Book, One Message
4 Interwoven with Christ	4 The Word of God
5 Starting Point	5 Social Media "Christianity"
6 Jesus and Jehovah	6 God's Word vs Man's Response
7 The Holiness of God	7 God, the Final Authority
8 The Existence of God	8 The Seriousness of the Gospel
9 The Study of God	9 The Missing Link
10 Created for His Pleasure	10 The Quantum Breakthrough
11 Retribution	11 Defilement by Association
12 Fingerprints of God	12 Opportunities and Outcome
13 Creation	13 Diversity and Inclusion
14 Means to an End	14 Nothing New Under the Sun
15 God, Our Great Reward	15 Gender Wars
16 Enshrined Captivation of God	16 Wealth Distribution?
17 The High View of God	17 Cancel Culture
18 Holy Spirit and the New Birth	18 Sickness and Fear
19 Striving against God's Spirit	19 Naming and Shaming
20 Baptism of the Holy Spirit	20 Chasing Careers, Losing Homes
21 Penetrating the Veil	21 The Hardening of the Heart
22 The Inward Witness	22 The Quest for the Origin of Life
23 Divine Discontent	23 Religion, Cults, and Identity
24 Proclamation of Truth	24 Social Justice and Absolute Truth
25 Make Alive	25 The Answer to Questions
26 God of the word	26 "Freedom" for All?
27 The Flow of the Spirit	27 Masculinity and Femininity
28 The New Creature	28 Abortion
29 The Holy Spirit	29 Education and Self-Reformation
30 Two Veils	
31 Without the Holy Spirit	

March		April	
1	All we need is "Love"?	1	Original Claim
2	Sin's Nature to Multiply	2	The Real Face of Sin
3	Tolerance and Truth	3	Conviction by Revelation
4	The Trap of Socialism	4	Yea, Hath God Said?
5	Born "this" Way?	5	Not Religion
6	Judgement Upon Sin	6	Point in Time Decision?
7	Modesty and Character	7	Repentance and Salvation
8	A Real Enemy	8	Contrasting Truth
9	Irrevocable Damage	9	Fruits Meet for Repentance
10	Sinful Lifestyle and Influences	10	Worthless Faith
11	Drawn unto Death	11	The Narrow Way
12	A Stark Reminder	12	Turn from Sin
13	Compassion and Wrath	13	Intellectual vs Supernatural
14	Purpose Driven Development	14	Depravity of Man
15	The Gospel of Confusion	15	Provision of the Law
16	The Nature of Lies	16	Conviction of Sin
17	Divine Author	17	Saving Faith vs Natural Faith
18	Restoration of Relationship	18	Regeneration, the Turning Point
19	Sin and Sinners	19	Is Salvation Free for Nothing?
20	Christ, the Conquering King	20	Truth, Fallen in the Streets
21	Everything has been Received	21	Finding Fault
22	The Gift of Faith	22	Why Repentance?
23	Examine Yourselves	23	God's Sovereignty and Man's Responsibility
24	Crucial Distinctions Required	24	The Lord Jesus Christ
25	Repent and Believe	25	The Offense of the Cross
26	The Goodness and Severity of God	26	The Inner Person
27	Original Intent	27	Who is a Christian?
28	A New Heart	28	The Lordship of Christ
29	Defining Faith	29	The Call to Discipleship
30	Sin and the Gospel	30	Freedom in Christ
31	No Man Cared for my Soul		

May		June	
1	The Cultural Impact	1	The Greater Responsibility
2	The Proclamation of Adoption	2	Righteous Anger
3	Truth and Trust	3	Walking with God
4	Christ In You	4	God Molding Man
5	Judge Not?	5	Spirit and in Truth
6	The Sacredness of Marriage	6	The Journey of Knowing God
7	Revelation and the End Times	7	Soldier of Jesus Christ
8	Impatient Requests	8	A Changed Heart
9	Dead to Sin	9	Though He Slay Me
10	Truth vs Life	10	The Cross before Me
11	Restitution	11	As Little Children
12	Vanity Fair	12	Killing Agag
13	The Patience of Satan	13	Ownership
14	The Simple Life	14	Mercy and Truth
15	The Conquering of Sin	15	Still Small Voice
16	Doulos of Jesus Christ	16	Victorious Christian Life
17	Accountability Under Grace	17	Humility and the Crucified Life
18	Reaction vs Truth	18	Saved unto Righteousness
19	Response to Government	19	Getting Right with God
20	Living by Faith	20	End Goal, Disciples
21	Privileged to Serve	21	The Missing Jewel of Prayer
22	God in a Box	22	Prayer and Submission
23	Approachable vs Agreeable	23	Faith that Overcomes
24	Relevant for every Generation	24	Answers to Prayer
25	Who is my Neighbor?	25	Praying Through
26	God's Desire	26	God's Work and Man's Responsibility
27	The Receiving of Truth		
28	Grafted into Christ	27	Fasting
29	It is Finished	28	Alignment
30	Forsaking All	29	Unknown Expectations
31	God's Treasures	30	Costly Prayers

July		August	
1	Corporate Prayer Meeting	1	The Inconveniences of an Awakening
2	A Humble Plea	2	Unpredictable Moving's of God
3	Prayers of Abomination	3	The Gift of Tears
4	Call Unto Me	4	Spiritual Stronghold
5	The Way of Blessing	5	Two Kingdoms
6	Progression of Prayer	6	Organizing "Revival"?
7	Prayer and Holy Hands	7	The Making of a Prophet
8	Obedience Proves your Asking	8	How Desperate are We?
9	Examining our Motives	9	Fruit that Remains
10	To Whom Much is Given	10	The Workings of God
11	Justifying Selfish Motives	11	Baptism of Fire
12	The Eternal Journey	12	God Against Us
13	Pharisee and Subtle Sins	13	Altar unto God
14	Personal Holiness	14	The Time Factor
15	Dealing with Pride	15	The Mercy of God
16	The Self Problem	16	Are you Thirsty?
17	Weights and Hindrances	17	The Dilemma of Extremes
18	Much shall be Required	18	Crossroads
19	Three Altars	19	The Cry of Sin
20	Humility, the Beauty of Holiness	20	Stemming the Tide of Sin
21	The Battle for the Mind	21	The Gospel of Accommodation
22	Purity at all Cost	22	Discerning the Times
23	About You vs About God	23	Without the Camp
24	Sacred Music	24	Spiritual Discernment
25	Enjoying God	25	Judgement of Sin
26	The Love Factor	26	The Love of Christ
27	Desiring Holiness	27	Tolerated, but not Desired
28	The Knowledge of God	28	Restoring our First Love
29	The Curse of Words	29	Spontaneous Revivals
30	The Facets of Christian Living	30	Get Out of the Boat
31	Revival	31	The Prodigal

September	October
1 Wings as Eagles	1 Who moved the Truth?
2 Preaching and Revival	2 Americanized Christianity
3 Restraint on Sin	3 The Eastern Influence
4 A Grim Truth	4 Silencing the Pulpits
5 Fleshly Works during Revival	5 Biblical Christianity
6 A Ray of Hope	6 Same God, different Results?
7 The Hidden Forces of Evil	7 Rebirthing the Natural Man
8 The Burden of Revival	8 The Wrath of Almighty God
9 Rediscovering the God of the Bible	9 Spiritual Experiences
10 Aftermath of a Revival	10 Lowering our Expectation
11 Pure Religion Undefiled	11 Watchman of the Soul
12 The Call to Give Up	12 Church Unity
13 Spiritual Awakening	13 The Object of Worship
14 God's Garden	14 The Cycle of Corruption
15 Seeking God Perpetually	15 A Jealous God
16 A Cause for Anguish	16 The Fear of God
17 Filling the Void	17 The Judgement Seat of Christ
18 Marks of Genuine Revival	18 Compromise
19 Broken and a Contrite Heart	19 The Purity of the Bride
20 The Manifest Presence of God	20 Authority vs Authoritarian
21 What is Our Supreme Goal?	21 Goal of Missions
22 Serious Indictments to Consider	22 That which is Unseen
23 Conveying Truths	23 Taking Responsibility
24 Three-fold in Purpose	24 External vs Internal
25 Self-satisfied Christianity	25 The Reckoning of Eternity
26 The Need for Extreme Caution	26 Satan's End Goal
27 Waiting on God	27 Thick Skin, Tender Heart
28 God will Require of Us	28 ICHABOD
29 The World Stage	29 Smearing Christ's Name
30 Divine Judgement	30 Our Plague of Shallowness
	31 Moratorium on the Gospel

November		December	
1	True Love is Action	1	The Mode of Education
2	The Normal Christian Life	2	Deep Ploughing
3	Worship	3	Unction / Fullness of the Spirit
4	Children's Ministry	4	Plucking Unripe Fruits
5	Preaching	5	Focus of Missions
6	The Great White Throne Judgement	6	Cheerful Giver
7	The Persecution of the Church	7	Repentance toward God
8	The Counsel of Balaam	8	The Fullness of Sin unto Death
9	Separation	9	Hell
10	The Reproach of Jesus Christ	10	Packaging God's Methods
11	Purpose of Contending	11	Bearing Fruit
12	Obedience to Christ	12	Opening Blinded Eyes
13	The Dawn of Creation	13	Who Art Thou?
14	Baptism, Our Position in Christ	14	Regeneration
15	The Age of Illusion	15	Authority on Truth
16	Erosion of Truth	16	A Call to Repentance
17	Following God	17	Forgiveness and Restoration
18	Solemn Assembly	18	Knowing God
19	Changing Times	19	Looking unto Jesus
20	Statistical Christianity	20	Self-examination
21	Worshipping an Unknown God	21	Embracing our Cross
22	Pride and Prejudice	22	Obey God rather than Men
23	Preaching without the Spirit	23	The Eternal Purposes of God
24	Preservation of Truth	24	Being Thankful
25	Blending of the Lines	25	Steadfastness of Heart
26	The God who Gives	26	Counting the Cost
27	The Deceit of Riches	27	An Expected End
28	Exposing a Lie	28	Endureth to the End
29	Indoctrination of Evil	29	I Change Not
30	The Deafening Silence	30	The Three Pillars
		31	Path to Recovery

About the Author

Jabez Abraham is the founder and president of Desiring Revival Ministries, a ministry for the furtherance of the cause of revival and making God known to all generations and nations. The inception came as a call of God, burdening him in 2005 on the need for genuine revival among God's people and the Nation. Since then, God has seeded that burden with a desire for God's people to return to Biblical Christianity that is not just a theory or theology but something vibrant and authentic as exhibited in the book of Acts.

CPSIA information can be obtained
at www.ICGtesting.com
Printed in the USA
LVHW090038111221
705864LV00001B/84